EDWIN VENNARD, B.S.M.E. and E.E., Tulane University, served as power sales engineer for Gulf States Utilities Co. Later he became General Commercial Manager of Southwestern Gas and Electric Company. In 1933, he accepted the position as head of the Rate Department of Middle West Utilities Co., the predecessor of Middle West Service Company. For a number of years he was Vice President of this organization in charge of rates, new business, advertising, public and employee relations; then in 1953 he became President.

In 1956 Mr. Vennard was made Managing Director of the Edison Electric Institute, New York. In addition to developing courses and programs concerning the electric power industry, Mr. Vennard has written many articles and booklets and has given hundreds of addresses on the subject of government power. McGraw-Hill has also published a companion volume by Mr. Vennard: THE ELECTRIC POWER BUSINESS, covering all economic aspects of the industry.

Government in the Power Business

Government in the Power Business

EDWIN VENNARD

Managing Director
Edison Electric Institute
New York

McGRAW-HILL BOOK COMPANY

New York   St. Louis   San Francisco
London   Toronto   Sydney

Preface

To live and progress, man must work. To get work done, he must have energy. To increase the amount of work he can do and the goods he can produce, he must increase the energy he uses. But man's own energy—the energy in his muscles—is limited. Early in history, however, he learned to harness the energy of animals to aid him. He also found ways to use the energy of wind and falling water. Even as late as 1850 in America, some 65 percent of the work was done by human and animal energy.

Man's great leap forward came when he learned to build machines that could make use of the energy in fossil fuels—coal, gas, and oil—and better use of the energy in falling water. Now, nuclear power has added another source of energy. Today, some 98 percent of the work in this country is done with the help of these energy forms. Man's own limited energy has been multiplied many times over, production of goods has increased, and standards of living have risen.

To keep living standards going up, it is important that we always have an abundant supply of energy. The electric utility industry is in the business of converting the raw energy in coal, gas, oil, falling water, and the atom to a more convenient, flexible, and useful form. In the relatively few years since Thomas Edison developed his electric lamp, the industry has learned to carry out this process of energy conversion with increasing efficiency and economy. As a result, a larger and larger portion of our total energy supply is being used to produce electricity.

One significant characteristic of the electric utility business is that it requires large aggregates of capital—about $4.45 of capital for each $1 of annual revenue. In America, and in most industrial economies, investment in the electric utility industry is roughly equivalent to 12 percent of all the capital invested in all business. The problem of providing these large aggregates of capital has caused difficulties in many economies. Generally speaking, two methods have been followed to supply them:

1. *Free-market financing.* Under this method people are *encouraged* to save—that is, to deny themselves something in the hope of something better tomorrow. Their savings are invested in various ways, including in business enterprises through the free market. This is the traditional method used in America. People expect a reward for their self-denial or a satisfactory return on their investment, depending upon the degree of risk involved. Enterprises obtaining capital in this fashion must compete in the market place to meet their financial needs.

2. *Government financing.* Under this method people are *required* to deny themselves something today in the promise of something better tomorrow. Through taxes, they are required to provide their government with capital. Governments can and do use funds gathered in this fashion to build the machinery of production.

Both methods work. Both methods can provide the same kind of machinery. Both can finance the same methods of operation, make use of the same techniques, and employ the same kind of people.

In America today about 80 percent of the users of electricity are served by enterprises which use free-market financing and are under government regulation. About 20 percent are served by various local, state, and Federal governmental agencies. Sometimes these two approaches are described as private ownership and public ownership. However, these terms do not properly describe the two methods. The some 350 power companies financed in the market in this country are owned by more than 4 million direct stockholders. Indirectly almost every American has a financial interest in them through insurance companies, investment trusts, banks, and the other organizations which have invested large sums of money in the electric utility industry. For this reason, the financial community views these power companies as publicly owned, meaning that they are owned by large numbers of people and that ownership is open to all. A more descriptive term for this method of financing is investor ownership. The other method generally can be referred to as government ownership.

Many reasons are given for choosing one form of financing over the other. In some countries people believe in government ownership of the means of production as a matter of national policy. In others, such as England, one political party believes in government ownership of some of the principal means of production, including power, banking, steel, and the like. In such countries "nationalization" of these industries may be discussed as a matter of policy. The people debate the issue and elect the party of their choice. In this country there is no clearly defined movement or program calling for nationalization of industry. There is no general plan proposed for complete government ownership of the electric light and power business. Therefore, it does not seem appropriate in this book to argue the over-all merits or demerits of complete nationalization of all industry. A separate book could be devoted to this subject alone. Rather, the purpose here is to describe and analyze the principal reasons advanced in America for government ownership. Most of these are economic rather than philosophic. While I favor the investor-owned method of financing for many reasons, the aim here is to let the economic facts speak for themselves. I believe they form a convincing argument.

Through the years, four main reasons have been advanced for government financing or ownership of power facilities in this country. They are:

1. *Some government power is necessary.* The argument here is that the task of financing power facilities is so great that there is need for both free-market financing and government financing. Since energy is so important in a modern society, if some government financing is necessary, of course it would be wise to utilize this method. But is it necessary? To examine this question the book includes a rather complete appraisal of the investor-owned portion of the industry. Has it met the power needs? Has it been built and run efficiently? Is it well regulated? How has the customer fared? Has the industry been alert to innovations and new methods? Is it possible to finance in the free market not only the investor-owned portion of the industry but also that 20 percent now being financed by government? What about its plans for the future?

2. *Government power provides a necessary yardstick.* According to this argument, there is need for some government operation of power facilities as a yardstick to measure the efficiency of operation of the investor-owned segment. The assumption is that government regulation is not quite

adequate. Advocates of this view point out that government power is cheaper than investor-owned power—and it often is. To examine the reason for this, the book includes the results of exhaustive analyses of the principal government-financed power enterprises, such as Tennessee Valley Authority (TVA), Bonneville Power Administration (BPA), and the generating plants built by the Rural Electrification Administration (REA). These government-financed power projects do not pay an interest rate on capital equivalent to the value of that capital nor do they pay the same taxes as do investor-owned companies. Few people realize the magnitude of these two subsidies. An examination of government power is included, after adjusting for the subsidies in cost of money and taxes.

3. *Government power is needed to help pay for flood control, irrigation, and other governmental activities.* This argument, too, is a matter of economics. Exhaustive studies have been made to determine the economic benefits to the government of this method of financing as distinguished from a method whereby the government would finance functions such as flood control and irrigation but allow power facilities to be financed in the free market. Under the second method the government saves the capital, and therefore the interest charges, on the power facilities. Moreover, it sells falling water to a power enterprise and taxes the sale of electricity generated as a result.

4. *Government power helps in regional economic development.* This argument is that cheap government power enables people to use more electricity and that low-priced power attracts industry to a region, resulting in increased economic activity in the area. The question is, is this a fact? Have the areas with subsidized power facilities developed more rapidly than areas receiving elec-

tric service from facilities financed in the free market? If some industries have chosen to locate in areas where electric power is subsidized by government, has this been at the expense of areas where no subsidies are available?

The book concludes with what I believe to be some reasonable suggestions on the government power issue in the public interest.

Although the book has been in concentrated production through the past three years, it is really a product of more than 20 years. Over this long period, I have published many economic studies, analyses, articles, and booklets on the subject of the government in the power business. Wide use has been made of this material in an aim to assemble in one volume the principal facts and economic analyses of government power. Many people have helped. The Edison Electric Institute (EEI) maintains a very complete library on this subject. The EEI Department of Economics and Statistics, under John Thornborrow, now Assistant Managing Director of the Institute, and T. H. Burbank, present Director of the Department, provided many of the data and the analyses, and carefully checked and documented all the facts. H. J. Young, my assistant, has contributed to the research and the writing, particularly by polishing and editing the rough drafts I gave him. I am deeply indebted to the others on the Institute staff and the numerous people who have been kind enough to read the volume and give their valuable suggestions.

I am grateful for all this assistance. Naturally, however, final responsibility for the form and substance of this volume is mine. I hope the book will fill a need, as I believe it will, by presenting in one volume the answers to the questions most frequently asked about this important matter.

Edwin Vennard

Contents

Contents

Government in the Power Business

Chapter **1**

Electricity in the modern world

A century ago the store of energy available for men's use seemed severely limited. Most human effort was devoted to providing the physical essentials of living—food, clothing, and shelter. Even in the world today these three items may consume from 55 to 90 percent of the household expenditures, depending on the economy.[1] In a situation where a person must spend 90 percent of his effort in supplying his creature needs, there can be little time for developing the necessities of economic progress. He is caught in a circle.

People must have food, clothing, and shelter. Probably one of the first lessons prehistoric man learned was that he had to work to satisfy these needs. It is a simple enough lesson to understand, particularly when a person is acting alone. He must work to get food or he will starve. He must work to get clothing and provide shelter or he will freeze. The alternatives are brutally clear: he must work or he will die.

Group living presents a more complicated pattern, but the same principles apply. Work must be performed or the group cannot survive.

In order to escape from the trap of directing all their energy to providing minimum requirements for living, people have had to find ways to gain an advantage over nature. The first man to use a lever to pry a boulder loose found such an advantage. The first man who made a spear to help him hunt for food created another.

Step by step, people have learned to use tools to help them with their work. The more tools we have and the better use we make of these tools, the more we can multiply the effectiveness of human effort. But still, for centuries, the value of these tools was restricted because the energy seemed restricted. The tools were tied closely to their sources of motive power. Moreover, most work had to be done by muscle power. As late as 1850 some 65 percent of the work done in the United States of America was being done by animate energy—animal power and manpower—which is a very slow, costly way to produce goods.[2] On the whole, animal power probably costs from fifty to a hundred times as much as mechanical power, and manpower more than a thousand times as much.[3]   (Chart 1·1)

Chart 1·1

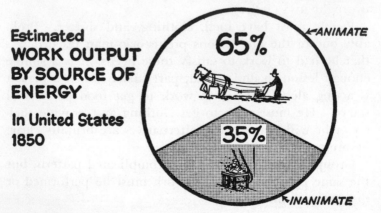

Estimated
**WORK OUTPUT
BY SOURCE OF
ENERGY**

**In United States
1850**

65%

35%

◢ANIMATE

◣INANIMATE

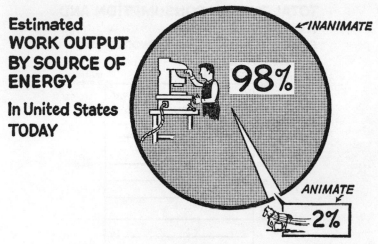

Estimated WORK OUTPUT BY SOURCE OF ENERGY In United States TODAY

Chart 1·2

Today, some 98 percent of the work done in the United States depends on inanimate energy—the energy found in fossil fuels, in falling water, in the wind, in the sun, and in the atom.[4]   (Chart 1·2)

The importance of this change can be seen in a study made by Mr. Fremont Felix, an engineering consultant, of the energy use in 153 countries throughout the world. Mr. Felix found a high degree of correlation between the use of energy per capita and national income per capita.   As the use of energy per capita goes up, the national income per capita rises.[5]   (Chart 1·3)

There is no better illustration of the way in which this principle operates than in the workings of the American economy.

Americans make up about one-seventeenth of all the people in the world.[6] Russia, China, and India all have populations that are much greater.[7] In terms of land area, the United States is far from being the largest nation in the world, nor is it particularly blessed with

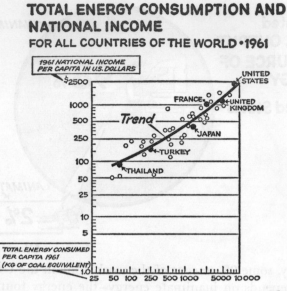

TOTAL ENERGY CONSUMPTION AND NATIONAL INCOME
FOR ALL COUNTRIES OF THE WORLD •1961

1961 NATIONAL INCOME PER CAPITA IN U.S. DOLLARS

TOTAL ENERGY CONSUMED PER CAPITA 1961 (KG OF COAL EQUIVALENT)

Chart 1·3

natural resources. The United States represents about one-fifteenth of the land surface of the world, just a little over 3½ million square miles.[8] (Chart 1·4) It has about the same proportion of the world's natural resources.

The characteristic that sets the American economy apart from most of the rest of the world is its use of energy. This country has built and uses one-third of all the electric power-producing capacity in the world.[9] A factory worker using 34,390 kilowatt-hours annually (the average annual usage per worker in 1965) had the equivalent energy of 513 men helping him on his job all year long.[10]

One corollary of this great use of energy is that the level of production and sale of durable goods is high. Americans own almost half of all the telephones in the world.[11] They own almost two-fifths of all the television

POPULATION and LAND AREA
U.S.A. COMPARED TO WORLD

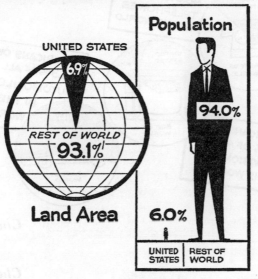

Population

UNITED STATES
6.9%

REST OF WORLD
93.1%

Land Area

94.0%

6.0%

UNITED STATES | REST OF WORLD

Chart 1·4

sets in the world.[12]   They own almost three-fifths of all
the automobiles in the world.[13]   And it has been estimated that America accounts for about 40 percent of the
net output of all goods and services in the world.[14]   (Chart
1·5)

During the past 100 years we have developed more and
more machines and found an increasing number of ways
to have them help us.   During this period income has
risen along with the increased horsepower-hours per man
hour worked.[15]   (Chart 1·6)   There has been a high degree of correlation over the past 30 years: As kilowatt-
hours per capita have gone up, per capita personal income
in constant dollars has continued to rise.[16]   (Chart 1·7)
That is, use of energy (including electric energy) is

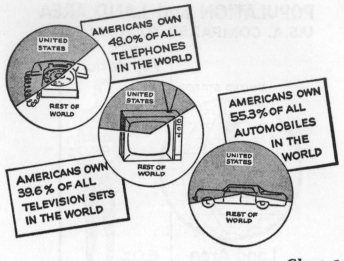

Americans own 48.0% of all telephones in the world

Americans own 55.3% of all automobiles in the world

Americans own 39.6% of all television sets in the world

Chart 1·5

Chart 1·6

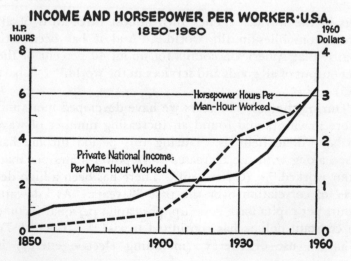

INCOME AND HORSEPOWER PER WORKER·U.S.A.
1850–1960

H.P.
HOURS

1960
Dollars

Horsepower Hours Per Man-Hour Worked

Private National Income Per Man-Hour Worked

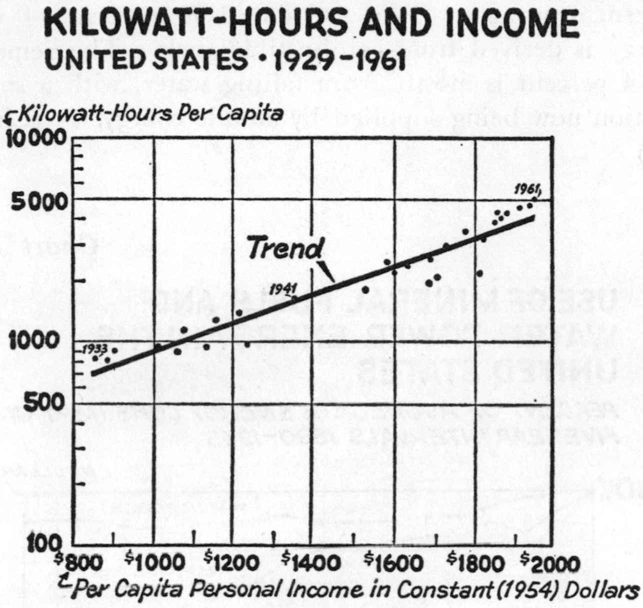
KILOWATT-HOURS AND INCOME
UNITED STATES • 1929–1961
Kilowatt-Hours Per Capita
10000
5000
1000
500
100
Trend
1933
1941
1961
$800
$1000
$1200
$1400
$1600
$1800
$2000
Per Capita Personal Income in Constant (1954) Dollars

Chart 1·7

closely connected with increased use of machines, advancing technology, and the national income.

Development of electric energy

In the United States our main sources of raw energy are coal, oil, gas, and falling water. Nuclear materials also provide a notable fraction, which promises to grow in the future. The energy drawn from these sources can be used in two ways: in its raw state or converted to electricity.

We use a great deal of raw energy in this country—more than any other nation. We use it to drive cars and fly planes, to heat homes and offices, and in hundreds of other ways. Of the total energy we use, about 23 percent is drawn from coal, about 40 percent from oil, about 33 percent from gas. That is, about 96 percent of our energy is derived from combustible fuels. The remaining 4 percent is mostly from falling water, with a small fraction now being supplied by atomic energy.[17]   (Chart 1·8)

Chart 1·8

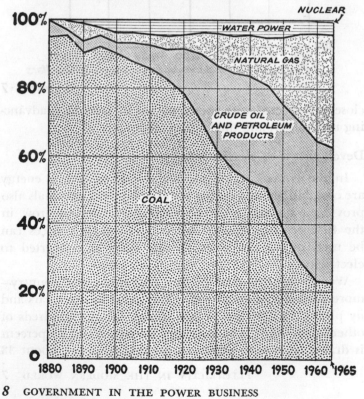

USE OF MINERAL FUELS AND WATER POWER ENERGY IN THE UNITED STATES
PERCENT OF AGGREGATE ENERGY CONSUMPTION FIVE YEAR INTERVALS 1880-1965

The use of energy is not stable. It presents a changeable picture. It is estimated that over three-fourths of the fuels used in this country are directed to industry, transportation, and electric generation. Households, commercial establishments, government, agriculture, and miscellaneous purposes take the rest.[18] However, except in certain instances where present technology is designed around liquid fuels or processes that require controlled chemical atmospheres and careful control of heat, each form of energy is competitive with the others. The manner and extent of their use depends upon economics and consumer preference.

In the metallurgical fields, coal is now the dominating fuel.[19] In transportation, oil is the principal supplier of energy.[20] Oil and gas have largely displaced coal in the heating market. With the extension of gas pipelines to more sections of the country, gas is limiting the growth of oil for heating; but with the continued improvement in the efficiency of converting raw fuel to electric energy, electricity is beginning to be used to a marked degree for space heating.

Over 50 percent of the total use of coal in this country is devoted to generation of electricity.[21] While coal has been losing the heating market to oil and gas, the industry now sees that as electric heating gains popularity coal will be in the heating business again—although one step removed from the consumer.

Presently over 20 percent of all the raw energy used in this country is used to make electricity.[22] But use of electric energy has been growing at about $2\frac{1}{2}$ times the annual rate of total energy use.[23] (Chart 1·9) By 1980, we expect that the generation of electricity will consume some 30 percent of the energy we use and by the year 2000 it may be in the range of 40 to 50 percent.[24] (Chart 1·10)

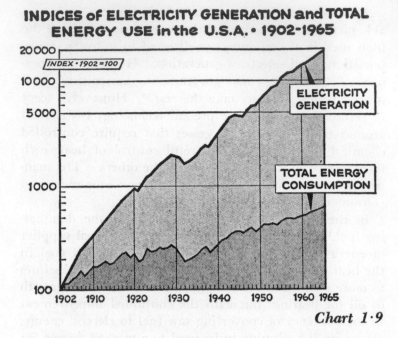

INDICES of ELECTRICITY GENERATION and TOTAL ENERGY USE in the U.S.A. • 1902-1965

INDEX • 1902 = 100

ELECTRICITY GENERATION

TOTAL ENERGY CONSUMPTION

Chart 1·9

Chart 1·10

FORECAST OF CONVERSION OF PRIMARY ENERGY TO
ELECTRICAL ENERGY
IN THE UNITED STATES · 1930-2000

PERCENT OF TOTAL ENERGY

There are a number of factors behind this trend. To begin with, electric energy has certain qualities which make it popular:

It is convenient. If you want it, all you need do is flip a switch or push in a plug.

It is flexible. It can run a motor, produce light, or provide heat. In a space capsule it can operate a tele-metering system no bigger than a dime, and in a steel mill it can operate a huge furnace at thousands of horse-power. It can serve people in hundreds of thousands of ways.

It is reliable. It is clean. It is efficient. It is quiet. And it is low in price.

Electric energy can be produced in small quantities or large. One of the first discoveries the pioneers of the electric industry made was that producing power in a large central station and then distributing it to a number of customers was more economical than having each cus-tomer provided with his own energy source. They found that customers used energy for different purposes and at different times and that this diversity in demand made it possible to operate power-producing machinery more eco-nomically by keeping the demand relatively steady. Then, through research, they were able to develop bigger gener-ating units, using higher temperatures and pressures, which could convert fuels into electricity more and more effi-ciently, and transmission systems that could move large blocks of power more and more effectively.

This has been the continuing pattern of evolution in the electric utility industry. The first power plants were relatively small and were built to serve individual com-munities. In some respects these isolated plants were similar to what is termed *on-site* generation today. As technology advanced, it became possible to construct transmission lines to interconnect the plants. Groups of plants were joined into small systems (Chart 1·11). Then, step by step, larger systems were formed and power companies began interconnecting their transmission lines one with the other, increasing reliability of service, and bringing the price of service down (Chart 1·12).

In this way a complex network of transmission lines has been formed that has spread across the country (Chart 1·13).

The energy industry

Together, electricity, coal, oil, natural gas, falling water, and nuclear fuels form the substance of what may be called the *energy industry*—the industry that provides the power to make an economy grow. This industry is particularly marked by its high capital requirements, and

Chart 1·11

High-Voltage TRANSMISSION LINES
60,000 VOLTS AND OVER

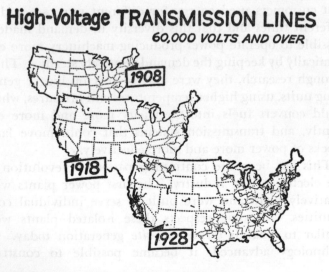

High-Voltage TRANSMISSION LINES

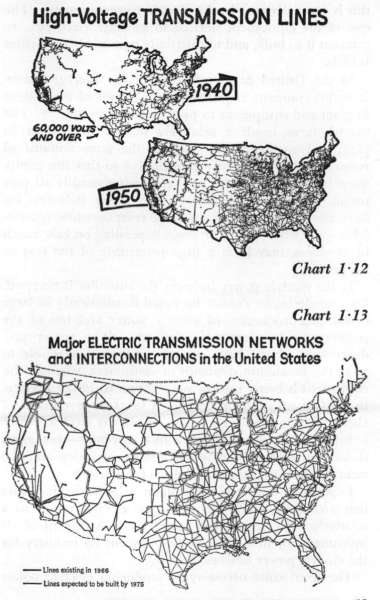

1940

60,000 VOLTS
AND OVER

1950

Chart 1·12

Chart 1·13

Major ELECTRIC TRANSMISSION NETWORKS and INTERCONNECTIONS in the United States

—— Lines existing in 1966
—— Lines expected to be built by 1975

ELECTRICITY IN THE MODERN WORLD   **13**

this is especially true in the electric power segment. The cost of the equipment needed to generate electricity, to transmit it in bulk, and to distribute it in usable quantities is high.

In the United States of America the average manufacturing company requires about 53 cents of investment in plant and equipment to produce $1 of revenue.[25] The manufacturer needs a relatively smaller investment in plant and equipment to produce the same amount of revenue and is frequently able to plan so that the equipment is used at a regular rate, producing steadily all year round. In relation to the electric power industry, his fixed costs are lower per dollar of revenue while his variable costs, which go up or down depending on how much he produces, may form a high percentage of the cost of his product.

In the electric power industry the situation is reversed. Because electricity cannot be stored economically in large quantities, production of electric power and use of the power must be almost simultaneous. The power producer must always have enough equipment available to meet the maximum demands of consumers, whether the equipment is being used or not. As noted in the Preface, in the United States of America it takes an investment of about $4.45 in plant and equipment in the electric power industry to produce $1 of annual revenue—over eight times that needed by manufacturing companies—and the ratio is at least the same throughout the world.[26]

Experience in the United States of America indicates that a country which has developed electric power to a relatively high degree may spend about 8 percent of all investment for new plant and equipment by industry for the electric power business.[27]

The fixed costs necessary to producing electric power

are higher than the variable costs and must be paid even during times when there is little demand for electricity. Because of this, the total costs of providing electric service may be relatively high although the incremental cost of providing additional service with the same equipment may be relatively small. Well before the turn of the century, the pioneers in the business of producing electric power had learned that as the volume of sales increases within the limits of an existing plant, the cost of each kilowatt-hour decreases. As the cost per kilowatt-hour goes down, electric energy becomes more competitive with other energy forms and use of electricity goes up.

The problem, of course, lies in the need for high capital investment. Before a nation can have electricity in sufficient quantities to mechanize its industry and its agriculture, it must have the means available for amassing large aggregates of capital. Even 80 years ago, when the power industry was in its infancy, when demand for electricity was small and generating plants were relatively inexpensive, the financial resources of individual persons were not sufficient for this purpose. Those men who tried to finance power systems on their own soon found themselves unwilling or unable to continue investing funds in costly equipment that tied up their capital for years.

The question of how to provide capital for expensive plant and equipment is faced to some degree by almost every industrial and commercial operation. It is of great importance in the power industry. In general, two answers have been found. One has been to provide the needed capital through a company in which investors may put as much or as little money as they choose. The alternative method has been to make use of the government or its agencies as the means for gathering the funds and for directing them into power facilities.

There have been variations to both approaches. Companies have been privately held, so that shares were not available to the public, or—and this is the general practice today—they may have had shares available for purchase by anyone who wished to buy them. A company may be chartered in such a way that the government is the sole shareowner, or it may have a combination of government ownership and investor ownership. Likewise, governmental financing may be through a specially organized corporation, it may be accomplished at the national level or at the local level, or it may make use of special districts or other units specifically organized to provide electric service.

It is also possible for industrial manufacturing organizations not primarily interested in producing electric power to become involved in generating or transmitting electricity and to offer it for sale at times when they have an oversupply. Large consumers of energy in areas where adequate utility service is not available might fall in this category, for example. In some cases these organizations are able to add considerable quantities of power to the public supply. Obviously they also require substantial amounts of capital.

The effect these alternative approaches to financing power facilities have in the equation of economic growth has been subject to considerable debate. Unfortunately, the lack of data has meant that the arguments have often been based on emotional rather than empirical grounds. The reason is clear. Economic growth takes time, and the power industry is relatively young. There was no body of experience on which to base judgments as to whether the use of voluntary investment or of government to finance power facilities was more in the public interest.

Enough evidence is now available, however, so that it is becoming possible to approach the problem more rationally.

The world picture

In 1964, electric energy production in the world reached 3.0 trillion kilowatt-hours.[28] Eighty-five percent of this energy, and about 83 percent of the world's installed

Table 1·1 Installed Generating Capacity,
Fifteen Highest Countries*

Country (by rank)	Installed capacity† (thousand kilowatts)
United States	240,471
U.S.S.R.	103,100
United Kingdom	45,899
Japan‡	38,051
Germany (West)	36,067
Canada	27,099
France	26,546
Italy	23,715
China (Mainland)	12,900
Sweden	11,515
Germany (East)	9,814
Spain	9,726
Poland	9,305
Norway	9,165
India‡	8,993
Subtotal (15 countries)	612,366
Other countries	121,644
Total for world	734,010

* Based on 1964 installed capacity.
† Year end except as noted.
‡ Year beginning April 1.
SOURCE: *World Power Data*, FPC, 1964, p. 5.

generating capacity, was provided by fifteen nations making up over 60 percent of the world's population. Four of these nations—the U.S.S.R., East Germany, Poland, and China (Mainland)—are Communist nations. Of the fifteen largest nations in electric generating capacity, only Japan, China, and India are not in either Europe or North America. No African nation is in this group.[29] (Table 1·1)

In 1964, Norway led the world in kilowatt-hour production per capita, followed by Canada, Luxembourg, Sweden, and the United States of America (Table 1·2).

Table 1·2 Countries Ranked by Kilowatt-hour
Production per Capita, 1964

Country	Kilowatt-hours per capita
Norway	11,896
Canada	6,969
Luxembourg	6,756
Sweden	5,836
United States*	5,641
Switzerland	3,852
New Zealand	3,702
Iceland	3,566
United Kingdom	3,170
Germany (East)	2,851

* Includes Alaska and Hawaii.
SOURCE: *World Power Data,* FPC, 1964, p. 4.

In terms of total production, the United States of America held the leading position, generating more than the next five nations combined. The power-producing capacity of this country was almost $2\frac{1}{2}$ times that of the Soviet Union, the second ranking nation.[30]

Of the nations outside the Soviet bloc, ownership of electric power facilities is divided so that about 60 percent of the installed generating capacity is provided by investor-owned utilities and industrial concerns and about 40 percent by government or governmental agencies (Chart 1·14). Within the Soviet bloc, ownership of power facilities is almost entirely in governmental hands. A few industries in Eastern European nations generate their own electricity, providing the exceptions to the rule.[31]

Among the nations outside the Soviet bloc, the approaches, or combinations of approaches, used in supplying power vary greatly. For example, in France, where electric energy is transmitted, distributed, and sold to ultimate customers by Electricité de France, a government agency, about 25 percent of the nation's generating

Chart 1·14

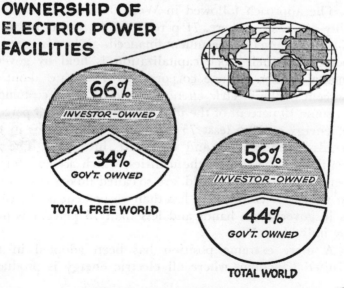

OWNERSHIP OF
ELECTRIC POWER
FACILITIES

66%
INVESTOR-OWNED

34%
GOV'T. OWNED

TOTAL FREE WORLD

56%
INVESTOR-OWNED

44%
GOV'T. OWNED

TOTAL WORLD

capacity is owned and operated by coal, oil, and other industries, which sell power in excess of their own needs to Electricité de France for distribution.[32] In Japan, on the other hand, where about 11 percent of the total electric generating capacity is provided by nonutility organizations, the law strictly prohibits them from contributing any of their output to the public supply.[33]

Methods of financing utility organizations are just as varied. In Japan, nine investor-owned companies supply nearly all the power offered for sale in the country. These companies own and operate their own generating plants, transmission facilities, and distribution systems. But a portion of the power produced in Japan is generated by a special corporation, the Electric Power Development Company, established for the principal purpose of developing large hydropower resources from which bulk power is sold to the nine companies. The majority of its invested capital is owned by the Japanese government.[34]

The approach followed in West Germany is considerably different. There, 71 percent of the utility organizations are largely government-financed. That is, over 95 percent of their stock capitalization is held by governmental bodies. These corporations distribute about 48 percent of the electric energy sold to ultimate customers. In some 19 percent of the utilities, selling about 3 percent of energy sold, at least 75 percent of the stock is in the hands of individual and corporate investors. The remaining 10 percent of the utilities, which account for 49 percent of the energy sold, are so-called mixed enterprises in which for each utility less than 95 percent of the stock is in government hands and less than 75 percent is held by individuals.[35]

A more extreme position has been adopted in the United Kingdom, where all electric energy is produced and transmitted by the Central Electricity Generating Board and two Scottish and one Northern Ireland electricity boards. Distribution to ultimate customers (except to railways) is carried out by area electricity boards—all under control of the national Power Ministry.[36]

The electric power industry in the U.S.

In the United States there are two basic methods of financing electric power supply systems. They can be business enterprises, operating under government regulation with capital obtained through the free market, or they can be government enterprises, operating without regulation and with capital obtained either through the imposition of taxes on citizens or through long-term bond financing in the free market. In both instances, of course, the capital needed to provide the power systems is obtained from individual citizens or from groups of citizens. The difference, from the individual's point of view, is that under the free-market system he may provide the capital voluntarily through investment of his savings in a company while under the other system he may have to provide the capital involuntarily, through taxes.

There is an important difference between the service provided by an investor-owned electric company and most government-financed agencies. An investor-owned company must serve anyone in its territory. It has what is known as *utility responsibility*. For the most part, government-financed agencies do not have utility responsibility since much of the electricity government produces is generated as an incidental by-product of some other function.

Traditionally, the United States depends on individuals rather than on government to operate business enterprises. When Thomas Edison began work on his electric light and power system, the system which resulted in the opening of a 720-kilowatt steam generating station in New York City in 1882, members of the New York financial community provided backing.[37] And when he began to put his system on the market, it was largely individuals rather than governmental bodies that responded. In 1966, some 77 percent of the installed generating capacity in the country was owned by investor-owned companies operating under governmental regulation and by industrial concerns which, in some instances, are also subject to government regulation. Of this, 70 percent was owned by utility companies and 7 percent by the industrial concerns. About 23 percent of the installed capacity was owned or financed by various governmental bodies, many of which are not subject to regulation.[38] (Chart 1·15)

Chart 1·15

OWNERSHIP OF ELECTRIC POWER CAPACITY
U.S.A. 1966

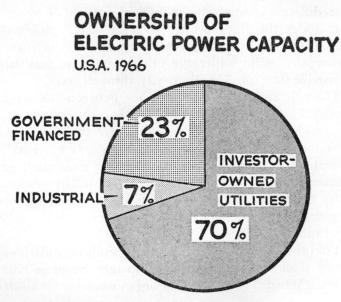

GOVERNMENT FINANCED — 23%

INDUSTRIAL — 7%

INVESTOR-OWNED UTILITIES 70%

Municipalities which own and operate power systems often try to make use of both the voluntary and involuntary methods of financing. Having found that local tax revenues alone cannot provide the large amounts of capital needed to have electric power facilities, these municipalities have gone to the market with revenue bonds. In many cases the method has been successful, and many municipalities now depend largely on revenue bonds to provide the capital they need.

Government or market financing?

In the final analysis, the choice between government financing and market financing may become a purely ideological matter affected by a multitude of noneconomic considerations. The history of power development in the United States of America, however, provides data which should be studied by all who are interested in economic progress.

The evidence indicates that it is possible to depend on free-market financing to build and operate a large and very advanced electric power supply system able to provide electricity reliably and economically to all areas of the nation and to all classes of customers.

Lionel D. Edie & Company has made a study comparing the average price of electricity in the six common-market countries in 1960 with the average price in the United States, which is interesting in this connection (Table 1·3). The study shows that the cost of electricity to the American residential consumer is the lowest of any of the countries.[39] When the fact that the American worker makes from three to five times as much as his European counterpart is considered, the hourly labor costs of electricity in this country are anywhere from a fourth to a sixth the cost to the European worker. Not only does

Table 1·3   Price of Electricity per Kilowatt-hour in U.S. Cents, Residential Customers, 1960

Country	Average
Belgium	4.68
Luxembourg	4.29
Italy*	4.16
France	3.72
Western Germany	3.50
Netherlands	2.90
United States	2.47

* Outside urban centers.
SOURCE: Lionel D. Edie & Co., Inc., *Outlook for Public Utilities,* May 29, 1963.

the American worker pay less for the power in absolute terms, but he earns more—so his real costs are even less.[40]

The electric utility industry is an important and fast-growing segment of any modern economy. Under sound management and government regulation it can provide an excellent location for savings. Investors understand this and are willing to provide the capital needed for continued growth of the industry.

Despite these facts, government financing of electric power facilities exists in this country. In the next two chapters we will examine the ways it has developed over the years.

REFERENCES

1. The National Industrial Conference Board, *The Economic Almanac,* 1964, pp. 507–508.
2. J. Frederick Dewhurst and Associates, *America's Needs and Re-*

sources, *A New Survey*, Twentieth Century Fund, New York, 1955, Appendix 25-3, Table L, pp. 908, 1116.

3. *Ibid.*, p. 910.
4. *Ibid.*, p. 908.
5. Felix Fremont, "Status and Growth of Electrical Energy, Total Energy and National Income . . .," *American Power Conference Proceedings*, Vol. XXVI, 1964, pp. 965, 976–977.
6. U.S. Bureau of the Census, *Statistical Abstract of the United States*, 1966, Table 1287, p. 898.
7. *Ibid.*, pp. 898–899.
8. *Ibid.*, p. 898.
9. FPC, *World Power Data*, 1964, p. 5.
10. EEI, *Questions and Answers about the Electric Utility Industry*, 1966, p. 22.
11. American Telephone and Telegraph Co., *The World's Telephones*, 1966, p. 2.
12. Television Digest, Inc., *Television Factbook*, No. 36, 1966, p. 872b.
13. Automobile Manufacturers Association, Inc., *Automobile Facts and Figures*, 1966, p. 28.
14. W. S. Woytinsky and E. S. Woytinsky, *World Population and Production*, Twentieth Century Fund, New York, 1953, p. 394.
15. Edwin Vennard and R. M. Winsborough, *The American Economic System*, Middle West Service Co., 1964, p. 24.
16. EEI.
17. U.S. Department of the Interior, Bureau of Mines, *Minerals Yearbook*, Vol. II, *Mineral Fuels*, 1964, p. 7.
18. U.S. Department of the Interior News Release, Bureau of Mines, for release 2-2-67, p. 3.
19. EEI, *Energy Resources of the United States*, 1966, p. 5.
20. *Report of the National Fuels and Energy Study Group to the Committee on Interior and Insular Affairs, U. S. Senate*, 87th Cong., 2d Sess., Sept., 1962, p. 20.
21. U.S. Department of the Interior News Release, Bureau of Mines, for release 2-2-67, Tables 3 and 4.
22. EEI, *Energy Resources of the United States*, 1966, p. 4.
23. EEI.
24. Federal Council for Science & Technology, *Research & Development on Natural Resources*, Washington, May, 1963, p. 5; EEI.
25. EEI.
26. *Ibid.*
27. *Ibid.*
28. FPC, *op. cit.*, p. 5.

29. *Ibid.*, p. 5.
30. *Ibid.*, p. 5.
31. Pacific Gas and Electric Co., *World Energy Use—Electric and Gas Utility Statistics,* 1959, pp. 32–33.
32. Charles Hochgesang, "Who 'Owns' Europe's Utilities?" *Electrical World,* vol. 158, pp. 47–50, July 2, 1962.
33. Overseas Electrical Industry Survey Institute, Inc., *Electric Power Industry in Japan,* 1966, pp. 6–7.
34. *Ibid.*, p. 3.
35. Hochgesang, *op. cit.,* p. 49.
36. *Ibid.*, p. 48.
37. Matthew Josephson, *Edison,* McGraw-Hill Book Company, New York, 1959, pp. 185–189.
    Edwin Vennard, *The Electric Power Business,* McGraw-Hill Book Company, New York, 1962, p. 8.
38. EEI.
39. Lionel D. Edie & Co., Inc., *Outlook for Public Utilities,* May 29, 1963, p. 1.
40. *Ibid.*

Chapter 2

The growth of government power

"I do not hold with those who advocate government ownership or government operation of all utilities. I state to you categorically that as a broad general rule the development of utilities should remain, with certain exceptions, a function for private initiative and private capital." [1]

So said Franklin D. Roosevelt, speaking as a presidential candidate in September, 1932. As he spoke, investor-owned electric light and power companies were generating about 94 percent of the electricity produced by the nation's utility industry. Municipal plants and local districts generated slightly less than 6 percent of the total that year, and the Federal government provided less than 1 percent.[2] Eight months later, in May, President Roosevelt signed the Tennessee Valley Authority Act of 1933— an action which gave powerful impetus to the growth of government ownership and operation of utilities throughout the nation.[3]

The causes for this growth are complex and often misunderstood. Their effect, however, is clearly visible: By 1966, government-financed agencies were providing

23.0 percent of the energy produced by the electric utility industry in this country—nearly four times the percentage of 1932.[4]

Government is in the power business in many forms. Municipalities sometimes own and operate power systems and generating plants. In certain parts of the country, particularly in the Pacific Northwest and in Nebraska, special districts have been organized to provide electric service. Elsewhere, state governments have entered the power business through the establishment of their own agencies, such as the New York State Power Authority, the Grand River Dam Authority in Oklahoma, and others. But it is the Federal government which, to an increasing degree, has come to represent government in the power business.

Actually, the Federal government itself acts in the electric utility business in a variety of ways. It owns and operates the Tennessee Valley Authority (TVA), a government corporation which has about 82 percent of its investment in electric power facilities.[5] Through the Department of the Interior's Bureau of Reclamation it constructs and operates power plants in the Western states and through the Defense Department's Corps of Engineers it constructs power projects throughout the country. The Bureau of Indian Affairs and the International Boundary and Water Commission operate hydroelectric dams. The Department of the Interior has created three agencies—the Bonneville Power Administration (BPA), the Southeastern Power Administration (SEPA), and the Southwestern Power Administration (SWPA)—which act as marketing agencies in certain areas for the electric energy produced at Federally owned hydroelectric dams. The Rural Electrification Administration (REA), an agency within the Department of

Agriculture, makes loans to rural electric cooperatives and others at special low interest rates and provides a number of services to its borrowers.

The development of the intricate structure of ownership, operation, financing, and regulation of power facilities which recurs at nearly every level of government is a story of strange gyrations growing out of a continuing misunderstanding by many Americans that any difference in price between government power and investor-owned power can be traced to the fact that government power projects do not pay an interest rate commensurate with the real (or market) value of capital or their full share of taxes. Survey after survey has revealed the lack of knowledge of the public concerning this aspect of government power. There is even less understanding of the differences between free-market financing and government financing, with its accompanying inequities in tax payments and cost of capital. And survey after survey has shown that when the public understands these complicated issues, it prefers investor ownership of electric power facilities.

Municipal ownership

The story began soon after the electric power industry was born. In the early years, during the 1880s and 1890s, when technological knowledge was limited, generating plants were small and the energy they produced could be transmitted for only relatively short distances. The plants were relatively expensive to build and the power lines were costly too. Enterprises organized to provide electric power tended to be in the more heavily populated centers—the towns and cities. In many cases financing of these pioneer power systems was accomplished through the free market, but in others it was done by municipalities eager for street lighting or wishing to use the new energy form in other ways. During the first 20 years of this century, hundreds of municipalities appropriated tax funds or issued bonds to provide capital to build generating or distribution equipment and to operate small power systems. By 1923, when municipal ownership reached its peak, there were 3,084 electric systems owned or operated by cities, towns and villages.[6]

Table 2·1 Municipal Electric Systems in the U.S.
(Electric Systems Owned and/or Operated by
Municipalities and Serving Ultimate Customers)

Period	Total number in existence	Period	Total number in existence
1882	4	1904	1,038
1883	8	1905	1,103
1884	10	1906	1,177
1885	16	1907	1,267
1886	25	1908	1,351
1887	36	1909	1,414
1888	52	1910	1,534
1889	82	1911	1,622
1890	107	1912	1,734
1891	138	1913	1,834
1892	190	1914	1,983
1893	221	1915	2,155
1894	276	1916	2,277
1895	355	1917	2,408
1896	413	1918	2,506
1897	459	1919	2,589
1898	567	1920	2,750
1899	623	1921	2,852
1900	728	1922	3,033
1901	783	1923	3,084
1902	847	1924	3,047
1903	932	1925	2,922

Table 2·1 continued

Period	Total number in existence	Period	Total number in existence
1926	2,655	1946	2,072
1927	2,367	1947	2,049
1928	2,191	1948	2,038
1929	2,026	1949	2,038
1930	1,928	1950	2,040
1931	1,874	1951	2,033
1932	1,863	1952	2,029
1933	1,878	1953	2,024
1934	1,890	1954	2,019
1935	1,906	1955	2,014
1936	1,913	1956	2,005
1937	1,921	1957	2,000
1938	1,942	1958	1,996
1939	1,999	1959	1,990
1940	2,019	1960	1,987
1941	2,052	1961	1,980
1942	2,078	1962	1,972
1943	2,078	1963	1,967
1944	2,079	1964	1,963 P
1945	2,086	1965	1,959 P

P: Preliminary.
SOURCE: EEI.

At the turn of the century regulation of the young electric utilities, as we now know it, was just beginning to take form. As a consequence, some communities found themselves with many small power producers competing with each other for limited business. As people came to realize that the very high investment cost required to produce a dollar of annual revenue in the electric utility business makes it desirable to have a single supplier providing power in an area, the sole supplier principle gained favor and government regulation was developed to give customers and investors necessary protection.

At the same time, technological developments were making it possible for power plants to be enlarged and linked into more efficient systems. Isolated municipal plants, severely limited in the areas they could serve, had difficulty keeping up with the advances. Even with the subsidies provided them in taxes and cost of money, they could not compete. Many municipalities decided that their citizens would be better served by the larger, more economical investor-owned systems and withdrew from the power business completely. Others decided to stay in the power business but to purchase power from neighboring investor-owned systems, thus participating in the economies becoming available through interconnection and pooling. By 1965, only 1,959 of the municipal systems remained, serving about 12 percent of the nation's electric ultimate customers (Chart 2·1). Of these, about 1,270 were purchasing all and about 300 were purchasing a portion of their energy requirements from interconnected systems. The trend is away from municipal ownership.[7] Of course, the basic reason for this trend has been the development of the large coordinated power systems, which are able to supply energy more economically than a small, independent municipal utility. It is the same reason the trend is away from isolated generating plants for industry, as was discussed in Chapter 1.

Economics and technology have not been the only factors affecting the development of the electric utility business in this country. The activities of a small number of men and women who have been committed to the idea of government control of utilities and other portions of the national economy have also had an effect. The evolution of municipal ownership became a matter of concern to this

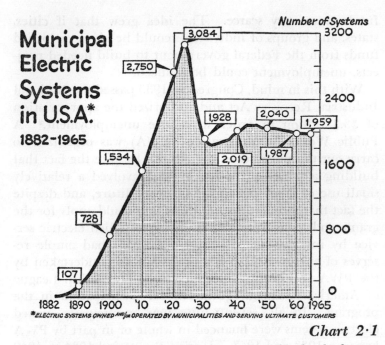

Municipal Electric Systems in U.S.A.*

1882-1965

Number of Systems

3,084

2,750

1,928   2,040   1,959

1,534   2,019   1,987

728

107

1882 1890 1900 '10 '20 '30 40 '50 '60 1965

3200

2400

1600

800

0

*ELECTRIC SYSTEMS OWNED AND/OR OPERATED BY MUNICIPALITIES AND SERVING ULTIMATE CUSTOMERS

Chart 2·1

group. One of their number, H. S. Raushenbush, for example, writing in *The New Leader* in 1927 as part of a Socialist symposium, reported: "We have set up municipal plants. Their status is changing and we should face that fact. Outside the large cities they can no longer compete in rates and efficiency with the new plants being established by companies having the benefit of the connected load of wide interconnection." [8]

The PWA. During the 1930s, well after it had become fully evident that municipal ownership was not the most effective form of power supply in most areas, an agency of the Federal government was created that began actively to promote municipal ownership of power facilities as a matter of policy. It happened this way.

In the long economic depression of the 1930s investible

funds were very scarce. The idea grew that if cities, states, and groups of individuals could be given or loaned funds from the Federal government to build needed projects, unemployment could be reduced.

With this in mind, Congress in 1933 passed the National Industrial Recovery Act and authorized the appropriation of $3.3 billion in order to relieve unemployment.[9] A Public Works Administration (PWA) was organized to carry out the purposes of the Act.[10] Despite the fact that building a power plant has always involved a relatively small use of labor per dollar of expenditure, and despite the fact that most cities and towns that could apply for the grants and loans were already being supplied electric service by investor-owned companies which had ample reserves of energy available, a campaign was undertaken by the PWA and groups like the Public Ownership League of America to encourage municipal participation in the program. In all, seventy-nine new municipally owned electric systems were financed in whole or in part by PWA between 1933 and 1943. During the period 1934 to 1940 some 209 existing municipal electric systems received money for additions and improvements in their facilities. Some twenty-seven large state, county, and district projects also were advanced sums by Federal agencies. In many instances, particularly those involving additions or improvements to existing systems, no loans were made: the Federal money was advanced as a grant or outright gift. Often, the grant or gift component of the allocations was as high as 45 percent, with the remaining 55 percent loaned at interest rates as low as 3 percent per year.[11]

One of the criteria established for receiving a loan or grant from the PWA was that each project was to be economically feasible and each loan self-liquidating. Obviously, when 45 percent of the system's capital was an outright gift and the remainder was loaned at very low interest rates, and when the project was excused from paying Federal income taxes, it became relatively easy to give the appearance of economic feasibility. Moreover, no consideration was given to the fact that when a municipality which had been purchasing power from a tax-paying power company began to generate its own power supply, the power company's income would be reduced and the tax income of government would go down accordingly. On this subsidized basis, many of the municipal systems were able to justify investing in small and relatively inefficient diesel engines to produce electricity.

As the PWA program progressed, the administrators began to follow a practice of informing an investor-owned company of a pending application for a grant or loan by one of its municipal customers and giving the company an opportunity to reduce its rates to the same level as those calculated for the proposed subsidized facility. The idea seemed to be that if a company managed to reduce its rates to these below-cost levels, the loan and grant would not be approved. Apparently, little consideration was given to the fact that Congress had not appropriated funds so that PWA could regulate the rates of local utility companies— which were already being regulated by other government bodies. The natural result of these policies, of course, along with the promotional efforts of the manufacturers of diesel engines, was a temporary increase in the number of municipal power systems.

An active advocate. For many years one of the most ardent and active advocates of municipal ownership of power facilities, as well as of government ownership of all key industries, was Carl D. Thompson. He is recorded as a member of the Socialist party in 1901. He became a member of the party's National Committee in 1905, serving as director of information from 1912 to 1916. He was campaign manager for the party in the national election of 1916. In 1914, while still director of information for the party, he formed the Public Ownership League of America.[12] He acted as secretary, or director, of the league until 1949.

The Public Ownership League was one of several organizations interested in government ownership of utilities which carried on active publicity campaigns during the 1920s. Another, the League for Industrial Democracy, provided lectures and literature, and set up special conferences in schools and colleges. Harry Laidler, Norman Thomas, Paul Blanshard, and Thompson were all active in this group.[13] The National Popular Government League, with Judson King as its executive director and guiding spirit,[14] and the People's Legislative Service, which operated in Washington with a legislative division, a statistical division, and a publicity division, were among the others.[15] Senator George Norris of Nebraska was active in several of the organizations, as were a number of other senators and congressmen.

In a typical year, 1922, Thompson was able to report to the 10,000 members of the Public Ownership League that during the previous 12 months he and his staff had conducted successful campaigns for municipal ownership of electric light and power plants in three cities; had given legal or engineering assistance with relation to utility matters to 50 additional cities; had prepared data on government ownership for 300 newspapers in South Dakota covering a 7-week campaign; had devoted 6 weeks to defeating a proposed measure in the Illinois State Constitution; had assisted debating teams in forty-four schools, colleges, and universities; had started a "superpower" movement in Wisconsin and Minnesota; had stimulated the public ownership movement in Oregon and Washington; had supplied the Commission of the City of Boston with information on municipal ownership; worked with the League of Municipalities of New Jersey; sent bulletins on municipal ownership of electric power plants to all members of the Oklahoma Legislature; prepared bulletins sent to 1,000 selected persons in North Carolina; took part in campaigns in California; published five new government ownership bulletins; and distributed the monthly magazine *Public Ownership*. Thompson himself gave more than 200 lectures on various phases of government ownership that year.[16]

The league also made a start at forming an investment company in order to help municipalities finance bonds for municipally owned plants. Although this project apparently never achieved the success desired, Thompson, in a history of the league, recalled that the league had helped one state "by selling a million dollars of its public project bonds." [17]

In 1923 the Public Ownership League held a convention in Toronto, Canada, and launched a movement to promote a government power system for the entire United States and Canada.[18] Activities began immediately. In March, 1924, a superpower bill was introduced into the Senate by Senator Norris and a committee was formed to aid in promoting the bill in both houses of Congress.[19] The following year Thompson published a book containing a map showing the outlines of the plan: interconnection of all existing municipally owned power plants with hydroelectric projects owned and operated by the Federal government, the Muscle Shoals projects on the Tennessee River, and projected steam and hydroelectric plants that could be built by the government.[20] It was a grandiose scheme, and he publicized it unremittingly (Chart 2·2).

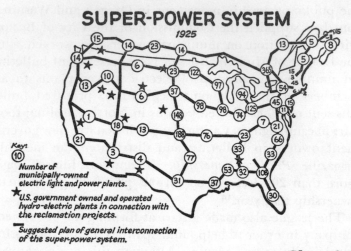

SUPER-POWER SYSTEM
1925

Key:
⑩ Number of municipally-owned electric light and power plants.

★ U.S. government owned and operated hydro-electric plants in connection with the reclamation projects.

— Suggested plan of general interconnection of the super-power system.

Chart 2·2

In 1933 Thompson reported to the members of the league that "a veritable revolution" was under way in Washington. To find out what was going on he went to visit members of the Senate and the House who were members of the Public Ownership League and, finally, the President.

We did not find it so difficult to make an appointment with and meet President Roosevelt . . .

. . . I began by way of introduction to say that I was Secretary of the Public Ownership League of America, etc., but the President interrupted in his jovial manner, saying, "I know all about it. You are doing a wonderful work. Someday I want to sit down and have a long talk with you . . ."

"Tell me," said the President, "how many municipal light and power plants are we gaining per year?"

"That," we said, "is rather difficult to determine. The power companies take some away from us—we take some away from them."

"Are we making a net gain?" the President put in.

"Oh yes, quite certainly."

"Good," he said, in his usual vigorous and emphatic manner.[21]

Two years later, in 1935, Secretary of the Interior, Harold L. Ickes, administrator of the PWA, set up a special three-man review board to speed up loans and grants of Federal funds to municipalities for light and power plants. The PWA was finding that many of the projects proposed by cities could not be described as economically feasible on any basis engineers in the Department of the Interior could approve. The special board was established to look over these applications and get them approved. Carl Thompson was one of the three men appointed to this task.[22]

By 1937, the Public Ownership League was able to look back and announce:

Step by step this plan which the Public Ownership League presented and published 15 years ago is being surely and steadily realized . . .

The Tennessee Valley has become an outstanding reality and its achievements steadily mounting. Boulder Dam has been finished and its power is flashing over the transmission lines to Los Angeles and the southwest. The Bonneville power system on the lower Columbia River is nearing completion and the Grand Coulee which will be the greatest power project ever undertaken in the history of the world is under construction and well on the way.

. . . One can see at a glance the extent to which our dream of 1922–25 has already taken form . . .[23]

In 1938 Thompson was employed by the Bonneville Power Administration, the U.S. Department of the Interior's power-marketing agency in the Northwest. His job was to encourage people in the cities, towns, and rural areas of Washington, Idaho, and Montana to organize, form utility and power districts, and otherwise prepare to take advantage of Federal power projects. In 1940, the Bonneville administrator still found him an effective advocate. "Well, regardless of his socialistic beliefs, he is a grand old man, and the farmers love him," he said. "He goes out to these meetings and they come to these meetings by droves to hear him talk." [24] It also was pointed out in congressional hearings that he was writing to people in Idaho on the letterhead of the Public Ownership League and signing himself as secretary of the league, urging government ownership of power facilities in Idaho while still on the Bonneville payroll.[25]

Economics of municipal ownership. The people of a municipality have a right to decide whether they will have municipal ownership of their electric utilities or whether their electricity should be provided by an enterprise financed in the free market. Before making their choice they should know the facts about each method.

As previously pointed out, the large investment required to produce each dollar of annual revenue in the power business means that the cost of money and taxes forms the largest element of the cost of furnishing electric service. On a project financed in the free market about half the revenue dollar goes for cost of money and taxes. Most municipal power systems depend largely on borrowing to raise the money they need for new equipment. Much of this borrowing is done in the form of revenue bonds, bonds that must be repaid from operating revenue of the electric system rather than from the general tax revenues. In some instances, general obligation bonds have also been issued to help finance power facilities. Investors find these municipal bonds attractive because they are not required to pay personal income taxes on the income they provide. Interest paid on bonds issued by investor-owned companies is generally subject to personal income taxes. As a result of this discrimination, municipal bonds enter the market with a lower interest rate than do the bonds of investor-owned companies. Furthermore, the municipal plants themselves are not required to pay

Federal taxes on the income they receive for the sale of electricity. These discriminations in the tax law result in a shifting of the burden of the cost of government from one taxpayer to another. When municipal plants are able to set electric rates lower than those of investor-owned companies, it does not mean that the municipalities are any more efficient or that they have found ways to provide power any more economically. All it means is that they are not including the true cost of money or their fair share of taxes. Their apparently lower costs are being obtained at the expense of the nation's taxpayers.

Periodically the Federal Power Commission issues a statistical report showing the cost of residential, commercial, and industrial electric service for consumers in communities of various sizes. The report indicates whether the community is served by an investor-owned company or by a government-financed project.[26] On the basis of these statistics it can be shown that some government-financed projects have lower prices than do some investor-owned companies. Some people then draw the erroneous conclusion that the government plants are more efficient and act more in the public interest than investor-owned companies. To avoid giving this misleading impression, the commission might add a footnote to these comparisons pointing out the subsidies in cost of money and taxes reflected in the prices of the government power suppliers.

Other Federal Power Commission studies make it possible to compare the expenses of investor-owned electric utility companies and government-owned electric utilities item by item. The record shows that there is nothing about government power that makes it more efficient than investor-owned power.

Production expense for the investor-owned companies is lower than that for the government-owned utilities.[27]

Trend in PRODUCTION EXPENSE

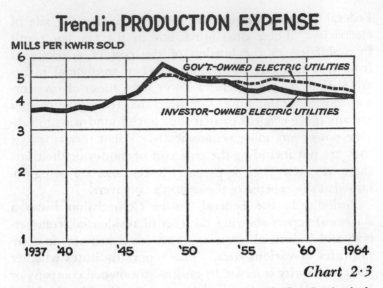

MILLS PER KWHR SOLD

GOV'T.-OWNED ELECTRIC UTILITIES

INVESTOR-OWNED ELECTRIC UTILITIES

1937 '40   '45   '50   '55   '60   1964

Chart 2·3

(Chart 2·3)   By putting the data on an index basis, it is possible to see that the over-all improvement shown by the investor-owned companies in production expense was greater than that of the government-owned utilities.[28] (Chart 2·4)

Distribution expense per customer has been nearly the same for the investor-owned and the government-owned utilities.[29] (Chart 2·5)   However, since 1954 it appears that the investor-owned companies have been able to control this expense slightly better.[30]   (Chart 2·6)

In government-owned utilities customer accounts expenses are often handled with other accounts, with the utility costs charged on an incremental basis.   As a result, this expense appears to be less per customer for the government-owned group.[31]   (Chart 2·7)

In recent years investor-owned utilities seem to have had better control of this expense item.[32]   (Chart 2·8)

As a rule, investor-owned companies are more aggressive

Index of PRODUCTION EXPENSE
Mills Per Kwhr Sold

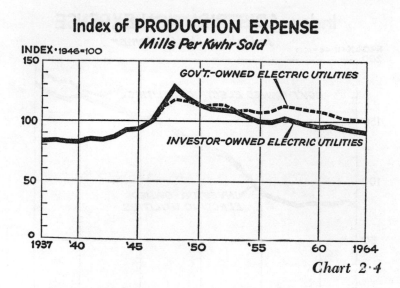

INDEX·1946=100

GOV'T.-OWNED ELECTRIC UTILITIES

INVESTOR-OWNED ELECTRIC UTILITIES

150

100

50

0

1937   '40   '45   '50   '55   60   1964

Chart 2·4

Chart 2·5

Trend in DISTRIBUTION EXPENSE

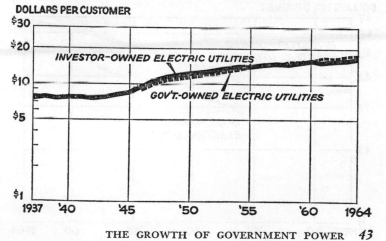

DOLLARS PER CUSTOMER

$30
$20

INVESTOR-OWNED ELECTRIC UTILITIES

$10

GOV'T.-OWNED ELECTRIC UTILITIES

$5

$1

1937   '40   '45   '50   '55   '60   1964

Index of DISTRIBUTION EXPENSE
In Dollars Per Customer

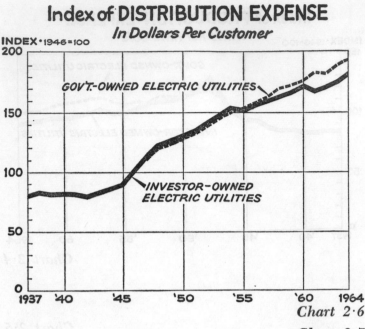

INDEX·1946=100

GOV'T.-OWNED ELECTRIC UTILITIES

INVESTOR-OWNED
ELECTRIC UTILITIES

Chart 2·6

Chart 2·7

Trend in CUSTOMER ACCOUNTS EXPENSES

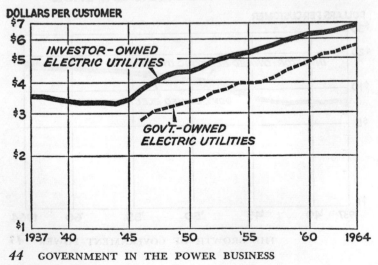

DOLLARS PER CUSTOMER

INVESTOR-OWNED
ELECTRIC UTILITIES

GOV'T.-OWNED
ELECTRIC UTILITIES

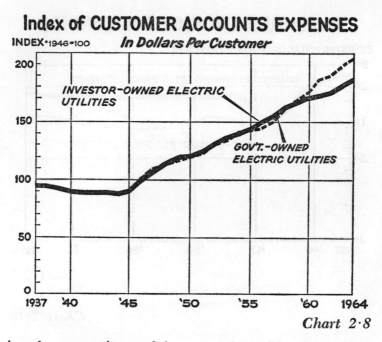

Index of CUSTOMER ACCOUNTS EXPENSES

INDEX·1946=100   *In Dollars Per Customer*

INVESTOR-OWNED ELECTRIC UTILITIES

GOV'T.-OWNED ELECTRIC UTILITIES

Chart 2·8

in sales promotion and in competing with other energy forms than are government power agencies, so their expense for this activity is higher.[33] (Chart 2·9) Between 1954 and 1964 the companies' sales expense per dollar of operating revenue increased about 8 percent—contributing to a near doubling of kilowatt-hour use per residential customer.[34] (Chart 2·10)

There has been no great difference between the investor-owned companies and government-owned utilities in administrative and general expense.[35] (Chart 2·11) Both seem to have good control of this item.[36] (Chart 2·12)

The ratio of operating expense before depreciation and taxes to gross revenues is a generally accepted measure of efficiency in the electric power business. On this basis, investor-owned companies have been doing a better over-all

Trend in SALES PROMOTION EXPENSE

CENTS PER DOLLAR OF OPERATING REVENUE

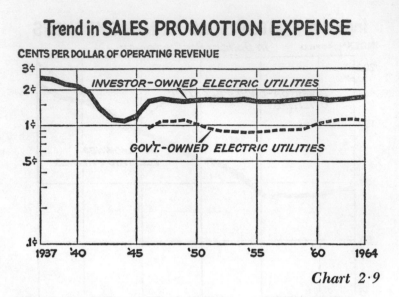

Chart 2·9

Chart 2·10

Index of SALES PROMOTION EXPENSE
In Cents Per Dollar of Operating Revenue

INDEX· 1946=100

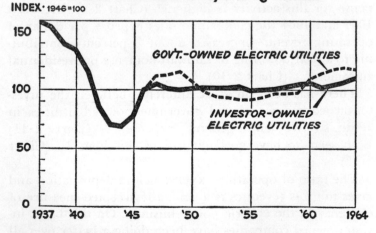

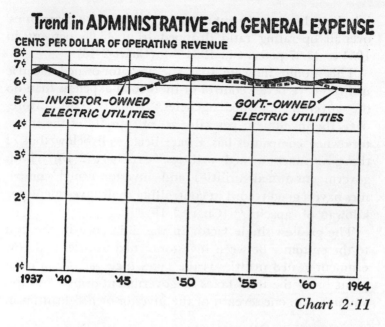

Trend in ADMINISTRATIVE and GENERAL EXPENSE

CENTS PER DOLLAR OF OPERATING REVENUE

INVESTOR-OWNED ELECTRIC UTILITIES

GOVT.-OWNED ELECTRIC UTILITIES

Chart 2·11

Chart 2·12

Index of ADMINISTRATIVE and GENERAL EXPENSE
In Cents Per Dollar of Operating Revenue

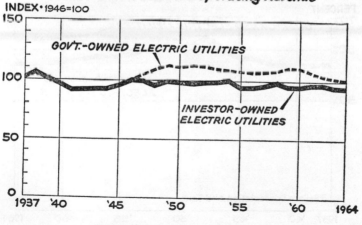

INDEX · 1946=100

GOVT.-OWNED ELECTRIC UTILITIES

INVESTOR-OWNED ELECTRIC UTILITIES

job than the government-owned agencies. The companies' over-all operating ratio dropped from 48.05 percent in 1954 to 43.97 percent in 1964.[37] (Chart 2·13)

This would indicate that the investor-owned electric utilities have better control of their total expenses than do the government-owned agencies.[38] (Chart 2·14) Moreover, the investment per kilowatt of capacity of the investor-owned companies has always been well below that of the government-owned utilities.[39] (Chart 2·15) Both government-owned utilities and investor-owned companies have a good record in controlling their investment per kilowatt of capacity.[40] (Chart 2·16)

The greatest single factor in the difference in the cost to the customer between investor-owned utilities and government-owned utilities is the taxes they pay. On a gross plant basis, the total taxes of government-owned utilities amounted to one-seventh of the investor-owned utilities in

Chart 2·13

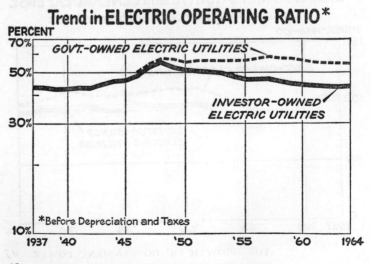

Trend in ELECTRIC OPERATING RATIO*

PERCENT

GOVT.-OWNED ELECTRIC UTILITIES

INVESTOR-OWNED ELECTRIC UTILITIES

*Before Depreciation and Taxes

1937 '40   '45   '50   '55   '60   1964

Index of ELECTRIC OPERATING RATIO*

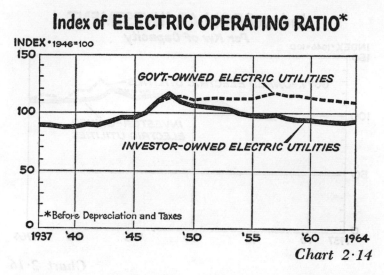

INDEX · 1946=100

Chart 2·14

1964.[41] (Chart 2·17) This represents a substantial loss of revenue to local, state, and Federal governments—a loss that must be made up through taxes of other kinds.

Chart 2·15

Trend in DOLLAR INVESTMENT PER KW OF CAPACITY

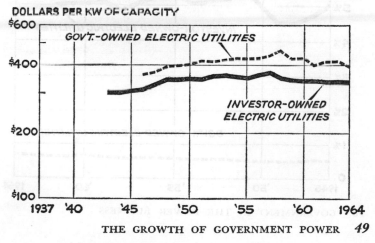

DOLLARS PER KW OF CAPACITY

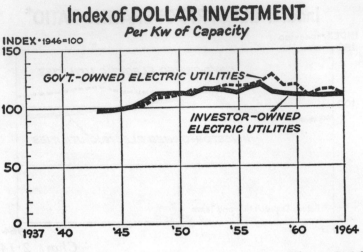

Index of DOLLAR INVESTMENT
Per Kw of Capacity

INDEX·1946=100

GOV'T.-OWNED ELECTRIC UTILITIES

INVESTOR-OWNED
ELECTRIC UTILITIES

Chart 2·16

Chart 2·17

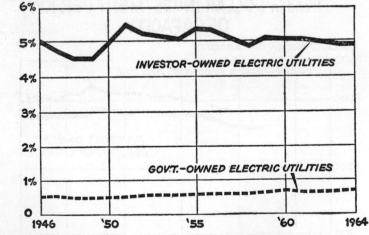

TOTAL TAXES As a Percent of Gross Plant

PERCENT

INVESTOR-OWNED ELECTRIC UTILITIES

GOV'T.-OWNED ELECTRIC UTILITIES

District, county, and state projects

During the 1930s and 1940s other government bodies entered the business of supplying electric energy. In the Pacific Northwest and in Nebraska there developed a movement to organize governmental units, often called public utility districts, for the purpose of producing or distributing electricity—just as a school district is a governmental unit set up for the purpose of operating schools. Financed by Federal grants and loans and by tax-free revenue bonds, encouraged by organizations devoted to the cause of government ownership of power facilities, by financial scavengers eager to profit from the dissolution of investor-owned power systems in the area, and by political considerations, public utility districts increased in number rapidly for a time. During recent years, however, no new public utility districts have been created (Table 2·2).

Table 2·2   Public Utility Districts

Name	Total capacity, kw	Hydro, kw	Steam, kw	Date of formation
Cowlitz County, PUD #1	96,640	70,000*	26,640	1936
Chelan County, PUD #1	974,100	974,100	....	1936
Douglas County, PUD #1	774,250†	774,250†	....	1936
Grant County, PUD #2	1,619,750	1,619,750	....	1938
Greys Harbor County, PUD #1	12,500	....	12,500	1938
Pend-Oreille County, PUD #1	60,560	60,560	....	1936

* Plant operated and power used by Pacific Power and Light Co.
† Generating station under construction.

In a few isolated instances counties have elected to supply their own power (Table 2·3).

Table 2·3   County Electric Systems

State	Name	Formation	Total, kw	Hydro, kw	Steam, kw
Georgia	Crisp County Power Commission	1930	32,700	15,200	17,500

In a number of cases governmental units formed for such purposes as irrigation have decided to include power supply among their activities. Most of these irrigation districts are located in the Western portion of the nation (Table 2·4).

As a rule, irrigation districts, public utility districts, and other similar agencies are not regulated as to their rates or their financing. They are autonomous bodies, operating under state laws. In the state of Washington, for example, public utility districts are managed by three commissioners elected for 6-year terms. These commissioners have the power to set electric rates, to issue bonds, to levy taxes, and to condemn and take over property at their own discretion. No Federal or state regulatory body has the power or is authorized to regulate them. Their customers have no redress, except to vote against the commissioners once every 6 years. Moreover, the law in Washington makes it virtually impossible for people to withdraw from operation of a public utility district. In a test case in 1938 in Pacific County, Washington, some 2,400 citizens signed a petition asking the county commissioners for an election to dissolve their public utility district. The attorney general ruled there was no way the question could be put to a vote—despite the fact that fewer than 2,400 votes had been cast to create the district in the first place.[42]

Table 2·4 Irrigation Districts

State	Name	Total, kw	Steam, kw	Hydro, kw	Internal combustion, kw
Arizona	Salt River Project Agricultural Improvement & Power Dist.	608,962	528,472	70,490	10,000
California	Imperial Irr. Dist.	210,676	130,000	67,400	13,276
California	Merced Irr. Dist.	90,900	......	89,100*	......
California	Modesto Irr. Dist.	27,000†	......	27,000†	......
California	Nevada Irr. Dist.	60,750	......	60,750	......
California	Oakdale-So. San Joaquin Irr. Dist.	81,090	......	81,090	......
California	Oroville Wyandotte Irr. Dist.	90,900	......	90,900	......
California	Turlock Irr. Dist.	3,732	......	3,732	......
California	Yuba County Water Agency	332,750§	......	332,750§	......
Nevada	Truckee-Carson Irr. Dist.	5,200	......	3,200‡	2,000

(Excludes irrigation districts in Nebraska)

* Under construction.
† Owned jointly with Turlock Irrigation District.
‡ Constructed by Reclamation.
§ 331,150 under construction.

During the 1930s the Public Works Administration (PWA), the Rural Electrification Administration (REA), and other Federal agencies provided funds to encourage establishment of public utility districts. In addition, the Federal agencies campaigned to further the idea of government ownership. During World War II this activity died down, but after the war it increased again. For example, in 1946 Dr. Paul Raver, Bonneville Power Administrator, was writing the Assistant Secretary of the Interior that he felt the program of first importance facing him was "revitalizing the public power movement in the Northwest" and that he had hired a man to head this activity. The program, he wrote, "involves fitting municipal ownership program with REA development in the rural areas into an existing PUD plan and enlisting the support of the PUDs in carrying it out." [43]

At the same time, a number of promoters were working to encourage government power agencies to buy out investor-owned power companies—so that they could line their pockets in the process. Even given the right to tax property in a district before starting its power operations, the public utility districts could not possibly accumulate enough capital to purchase an existing electric utility system or construct a new one without outside financial help. In large part, the necessary capital was raised by issuing general revenue bonds. To make these financial transactions possible a group of middlemen grew up. They were professional dealers in bonds who knew where to find customers for the bonds. The way one of the most active of these men, Guy C. (Flash) Myers, operated was described by U.S. Representative Ben Jensen in these words:

Here is the way Guy Myers' tax-capitalizing device works: Suppose I have a business that is worth only $100,000 on the basis of its net earnings after taxes, and suppose that business is now carrying $2,400 a year in Federal income taxes as part of its operating expenses.

Now, suppose some smart fellow comes along and says to you, "Look, you've got a nice little business here, and I know how you can get a fancy price for it. I've got a client who doesn't have to pay Federal taxes, and he's very anxious to buy you out. If you sell it to a taxpayer like yourself, you know very well that all you can get for it is $100,000, because that's as big an investment as it will carry.

"But if you will sell it to my tax-free client, he can take the $2,400 a year you now pay Uncle Sam and use that money to pay interest on a much bigger investment. That $2,400 will pay 6 percent on $40,000, which means that he can make the business carry an investment of $140,000 and still show the same net return.

"So here's what we can do. I'll get my client to pay you $130,000 for the business, and pay me $10,000 for fixing up the deal, and we'll both make a nice piece of change."

Yes; that is exactly the way Guy Myers works . . . Only he is not working for small change. He is dealing in millions and hundreds of millions, and his commissions run into seven figures.[44]

Several financial syndicates made a speciality of marketing public utility district bonds, and groups of lawyers, consulting engineers, accountants, and other advisory companies developed which made a business of helping change over tax-paying investor-owned enterprises to government-owned operations which paid no Federal income taxes. For their own reasons, all these interests played an important part in the development of government power systems.

Grand River Dam Authority. In 1935 the Legislature of the state of Oklahoma created the Grand River Dam Authority, among other things, to build and operate hydroelectric projects along the Grand River [45] although investor-owned companies had shown interest in developing a dam at the site with market financing.[46] In 1939, the authority received a license from the Federal Power Commission to build a major hydroelectric project near Pensacola in northestern Oklahoma.[47] At the same time the Army engineers were recommending a three-dam coordinated flood control and power development plan involving dams at Pensacola, Markham Ferry, and Fort Gibson, Oklahoma.[48] Ignoring this report, the PWA went ahead with a program of loans and grants to the authority for construction of the Pensacola Dam, primarily for hydroelectric production. As Representative D. D. Terry of Arkansas said in 1941:

"The Pensacola Dam, in effect, was lifted out of the flood control program . . . and taken from the jurisdiction of the United States Army engineers by the action of the G[rand] R[iver] D[am] A[uthority], and it was not built in accordance with the report plan of the Army engineers in a number of structural details, and its flood-control capacity was greatly reduced.

"Mr. Speaker, I am in favor of making these reservoir dams for the dual purpose of hydroelectric development and flood control," he continued, "but I do not want to see flood control, which so vitally affects the destinies of my State, sacrificed for power development, when such power development can be provided for on streams where the flood-control feature is not so vitally important, and I think that all due care should be taken by the builders of such reservoir dams to see that the essential benefits of hydroelectric power and flood control are properly conserved. I do not believe that in the instance of the Pensacola Dam, which was erected by the G.R.D.A., that the flood-control features were sufficiently considered, and that they were largely sacrified in the interest of power. I believe that the United States Army engineers protested against the serious reduction in the flood control features of this dam, but that their protests were disregarded.

"I understand that several months ago a serious flood came down the Grand River by reason of the reservoir not being in readiness to take care of the additional flood waters, and that but for the fact that the Arkansas River was comparatively low at that time, a serious major flood would probably have occurred on the lower reaches of the Arkansas. I am also informed that the flood that is at this moment raging down the Arkansas River could have been considerably reduced if the Pensacola Dam had been properly constructed to take care of floodwaters . . ." [49]

Most hydroelectric projects are used more economically when operated to provide power during periods of peak demand, with steam-generating stations supplying the base load. This is the case when they are integrated with an interconnected power system composed mostly of steam plants. Operated around the clock, the Pensacola Dam could supply approximately 25,000 kilowatts of capacity, but operated during 4 to 6 hours a day of peak demand it could supply 60,000 kilowatts. Therefore, its maximum benefit would have been derived by operating in conjunction with the existing steam plants in the area owned by power companies. This was not done.

In 1941, the Office of Production Management, a Federal wartime agency, decided to have an aluminum plant built near Malvern, Arkansas.[50] Aluminum production requires a great deal of electricity and so some of the principal electric utilities of the Southwest were called to Washington to discuss plans for supplying the new plant.[51] At the time, Arkansas Power & Light Company, which served the vicinity, did not have enough reserve power available to serve the plant itself while maintaining an ample supply of power for all its other customers. However, its power system interconnected with those of companies in Louisiana, Texas, Oklahoma, and Kansas. The companies agreed to pool their facilities to meet the needs of the aluminum plant. They also agreed to interconnect with the Pensacola Dam so that the 60,000 kilowatts of peaking power could be made available.[52]

As this proposal was being discussed, a group of rural electric cooperatives announced that it wanted to form a super-cooperative that would contract to furnish power to the aluminum plant despite the fact that the REA was created to give a subsidy to rural electric customers, not industries. The cooperatives had no power-producing capacity of their own. They were distributors of electricity, not producers; and they had always purchased their relatively small requirements from the investor-owned companies. Despite this, a full-blown controversy developed. Then on November 19, 1941, President Roosevelt, acting under his wartime powers, issued an executive order seizing the Pensacola Dam from the state of Oklahoma. He ordered the Federal Works Administrator to take over the Grand River Dam Authority and to operate it for the duration of the war.[53] The next steps came swiftly. Within a month the rural electric cooperatives formed their super-cooperative, the Ark-La Electric Cooperative, which was given a contract to supply 32,000 kilowatts of power to the aluminum plant.[54] It was agreed that Ark-La would obtain its power from the Grand River Dam Authority, although this would mean that the hydroelectric capacity of the authority would not be used in the most economic fashion. The super-cooperative then built 200 miles of expensive transmission lines from the Pensacola Dam in Oklahoma to the aluminum plant site in Arkansas, although the power could have been delivered over the utility companies' existing lines. Copper was in great demand for war production—in such great demand that some power companies were actually forced to use silver in their switchboards—yet the War Production Board allocated all the copper needed to build the unnecessary line.

To confuse the tangled situation still more, the Federal Works Administration on May 7, 1942, arranged for the two investor-owned power companies in Oklahoma, the Oklahoma Gas & Electric Company and Public Service

Company of Oklahoma, to provide reserve capacity for the Grand River Dam Authority and supply the authority's entire commitments for electric power between the hours of 9 P.M. and 8 A.M.[55]

Complaints about the neglect of flood control at Pensacola continued. In a letter to Senator Styles Bridges in 1943, the Arkansas Department of Public Utilities, the state regulatory body, noted that it was sorely distressed over the matter. After pointing out that little, if any, power from Grand River had been needed for the aluminum plant, the department stated:

After the [REA-financed] line was built and the aluminum plant was in operation, the super-cooperative's line went out and could not be used for 86 hours. Notwithstanding this outage, the power [companies'] pool picked up the entire aluminum plant load immediately and carried it for approximately 36 hours without any aid from the Grand River Dam power. During the remainder of the 86-hour period, Grand River power was delivered to the aluminum plant through the pool's facilities.[56]

Here was proof that the companies' plan would have worked.

The super-cooperative could not supply all the power needed by the aluminum plant even under normal conditions, and the investor-owned companies were asked to provide the balance. This they agreed to do. When the Military Affairs Committee of the House of Representatives investigated the situation, it reported that the construction of the transmission line had been unnecessary, that critical war materials had been wasted, and that the Rural Electrification Administration had been misleading the public by propaganda.[57] After the war the cooperatives sold the Ark-La line to the power companies, which now own and operate it. In 1946 the Grand River Dam Authority was returned to the state of Oklahoma.[58]

Today, the authority consists of the Pensacola Dam, with an installed capacity of 86,400 kilowatts, and a steam generating station, some of the units of which were acquired in 1949 from the War Assets Administration, with a total capacity of 45,000 kilowatts. At the end of 1964 it was operating about 800 miles of high-voltage transmission lines, including approximately 390 miles of 69,000-volt lines which it leases from KAMO Electric Cooperative. In 1961 it sold $50 million in revenue bonds to refund all outstanding debt and to finance the Markham Ferry Project. The project is now in operation with a power-producing capacity of 100,000 kilowatts.[59] (Table 2·5)

Table 2·5 Grand River Dam Authority, Vinita, Oklahoma

Project	Hydro, kw	Steam, kw	Total, kw
Chouteau*		45,000	45,000
Pensacola†	86,400		86,400
Markham Ferry‡	100,000		100,000

* Purchased from U.S. government (War Assets Administration) as surplus at Oklahoma Ordnance Works. Capacity increased by authority from 20,000 to 45,000 kw.

† Operation of Pensacola was taken over by the U.S. government on Nov. 20, 1941; operation returned to authority Sept. 1, 1946. Government made grant to authority of $11,113,636 and purchased authority's revenue bonds of $14 million at 4% interest. Under special act of Congress interest rate on bonds was reduced from 4% to 2½%. In addition, Corps of Engineers expended $2,090,000 for flowage easements.

‡ P L 476 (83d Cong., 2d Sess.) of July 6, 1954 rescinded authorization for the Corps of Engineers to build Markham Ferry. The authority obtained a license from the Federal Power Commission on June 22, 1955, for construction. (The Federal government contributed $6,909,000 toward construction.)

In 1957 the Authority and Public Service Company of Oklahoma agreed to integrate the operation of their existing and future electric facilities. Under the contract, the entire systems of the authority and the company will be completely coordinated. Switches at all points of interconnection remain closed at all times so that the electric energy may flow back and forth from one system to the other as the loads require. The agreement provides the authority with an additional supply of firm power, energy as needed beyond its own generating resources, and an assured market for any surplus power it may produce. It provides the company with a supply of hydroelectric peaking capacity which helps it provide for peak periods of demand at a relatively low cost. The contract also provides that during flood times the company will shut down any of its generating units where the fuel cost is more than $1\frac{1}{4}$ mills per kilowatt-hour and purchase energy during all hours of the day—energy that would otherwise be wasted over the dams.[60]

The Nebraska power system. In 1937 some 85 percent of the electric power output in Nebraska, the home state of Senator George Norris, was provided by investor-owned companies.[61] By 1942 there remained only one investor-owned power company in the state, serving Omaha and its environs.[62] Four years later, in 1946, not a single investor-owned power company was left.[63] The swift dissolution of the investor-owned electric utility systems culminated a long period of struggle which provides examples of all the varied pressures at work in the growth of government-owned power systems.

In Nebraska, as in many areas, investor ownership and government ownership of power facilities started at about the same point in history. The first investor-owned power plant in the state was established in 1883, and the first municipally owned plant began operation just a year later. Both forms of ownership grew rapidly. By 1902 there were forty-three investor-owned companies and eleven municipal plants.[64] As technology progressed, it became possible for the investor-owned central stations in the state to interconnect and develop systems, thus opening the way to greater efficiency of production and enabling prices to be lowered. Making use of the financial backing of such holding company systems as the Electric Bond and Share Company, Middle West Utilities, United Light & Power, and Stone & Webster, the investor-owned enterprises were able to consolidate in ways that improved service greatly.

In the smaller communities of the state, however, municipal plants continued to be established, reaching an all-time peak of 281 in 1925. The continued growth of these plants seems to have been caused by the fact that they often provided electricity at lower rates than investor-owned companies, even though their costs were higher; and because suppliers of diesel generating equipment, such as Fairbanks, Morse & Company, were promoting the idea that small towns should establish their own power facilities.[65] Of course, sometimes rates of municipalities were higher than those of the investor-owned companies for in some cases local governments used their power systems to supply funds for their treasuries.

Despite these factors, the number of municipal plants declined sharply from 1925 to 1932.[66] Then came the New Deal. In order to take advantage of Federal funds being made available through the Reconstruction Finance Corporation, C. A. Sorenson, the state attorney general, and others worked to change Nebraska law to make it possible for groups to be formed that could borrow the money.[67] In 1933 they worked to pass an Enabling Act which permitted 15 percent of the voters in a political subdivision of the state to petition the State Department of Roads and Irrigation for permission to form a district. Once certified, the district became a government corporation with the right to acquire and operate utility properties. The districts were exempt from taxes and from any state regulation, and they were authorized to sell revenue bonds. Moreover, once the districts entered the utility business, the law made it impossible for them to get out. It was made illegal for them to sell their facilities to investor-owned companies no matter what happened.[68]

Five projects were organized under the Enabling Act, with financing provided by the PWA. Two were single-purpose irrigation projects which eventually failed financially. The others were the Loup River Public Power District, the Platte Valley Public Power and Irrigation District, and the Central Nebraska Public Power and Irrigation District. All three were hydroelectric developments, and together their planned power production was to be equal to about 85 percent of all the electricity used in the state.[69] With this large supply of power available the districts had three courses open to them: they could sell power at wholesale rates to existing investor-owned companies with established distribution systems, they could try to compete with the companies, or they could acquire the investor-owned companies and establish a complete government-owned power system. The companies made it clear that they were willing to cooperate with the districts in distributing power. The president of the Nebraska Power Company told the people that: "If Nebraska's hydroelectric projects can produce a cheap power, the people will reap the benefits. The Nebraska Power Company always has been and is now ready and willing to buy power from these projects. If any savings would be made by such a purchase, we will pass on to our customers every dollar of those savings." [70]

The advocates of government ownership, including Senator George Norris, objected to selling power to the companies. During 1937, 1938, and 1939 a number of attempts were made to purchase the companies, either by individual districts or by groups.[71] John D. Ross, who was later to become the first Administrator of the Bonneville Power Administration, urged that the only way for the districts to secure a market for their output would be for them to take over the property of the companies. On his recommendation the three districts brought Guy Myers to Nebraska.[72]

Myers saw that, to provide the financing needed to acquire the companies' properties, a new super-district would need to be formed which, independent of the existing districts with their financial obligations to the PWA, would be freer to act. As a result, the Consumers Public Power District came into being in 1939 with Guy Myers as its fiscal agent. Myers was able to sell bonds of this new district to private bankers, pledging as security the revenues to be earned from the properties he expected to acquire—with a tax-exempt status that would add substantially to the net revenues. Between 1940 and 1942 over $40 million worth of property was purchased in this fashion.[73] The process did at least two things: it reduced the tax revenue of the Federal government and it benefited Guy Myers.

Acquisition did not bring an end to conflict, however. In the ensuing years the districts and rural electric cooperatives financed by the REA in Nebraska had a series of difficulties. Without a regulatory commission to help settle the differences of these groups, controversies dragged on and on. For instance, in 1955 the Platte, Loup, and

Consumers Districts agreed that they would form two integrated power systems in the state. Nothing came of the agreement because of continued objections from the city of Kearney, which did not want any change in its distribution system, and because the rural cooperatives feared an integrated competitor in distributing energy.[74] The state government has not been able to resolve these conflicts, but in 1961 the Legislature created a Legislative Council Study Committee on Public Power to evaluate power problems and, at the same time, requested the districts to form a committee to be known as the Nebraska Public Power Committee to suggest improvements.[75] Possibly these groups will be able to work out a plan that will help the people of Nebraska avoid the economic loss that has come from continued conflict among the government-owned systems (Table 2·6).

Lower Colorado River Authority. The Lower Colorado River Authority (LCRA) is an agency of the state of Texas. It controls and operates a system of dams, irrigation works, reservoirs, hydroelectric plants, steam generating plants, transmission lines, and distribution lines in a 31,000-square-mile area in the central part of the state. The system has a power-producing capacity of some 387,250 kilowatts, of which about 202,250 kilowatts is produced in six major hydroelectric plants along the Lower Colorado River.

The authority was created in 1934 by an act of the Texas State Legislature.[76] The complex series of events which eventually led to its formation exemplifies the variety of factors that have influenced the development of government power operations in other areas as well.

Beginning about the middle of the nineteenth century a number of men had dreamed of the possibility of building a series of dams on the Lower Colorado River, above

Table 2·6 Nebraska Power System

District	Total, kw	Hydro, kw	Steam, kw	Internal combustion, kw
Consumers Public Power District*	177,262	7,262	159,450	10,550
Nebraska Public Power System†	120,250	1,900	117,000	1,350
Loup River Public Power District‡	47,748	47,748	....	....
Platte Valley Public Power and Irrigation District§	26,100	26,100	....	......
Central Nebraska Public Power and Irrigation District#	154,000	54,000	100,000	......
Omaha Public Power District	620,600	......	620,600	......
Norris Public Power District	720	720	....	......
Southwest Public Power District	756	....	....	756

* Formed to utilize hydroelectric energy developed by Loup River Public Power District, Platte Valley Public Power and Irrigation District, and Central Nebraska Public Power and Irrigation District. Also purchased other generating properties.

† Established to transmit and market, principally at wholesale, power generated by districts included in Consumers Public Power District.

‡ Received Federal PWA grant of $4,644,000 and loan of $10,268,000; also REA loans of $24,662,000.

§ Received Federal PWA grant of $2,494,000 and loan of $9,166,000.

Received Federal PWA grant of $19,372,510 and loan of $24,168,000. Also received loans from REA in amount of $15,915,789. Entire output sold to Nebraska Public Power System.

Austin, Texas. In 1909, in fact, a dam was built about a third of the way across the river just below Marble Falls, but it was not completed.[77] In 1927 Martin J. Insull, president of the Middle West Utilities Company in Chicago, let it be known that his company was considering investing a total of some $15 million in building dams above Austin. When this news became public, citizens of the lower river valley were pleased. Some even sent Insull telegrams urging that the dams be built. In the upper river valley, however, opposition developed. The people were afraid that dams downstream might take so much of the flow of the river that the cities upstream would suffer. After spending nearly $500,000 in purchasing overflow rights and making studies, Insull felt the opposition to be too strong and announced his company would not continue the project.[78]

In 1929 the Emery, Peck and Rockwood Development Company obtained the water-right permits needed to build dams on the river and immediately set to work making surveys, buying land, and designing dams. In April, 1931, a construction contract for the main dam, to be called the Hamilton Dam, was awarded. It was to be completed by March 1, 1933. In the fall of 1931 Emery, Peck and Rockwood sold the Hamilton Dam properties to the Central Texas Hydro-Electric Company, an Insull subsidiary. Work continued on the dam until April, 1932, when, with the dam about 45 percent completed and over $3 million already spent on the project, construction stopped. Central Texas Hydro-Electric Company, along with other Insull properties, was in the hands of receivers.[79]

In the fall of 1932 Ralph W. Morrison, a Texas financier, went to Chicago and convinced a receiver of the Mississippi Valley Utilities Company, an Insull subsidiary which was a major bondholder of the Central Texas

Hydro-Electric Company, that there was a way to finance and complete Hamilton Dam. In accordance with this plan, Morrison organized the Colorado River Company and applied to the Reconstruction Finance Corporation (RFC) for a loan of $4.5 million to complete the project. The application was turned down. In August, 1933, Morrison's company applied to the PWA for the same amount, but there were soon indications that the loan would not be approved.[80] A movement thereupon developed to create a government agency to finance completion of the Hamilton Dam. First in October, 1933, and again in 1934 bills were introduced into the Texas Legislature to create a Colorado River Authority. Neither came to a final vote. The question of financing was too uncertain.[81]

The uncertainty was removed on June 28, 1934, when President Roosevelt, upon the urging of Representative J. P. Buchanan, then Chairman of the powerful House Appropriations Committee, conditionally approved the Colorado River Company's PWA loan application, with the understanding that three of the nine directors of the company should be appointed by the Texas Board of Water Engineers, five by the PWA Administrator, Harold Ickes, and one by the company stockholders. A second condition of the loan was that the company agree to sell all its property at "a prudent investment cost" to a state agency that the Legislature could create.[82]

At a celebration sponsored by the Austin Chamber of Commerce and the Colorado River Improvement Association it was unanimously voted to rename the half-completed dam Buchanan Dam. Congressman Buchanan took the occasion to urge speedy creation of a Colorado River Authority to administer the project and to assure the gathering that, when the authority had been set up, the Federal government would not only aid in completing

Buchanan Dam but also help build four more dams above Austin. Congressman J. J. Mansfield, then Chairman of the House Rivers and Harbors Committee, representative of another lower Colorado district, also spoke in support of the plan.[83]

Meanwhile, steps were being taken to transfer property rights for what was now to be called Buchanan Dam to Morrison's Colorado River Company. The properties of Central Texas Hydro-Electric Company were sold at public auction to a receiver of the Mississippi Valley Utilities Company for $3,550,000. Most of the purchase price was met by depositing the company's bonds with the court. At the same time, the Mississippi Valley Utilities Company's receiver obtained permission from a U.S. District Court to make an agreement with the Colorado River Company to complete the dam in return for the properties, giving the receiver 49 percent interest in the Colorado River Company. The court explained that, in its opinion, this was the best way to get some repayment for the bondholders.[84]

In October, 1934, the Texas Legislature passed the Lower Colorado River Authority measure over the objections of some who contended that government financing would result in large promoters' profits for the Colorado River Company.[85] Certainly, among the important factors contributing to formation of the state-owned authority were (1) the economic depression, which made it impossible for investor-owned companies to complete construction of Hamilton Dam as scheduled, (2) the spectacle of the half-completed dam itself, (3) the support of such powerful people as the Chairman of the Appropriations Committee and the Rivers and Harbors Committee of the U.S. House of Representatives, (4) the backing of people in the lower river valley who wanted flood protection, and

(5) the interest of the PWA in making loans for large public works projects, particularly for generation of electric power.

Formation of the LCRA made it possible for PWA grants and loans to be obtained to buy existing investor-owned hydroelectric facilities and to build others whose primary purpose claimed to be flood control. The power companies of the area offered to distribute the energy produced at these multipurpose dams, pledging to pass on any savings resulting from the purchase to their customers. In this way, the companies pointed out, benefits of the authority's power operations would reach the greatest number of consumers and the authority would be gaining the greatest amount of revenue, thus enabling a speedier repayment of the Federal loans. The authority, however, decided to sell its power only to municipalities and rural electric cooperatives, and soon its representatives had begun an active campaign to promote municipal ownership of power systems.[86]

The Federal Power Commission was also interested in the new authority. Its engineers undertook a survey examining the possibility of distributing Lower Colorado River Authority power to the city of Fort Worth. Armed with this survey, proponents of the authority tried to convince the city to organize a municipal power system and purchase energy from LCRA. PWA loans and grants were offered as an inducement, but the city refused them and elected to continue receiving service from an investor-owned company.[87] Not all the municipalities were able to withstand the blandishments of the LCRA spokesmen, however. Town after town decided to follow their advice.[88] Finally, in desperation, the president of one of the investor-owned power companies, Texas Power & Light Company, wrote to the authority offering to sell a large section of the company's service area.

"The difficulties which confront power Companies, faced with competition from power projects which are heavily subsidized by gifts of Federal funds, compel us to endeavor to work out with you some plan to prevent the destruction of our properties in that part of Texas where you advise us you desire to establish your market; consequently we must yield to your requirements that substantial markets be surrendered to you. However, we respectfully point out to you that the methods which your representatives have employed to accomplish your desired ends are destructive of the best interests of the people in Texas whom you hope to serve and also of the Authority itself. While our negotiations with you have been in progress, your representatives have endeavored to persuade the municipalities served by us to apply for PWA loans and grants, which loans and grants, if secured, could not be used to purchase existing facilities and could only be used to construct duplicate and competing distribution systems."

"Our company has constructed a large network of transmission lines, costing many millions of dollars to serve in excess of 500 communities and 63 counties of Texas with electricity, and has spent large sums of money to develop the markets for power in this territory. This system has been developed as a unified whole, all cities and towns being interconnected and, in addition, such system is interconnected with adjoining systems of other Companies, so as to serve a large part of the State most effectively and economically. If certain of these communities should decide to distribute Colorado River power and should purchase from us the distribution system within their boundaries, our investment burden in this transmission system would have to be borne by those communities which remain a part of our system. If, in like manner, certain other communities now served by us should elect to buy your power and distribute it in competition with us, a similar effect would result, detrimental to the interests of those consumers who continue to be served from our system.

"We have been able to make numerous and frequent rate reductions as a result of our intensive effort to increase the uses of electricity. Every community which we serve is receiving electric service today at materially less cost, most of them at less than half the cost of a few years ago. If our company is permitted to continue to develop in an economically sound manner, we will be able to continue to make such reductions in the future. If, on the other hand, we should be deprived of the business of the towns here, and of half the business of the towns there in a scatter-shot manner our investment and operating expenses would be practically the same as those necessary to serve our system as presently constituted. Obviously, this would make it much more difficult for us to continue to make rate reductions in the future as in the past. A great injustice will thereby result to all of our 138,000 electric consumers." [89]

Having negotiated with the authority for years, having tried every way it could to continue sound operations, the company was forced to sell all its electric properties in sixteen counties. The authority borrowed $5 million from the Federal government, through the Reconstruction Finance Corporation, and made the purchase.[90]

While acquiring a marketing area almost as large as Vermont, New Hampshire, Massachusetts, and Connecticut combined, the authority was facing serious difficulties on another front. Established as a flood control project, the authority had proceeded to build multipurpose dams and committed itself to the generation of electricity. In the summer of 1938 a devastating flood occurred, causing property damages of between $5 and $10 million.[91] After studying the causes of the flood, a special Texas State Senate Committee reported that, assuming that the primary purpose of the dams was to be flood control, "the management of the Authority was negligent in allowing the reservoir to remain nearly full of water because such a plan of operation left no empty storage to catch flood waters which might come at any time." [92] The committee stated that dams cannot be used satisfactorily for both flood control and for generation of electricity, but that the management of the authority refused to make any commitment of any definite amount of empty storage that would be kept available for flood protection. It demanded that a clear-cut policy be formulated for operation of the dams and that the policy be observed.[93]

In 1965, according to an estimate made by *Moody's Public Utility Manual,* the Lower Colorado River Authority represents an investment, in terms of reproduction cost of its properties, of over $150 million. Its power is supplied at wholesale and retail to municipalities and cooperatives and it interconnects with the systems of its neighboring investor-owned companies. Firm power and energy are being sold at wholesale under long term contracts to these companies, to 30 municipalities, 11 rural cooperatives, and some 250 smaller communities. Additional amounts of power and energy are sold at retail through three city distribution systems which the authority owns and operates.[94] (Table 2·7)

Table 2·7   Lower Colorado River Authority

Total, kw	Hydro, kw	steam, kw
531,250	202,250*	329,000†

* 56,000 kw originally financed by grants from Federal government (PWA) ($20,630,000) and Federal government loans secured by 4 percent revenue bonds, later refinanced with new revenue bonds at 2.88 percent.
† Represents 60,000 kw in leased plant and 144,000 kw under construction financed by REA at 2 percent interest.

Santee-Cooper. The South Carolina Public Service Authority is a state agency, established in 1934, to construct and operate a navigation and power development on the Santee and Cooper Rivers in South Carolina.[95] Using grants and loans from the PWA, the agency constructed a large hydroelectric dam, known as the Santee-Cooper project, and then set about trying to acquire the properties of the South Carolina Electric & Gas Company and the Lexington Water Power Company. After years of negotiations, the agency and the companies agreed to a proposal that the company properties be turned over to Santee-Cooper for $40 million—only to have the State Supreme Court hold in 1942 that the South Carolina Public Service Authority did not have authority to acquire the properties.[96] In appealing the decision, the authority called upon the court to take judicial notice of the situation confronting the Congress and state legislatures during the early thirties respecting the constitutionality of legislation which was intended to carry into effect certain New Deal policies.

"One of these policies was and is the bringing of the business, manufacture and sale of electric power into public ownership, for the avowed purpose of eliminating the financial and managerial abuses of private management, and so reducing the cost of electric energy as to bring the benefits of its use in industry and in agriculture and in domestic affairs to every home and farm and factory in the United States.

"To assert in legislation in 1934 that this was the purpose of a statute would have been considered folly, because of the composition of the Supreme Court of the United States at that time and the tendency of decisions of that Court. It was sought to escape the constitutional questions involved in the policy above stated by declaring a more generally accepted 'public purpose' in the applicable legislation of both Congress and also of the state legislatures, but to encompass within such legislation additional provisions to give effect to this new social policy.

"In the great national projects like the Bonneville Dam, the Boulder Dam, and the TVA, the improvement of navigation, reclaiming waste lands, and the creation of a 'yardstick' for electric rates are illustrations of legislative declarations intended to overcome the probable hostile attacks, while at the same time everybody understood and now knows it as a fact that the object of the named projects, and of scores of others that have since been undertaken, was to socialize, so to speak, the business of producing and distributing electric energy through public grants and public ownership.

"In South Carolina the policy is represented in the South Carolina

Public Service Authority, the Rural Electrification Authority, the County Cooperatives, the Buzzard's Roost hydro-electric plant, and widespread municipal ownership financed through the Reconstruction Finance Corporation or created independently under the State Constitution and statutes." [97]

Despite this frank statement of the authority's purpose, the court decision was upheld. The authority was restricted from broadening its activities, and investor ownership was given a new lease on life in South Carolina.[98]

Thwarted in the attempt to move directly into ownership and operation of a large power system, Santee-Cooper officials approached officials of the state's rural electric cooperatives with a plan. They suggested that the cooperatives should organize themselves into a super-cooperative which could borrow money from the Rural Electrification Administration to build a network of transmission lines in central and lower South Carolina where investor-owned companies were then operating. They pointed out that for several years the companies had been purchasing power from Santee-Cooper and had been making plans for the future on the assumption that they could continue to do so. Their wholesale contracts with the rural electric cooperatives were built on this assumption. However, Santee-Cooper had begun to terminate contracts with the companies during the 1940s, and the rural cooperatives might no longer have felt assured that they could continue to depend on the companies to supply the power they required. Of course, there was no reason for the cooperatives to feel this way. The companies had plenty of power. Nevertheless, the Santee-Cooper proposal seemed convincing. The cooperatives formed the Central Electric Power Cooperative. It was given a $7,595,000 REA loan and the transmission lines were built—and operated by Santee-Cooper.[99]

Over the years, REA has loaned additional sums to the Central Electric Power Cooperative. By 1963, the total came to $14,191,248.[100] In that year a further step was taken. The super-cooperative obtained a single loan for $32.9 million from REA. Some $5.3 million of this is to finance additional transmission facilities and the remaining $27.6 million is to be used to construct a 150,000 kilowatt steam generating station—to be operated by Santee-Cooper for 35 years, at which time the plant and the transmission lines will be deeded to Santee-Cooper without cost.[101]

In discussing Santee-Cooper's future, R. M. Jefferies, general manager of Santee-Cooper since the 1930s, told a newspaper in 1962 that any attempt to finance a steam station through the free market would require payment of an interest rate possibly twice the 2 percent charged by REA.[102] (Table 2·8)

Table 2·8   South Carolina Public Service Authority
("Santee-Cooper")

Project	Hydro, kw	Steam, kw	Total, kw
Pinopolis	132,615	100,000	232,615
Spillway	1,920	....	1,920
Myrtle Beach	....	22,500	22,500
Conway*	....	150,000	150,000
Total	134,535	272,500	407,035

Operates about 1,000 miles of transmission line, leased from Central Electric Power Cooperative, Inc.
Loans from Federal government (at 2½%): $29,494,000.
Grants from Federal government: $24,131,000.

*Leased from Central Electric Power Cooperative, Inc.

New York State Power Authority. The Power Authority of the state of New York was created in 1931, during Franklin Roosevelt's term as governor. It was empowered to construct hydroelectric projects in the International Rapids section of the St. Lawrence River and in the Niagara River and to operate and maintain the projects in cooperation with appropriate United States and Canadian authorities. However, it was more than 20 years before construction of a dam actually started.

In 1957 President Eisenhower signed a bill directing the Federal Power Commission to issue a license to the authority for construction and operation of a power project on the Niagara River, under a treaty signed with Canada in 1950.[103] Construction began in January, 1958, and the project was completed on November 30, 1963.[104]

The authority today takes part in two power projects: the St. Lawrence Power Project, a joint development with the Hydroelectric Power Commission of Ontario, and the Niagara Power Project. All the power for the St. Lawrence Project is presently generated at the Robert Moses–Robert H. Saunders Dam, which straddles the international boundary about 74 miles up the St. Lawrence River from Montreal. The project, which was completed in 1960, has an installed capacity of 1,824,000 kilowatts, of which 912,000 kilowatts is installed on the United States side. Power is sold to the Public Service Board of Vermont, to municipalities in New York State, to investor-owned electric utility companies, to the U.S. Air Force, to rural electric cooperatives, and to several large industrial customers.[105]

Power for the Niagara Project is provided by the Robert Moses Niagara Power Plant, with a 1,950,000-kilowatt capacity, supplemented by a 240,000-kilowatt plant. The project also has transmission lines which carry power to neighboring investor-owned electric utility companies. Energy is sold at wholesale to the companies, to the Public Service Board of Vermont, and to a number of municipalities.

Rates for electricity sold by the authority are not subject to regulation by any state agency.[106] (Table 2·9)

Table 2·9   New York State Power Authority

Project	Hydro, kw	Steam, kw	Total, kw
St. Lawrence	1,824,000*	....	1,824,000*
Niagara	2,190,000†	....	2,190,000†
Total	4,014,000	....	4,014,000
Operates 350 miles of transmission line.			

*Includes 912,000 kw installed on Canadian side.
†Includes pump generating plant of 240,000 kw.

Brazos River Authority.   In Texas, the Brazos River Authority (formerly named the Brazos River Conservation and Reclamation District), financed by a WPA grant, an RFC loan, and state tax remissions, operates the Possum Kingdom Dam on the Brazos River.   All the output of the authority is sold to the Brazos River Transmission Electric Cooperative, Inc., a super-cooperative.[107] (Table 2·10)

The Brazos River rises in the eastern part of New Mexico, approximately 30 miles west of the Texas–New Mexico boundary and runs southeast to the Gulf of Mexico, near Freeport, Texas.   The Possum Kingdom Dam is located on the upper reaches of the river.   Investor-owned power companies serving northwest Texas have transmission lines near the dam, taking power to cities and rural electric cooperatives in the area.   When the dam was be-

Table 2·10   Brazos River Authority
(Formerly Brazos River Conservation and Reclamation District)

Project	Hydro, kw
Possum Kingdom	22,500
(Morris Shepard)	

Entire output sold to Brazos River Transmission Electric Cooperative, Inc.
Loan from Federal government (at 4%): $4,200,000.
Grant from Federal government: $4,500,000.

ing built, the companies offered to buy all the power it produced and distribute it over their lines. Just as they were about to sign a contract with the Brazos River Authority, the REA stepped in.[108]

REA headquarters in Washington caused a new corporation to be formed that could bid for the Possum Kingdom power. This corporation, the Brazos River Transmission Electric Cooperative, Inc., was organized as a transmission company. The REA put up all the money to form the corporation. It could buy electricity and then sell it to the rural electric cooperatives which are its stockholders. All the money needed to form the corporation was put up by the REA.

The first bid which the super-cooperative made for power from Possum Kingdom Dam was for over $100,000 a year less than the bid submitted by the investor-owned companies. At the same time, the companies offered to buy the power, carry it over their lines, and deliver it to the cooperatives at 6.35 mills per kilowatt-hour. The super-cooperative said it would have to charge the cooperatives at least 15.0 mills per kilowatt-hour.[109]

Despite the fact that if the authority were to sell its

power to the super-cooperative it would lose over $100,000 a year and that the cooperatives would then be forced to buy their power at a higher rate, the power committee of the authority board recommended that all Possum Kingdom power be sold to the Brazos River Transmission Electric Cooperative, Inc. The meeting at which this arrangement was decided occurred on March 25, 1941. The Fort Worth *Star-Telegram* reported that the directors

apparently were more deeply impressed by repeated warnings . . . that failure to approve the contract with the transmission co-operative would result in the district being "disowned" by the Federal government and shut off from future aid in the construction of other dams contemplated for flood control purposes.[110]

On March 31, 1941, the same newspaper reported that, despite the apparently better terms offered by the investor-owned companies, the board of the Brazos River Conservation and Reclamation District instructed its president and secretary to sign a contract giving the cooperative exclusive rights to the energy generated at the new hydroelectric plant for 25 years. It was stated at the time that the board's action had been unanimous, but the president, L. Mims, of Houston, later reported that his own vote had been in the negative, making the vote 19 to 1.

The newspaper quoted Mims as saying that 12 or 15 of the board members realized that acceptance of the cooperative contract was a bad thing to do, from a strictly business standpoint.

"They simply surrendered to the recommendations of the power committee," he said, "because they were afraid if they accepted the offer of the private utility we would get no further aid from the Federal Government for other projects in the Brazos River flood control program." . . .
Mims also revealed that Vincent D. Nicholson of Washington, chief counsel for the Rural Electrification Administration, had ap-

peared before the board after it went into executive session. He did not divulge what Nicholson said.

"Rightly or wrongly," Mims said, "the board was led to believe that with the acceptance of the cooperative contract, additional aid will be forthcoming immediately." [111]

Other state agencies. A number of other state power agencies have been created during the years. The Colorado River Commission of Nevada is the authority set up by the state of Nevada to hold and administer all rights and benefits pertaining to the distribution of the power allocated to the state including that from Hoover Dam.[112] Another state agency is the Public Service Board of Vermont, which contracts to buy power from the Power Au-

Table 2·11   Miscellaneous Government Power Agencies

State	Name	Hydro, kw	Steam, kw
Calif.	California Dept. of Water Resources	758,600*	....
	East Bay Municipal Utility District	15,000	....
	Escondido Mutual Water Co.	760	....
	Public Utility Commission of San Francisco (Hetch-Hetchy)	208,600	....
	Placer County Water Agency	210,870	....
Mass.	Metropolitan District Water Commission	9,060	....
N. J.	Passaic Valley Water Commission	2,400	....
Texas	Guadalupe-Blanco River Authority	16,080	....
	Red Bluff Water Power Control District	2,300	....
Wash.	Washington Public Power Supply System	26,125	786,000
Subtotal	....	1,249,795	786,000
Total	....	2,035,795	

* Under construction.

thority of the state of New York for resale to suppliers of electricity within the state.[113]

The most recent state power agency to be formed is the Sabine River Authority, through which Texas and Louisiana plan to build the Toledo Bend Dam and Reservoir on the Sabine River in east Texas. When completed, the $80-million project is expected to include one of the largest man-made lakes in the nation. Three investor-owned electric light and power companies have agreed to purchase the entire output of the project.[114]

REFERENCES

1. The *New York Times,* Sept. 22, 1932.
2. EEI.
3. *Tennessee Valley Authority Act of 1933,* Public Law 17, 73d Cong., H.R. 5081, approved May 18, 1933.
4. EEI, *Historical Statistics of the Electric Utility Industry,* Table 10, p. 10.
   EEI, *Statistical Year Book of the Electric Utility Industry for 1966,* advance release, Table 10S.
5. Tennessee Valley Authority, *TVA Annual Report,* 1966, p. A4.
6. EEI, *Pocketbook of Electric Utility Industry Statistics,* 1967 p. 25.
7. *Ibid.,* p. 25; EEI, *I Want To Know About the Electric Utility Industry,* 1966, p. 36.
8. H. S. Raushenbush, *The New Leader,* Mar. 12, 1927, p. 4.
9. *The National Industrial Recovery Act,* Public Law 67, 73d Cong., H.R. 5755, June 16, 1933.
10. Letter from the Administrator of Public Works to the U.S. Senate, Mar. 22, 1934, p. 9. (Senate Document 167, 73d Cong., 2d Sess.)
11. H. S. Bennion, "Testimony Offered in Federal Power Commission Hearing on Accounting for Costs of ECAP," Nov. 23–24, 1959.
12. *Congressional Record,* 77th Cong., 1st Sess., Vol. 87, Part I, Jan. 8, 1941, pp. 57–58.
13. New York *Call,* Nov. 19, 1921; The League for Industrial Democracy, "The College Student as a Rebel," New York, 1927.
14. Judson King, *The Conservation Fight,* Public Affairs Press, Washington, 1959, pp. vi and 171.

15. Robert La Follette, *United Farmers Forum,* June 1921, p. 13.
16. *Digest of Proceedings, Public Ownership Conference,* 1923, pp. 14–15.
17. Carl Thompson, "What the Public Ownership League Has Done—Is Doing—Plans to Do," *Public Ownership,* Public Ownership League of America, Chicago, 1929, p. 14.
18. *Digest of Proceedings, Public Ownership Conference,* 1923, pp. 8–9, and Resolution, pp. 1–2.
19. *Congressional Record,* 68th Cong., 1st Sess., Vol. 65, Part 4, Mar. 10, 1924, p. 3874.
20. Carl Thompson, *Public Ownership,* Thomas Y. Crowell Company, New York, 1925, p. 371.
21. Carl Thompson, "A Week in Washington," *Public Ownership,* June, 1933, p. 90.
22. "Activities of the League," *Public Ownership of Public Utilities,* June, 1935, p. 108.
23. Carl Thompson, "Our Dreams Come True," *Public Ownership, of Public Utilities,* Sept., 1937, pp. 116–117.
24. *Hearings before the Subcommittee of the Committee on Appropriations on the Interior Department Appropriation Bill for 1941, House of Representatives,* 76th Cong., 3d Sess., Part I, Jan. 30, 1940, p. 267.
25. *Ibid.,* pp. 266–267.
26. FPC, "Typical Electric Bills," Washington, 1966.
27. FPC, *Statistics of Electric Utilities in the U.S., 1964, Privately-Owned,* Table 15, p. XXXI, and Table 18, p. XXXVII; *Statistics of Electric Utilities in the U.S., 1964, Publicly-Owned,* Table 10, p. XIII, and Table 13, p. XIV.
28. *Ibid.*
29. *Ibid.*
30. *Ibid.*
31. *Ibid.*
32. *Ibid.*
33. *Ibid.*
34. *Ibid.*
35. *Ibid.*
36. *Ibid.*
37. *Ibid.*
38. *Ibid.*
39. FPC, *Statistics of Electric Utilities in the U.S., 1955, Privately-owned,* Table 22, p. XXXIII; *Statistics of Electric Utilities in the U.S., 1964, Privately-owned,* Table 21, p. XL, and Table 8, p. XX; *Statistics of Electric Utilities in the U.S., 1954, Privately-owned,* p. XXVIII, *Statistics of Electric Utilities in the U.S.,*

1937–1943 Yearly Editions, Privately-owned; Statistics of Electric Utilities in the U.S., 1956, Publicly-owned, Table 11, p. XV, and Table 15, p. XVII; Statistics of Electric Utilities in the U.S., 1964, Publicly-owned, Table 21, p. XVIII, and Table 17, p. XVI.

40. Ibid.

41. FPC, Statistics of Electric Utilities in the U.S., 1964, Privately-owned, Table 18, p. XXXVIII, and Table 8, p. XX; Statistics of Electric Utilities in the U.S., 1955, Privately-owned, Table 17, p. XXVIII.; Statistics of Electric Utilities in the U.S., 1945, Privately-owned, p. XV; Statistics of Electric Utilities in the U.S., 1964, Publicly owned, Table 13, p. XVI, and Table 17, p. XVIII; Statistics of Electric Utilities in the U.S., 1956, Publicly-owned, Table 11, p. XV.

42. Washington Water Power Co., The PUD's of Washington State, p. 24.

43. Congressional Record, 81st Cong., 1st Sess., Vol. 95, Part 3, Mar. 29, 1949, pp. 3420–3421.

44. Ibid., p. 3419.

45. State of Oklahoma, Session Laws, 1935, Article 4, Chapter 70, as amended (Grand River Dam Authority Act).

46. H. D. Robards, "Pensacola Dam Completed," Power Plant Engineering, February, 1941, p. 72.

47. Grand River Dam Authority, A Public Corporation v. Grand-Hydro, A Private Corporation, U.S. Supreme Court, No. 6, October Term, 1948, pp. 5–6.

48. Letter from Secretary of War to the Speaker of the House of Representatives, Document 107, 76th Cong., 1st Sess., Jan. 12, 1939, p. 5.

49. Congressional Record, 77th Cong., 1st Sess., Vol. 87, Part 8, Nov. 7, 1941, p. 8684.

50. Preliminary Hearings before the Subcommittee of the Committee on Appropriations, House of Representatives, on the Agriculture Department Appropriation Bill for 1943, 77th Cong., 1st Sess., p. 325.

51. Investigation of the National Defense Program—Interim General Report of the Committee on Military Affairs, House of Representatives, pursuant to H. Res. 162, 77th Cong., 2d Sess., p. 174.

52. Federal Works Agency Release No. 674, June 21, 1943.

53. F. D. Roosevelt, Executive Order: Directing the Federal Works Administrator to Take Possession of and Operate a Certain Project of the Grand River Dam Authority, Nov. 19, 1941.

54. U.S. Department of Agriculture Release No. 355, Dec. 12, 1941.

55. *Public Utilities Fortnightly*, June 4, 1942, p. 782.
56. *Congressional Record*, 78th Cong., 1st Sess., Vol. 89, Part 4, May 27, 1943, p. 4936.
57. *Investigation of the National Defense Program—Interim General Report of the Committee on Military Affairs, House of Representatives, pursuant to H. Res. 162*, 77th Cong., 2d Sess., pp. 183–184.
58. U.S. Code Congressional Service, 79th Congress, 2d Session. 1946, Grand River Dam Project, Chap. 10, Public Law 573, p. 709.
59. *Moody's Municipal and Government Manual*, 1966, pp. 1773, 1774; FPC data.
60. Markham Ferry Dedication book.
61. Harry M. Trebing, "Nebraska's Continuing Power Problems, Part I," *Public Utilities Fortnightly*, Mar. 29, 1962, p. 441.
62. *Ibid.*, p. 443.
63. *Ibid.*, Part II, Apr. 12, 1962, p. 512.
64. *Ibid.*, Part I, p. 434.
65. *Ibid.*, pp. 434–435; see also: *Public Service Magazine*, April, 1933, p. 101.
66. Trebing, *op. cit.*, pp. 434–435.
67. *Ibid.*, pp. 438–439.
68. *Ibid.*, pp. 438–439, 445. (In a note on p. 445, Trebing comments that although previous legislation dating back as far as 1895 permitted creation of irrigation and water power districts, these laws proved unworkable in practice as a basis for district organization and operation.)
69. *Ibid.*, pp. 440–441.
70. Omaha, Nebraska *World Herald*, Mar. 3, 1938.
71. *Ibid.*, Oct. 14, 1938; the *New York Times*, Sept. 5, 1937; Omaha, Nebraska *World Herald*, Feb. 7, 1934, and other newspaper reports of the period.
72. Trebing, *op. cit.*, pp. 442–443.
73. *Ibid.*, p. 443.
74. *Ibid.*, p. 520.
75. *Ibid.*
76. Chapter 7, Acts of 1934, 43d Texas Legislature, and *Moody's Municipal and Government Manual*, 1966, p. 2079.
77. Comer Clay, "The Lower Colorado River Authority," *Public Administration and Policy Formation*, pp. 203–204.
78. *Ibid.*, p. 204.
79. *Ibid.*, pp. 204–205.
80. *Ibid.*, p. 205.
81. *Ibid.*
82. The *Austin American*, June 30, 1934, quoted in Comer Clay, *Ibid.*, pp. 205–206.

83. The *Austin American,* July 18, 1934, quoted in Comer Clay, *Ibid.,* pp. 206–207.
84. The Chicago *Daily Tribune,* Sept. 25, 1934, quoted in Comer Clay, *Ibid.,* p. 206.
85. Clay, *Ibid.,* pp. 207–208.
86. Letter of J. W. Carpenter, President, Texas Power & Light Co., to Executive and Power Committee, Lower Colorado River Authority, Sept. 6, 1938.
87. The New York *Herald Tribune,* Aug. 2, 1938; Fort Worth, Texas *Morning Star Telegram,* Oct. 1, 1938.
88. Letter of J. W. Carpenter.
89. *Ibid.*
90. The *Wall St. Journal,* Feb. 3, 1939.
91. *Report of (Texas State) Senate Investigating Committee concerning Colorado River Authority,* to the Governor of Texas, T. J. Holbrook, Chairman, Feb. 1939, p. 3.
92. *Ibid.,* p. 5.
93. *Ibid.,* pp. 5, 6.
94. *Moody's Public Utilities Manual,* 1966, p. a69.
95. *Moody's Municipal and Government Manual,* 1966, p. 2001.
96. The New York *Herald Tribune,* June 4, 1942.
97. *Petition for Rehearing and for Alternate Relief, F. B. Creech et al. v. South Carolina Public Service Authority,* The State of South Carolina, in the Supreme Court, 1942.
98. The *New York Times,* Dec. 24, 1943.
99. Charleston, South Carolina *News & Courier,* Oct. 13, 1948, Mar. 2, 1949, Mar. 12, 1949, and Mar. 14, 1949.
100. U.S. Department of Agriculture, Rural Electrification Administration release, June 28, 1963.
101. *Ibid.*
102. Charleston, South Carolina *News & Courier,* Sept. 5, 1962.
103. *Moody's Municipal and Government Manual,* 1966, p. 1452.
104. *Ibid.*
105. *Ibid.*
106. *Ibid.,* 1967, p. 1505.
107. *Engineering News-Record,* June 8, 1939, p. 72; Federal Loan Agency Release, FLA-9, Nov. 1, 1939; FPC Release No. 1463, Mar. 15, 1941.
108. *Christian Science Monitor,* Mar. 29, 1941; *Fort Worth Press,* Mar. 27, 1941; The *Wall St. Journal,* Apr. 4, 1941; *House Document 535,* 81st Cong., 2d Sess., Brazos River and Tributaries, Oyster Creek and Jones Creek Texas, Mar. 23, 1950, p. 120.

109. *Fort Worth Press,* Mar. 27, 1941; *Christian Science Monitor,* Mar. 29, 1941.
110. Fort Worth, Texas *Star-Telegram,* Mar. 26, 1941.
111. *Ibid.,* Mar. 31, 1941.
112. State of Nevada, *Report of Colorado River Commission of Nevada,* Jan. 1, 1927, to Sept. 1, 1935, p. 92.
113. State of Vermont, *Biennial Report of the Public Service Board,* July 1, 1964 to June 30, 1966, p. 40.
114. The *New York Times,* Jan. 12, 1964.

Chapter **3**

The Federal government
in the power business

From the time this nation was formed, navigation and flood control have been understood to be constitutional functions of the Federal government.   Problems of irrigation, soil erosion, and reclamation all bear on river development and the sound conservation of natural resources.   Thus, passage of the Reclamation Act of 1902 to develop Federal irrigation projects in the seventeen states west of the 100th meridian met general approval. Within the next 5 years thirty-nine irrigation projects were approved for construction in the sparsely settled, semiarid Western states.[1]   These early projects were designed with a single purpose in mind: irrigation.   In some, however, incidental amounts of electricity were produced for use around the dams and for water pumping.   Excess energy produced in this way was sold wherever possible, and the revenue applied to the operation of the project.   In order to make clear how this incidental power should be disposed, Congress gave the matter specific attention in the Reclamation Act of 1906.   Section 5 of that act reads:

Sec. 5. That whenever a development of power is necessary for the irrigation of lands under any project undertaken under the said Reclamation Act, or an opportunity is afforded for the development of power under any such project, the Secretary of the Interior is authorized to lease for a period not exceeding 10 years, giving preference to municipal purposes, any surplus power or power privilege, and the moneys derived from such leases shall be covered into the reclamation fund and be placed to the credit of the project from which such power is derived: *Provided,* That no lease shall be made of such surplus power or power privilege as will impair the efficiency of the irrigation project.[2]

That is, Congress stated that power at reclamation dams could be sold, giving preference to "municipal purposes" such as street lighting and water pumping. The purpose for which the power would be used, not the purchaser of the power, was what concerned Congress. More important, Congress underlined that in no case should power development impair the efficiency of a project for carrying out its primary function of irrigation. Irrigation dams were to be primarily for irrigation, and nothing else.

The policy worked smoothly for years. But developments in the Southeastern section of the country, along the Tennessee River, brought Federal interest in power on a different basis.

The first tries at TVA

People living along the Tennessee River had long been troubled by a section of the river known as Muscle Shoals, which had always been a serious obstacle to transportation. Attempts were made to solve the difficulty with canals, but they were largely unsuccessful.[3] Then, during World War I, the Federal government decided to build an experimental nitrate plant at The Shoals. The process of producing nitrate can require large amounts of electricity and so a hydroelectric plant was planned. Although construction of the nitrate plant was rushed to meet the necessities of national defense, the plant never contributed to the war effort. The armistice was signed before it was completed.* Construction on the hydro-electric stations was halted soon after it had begun and Congress lost interest in the project, despite the efforts of Senator George Norris of Nebraska to keep it in the public eye.[4]

* Power development at Muscle Shoals had been a matter of dis-cussion since at least 1898, when the first of a series of bills was introduced in Congress to authorize construction of a dam and power facilities by a group of investors. Congress authorized a number of these bills but the companies to which development privileges were granted apparently were unwilling to accept the exact terms. The second of the series was vetoed by President Theodore Roosevelt in 1903. Other attempts were made to de-velop the site for power purposes during the next 15 years, with no success. As one approach to the problem, Frank S. Washburn, then President of American Cyanamid Co., suggested in hearings on the National Defense Act of 1916 that the Federal government develop the power resource at Muscle Shoals and make the energy available to the Cyanamid Co. for use in a proposed munitions plant (J. King, *The Conservation Fight*, Public Affairs Press, 1959, pp. 1, 4, and J. S. Ransmeier, *The Tennessee Valley Authority*, Vanderbilt University Press, Nashville, Tenn., 1942, pp. 41–44.)

On March 10, 1916, Senator Ellison D. Smith of South Carolina introduced a bill (S 4971) into the Senate to authorize the President to build works on navigable streams for the production of power and other products necessary for manufacturing munitions in war-time or fertilizers in time of peace. After much debate, this bill was incorporated into the National Defense Act of 1916 as Section 124, saying:

The President of the United States is hereby authorized and empowered to make, or cause to be made, such investigation as in his judgment is necessary to determine the best, cheapest, and most available means for the production of nitrates and other projects for munitions of war and useful in the manufacture of fertilizers and other products by water power or any other power as in his judgment is the best and cheapest to use; and is also hereby authorized and empowered to designate for the exclu-sive use of the United States, if in his judgment such means is best and cheapest, such site or sites upon any navigable or non-navigable river or rivers or upon the public lands, as in his opinion will be necessary for

In 1921 Senator Norris, a long-time advocate of government ownership of electric power facilities, began a 12-year struggle to bring the Muscle Shoals power plant under Federal operation. His first attempts attracted little attention. Construction of the plant remained at a standstill. When Henry Ford expressed interest in the Muscle Shoals site, however, construction resumed.[5] Wilson Dam, as the plant was called, began operation in 1925 and three electric generating units were put in operation.[6]

The question of what to do with the dam began to reach headline proportions by the middle of the 1920s.

---

carrying out the purposes of this Act; and is further authorized to construct, maintain, and operate, at or on any site or sites so designated, dams, locks, improvements to navigation, power houses, and other plants and equipment or other means than water power as in his judgment is the best and cheapest, necessary or convenient for the generation of electrical or other power and for the production of nitrates or other products needed for munitions of war and useful in the manufacture of fertilizers and other useful products.

The sum of $20,000,000 is hereby appropriated, out of any money in the Treasury not otherwise appropriated, available until expended, to enable the President of the United States to carry out the purposes herein provided for.

The plant or plants provided for under this Act shall be constructed and operated solely by the Government and not in conjunction with any other industry or enterprise carried on by private capital. [Act of June 3, 1916, ch. 134, 39 Stat. 215, 50, USCA 79]

Under the authority of this act, President Wilson established a Federal reservation at Muscle Shoals and ordered that an experimental process plant be built. This was later expanded to include an order to construct a cyanimid process nitrate plant, steam power stations, a railroad, a quarry, workers' housing, a transmission line to a temporary power source provided by the Alabama Power Co., and a large hydroelectric project. The President's decision that these facilities be built at Muscle Shoals disregarded a recommendation by the Chief of Ordnance that the site be North Chattanooga, Tennessee (U.S. Congress, House of Representatives Hearings, Serial 6, Ordnance 3, before Subcommittee No. 5 of Select Committee on Expenditures in the War Department, 66th Cong., 2d Sess., 1920, and House Report 998, 66th Cong., 2d Sess., Finding Number 11).

Ford offered to lease it and to purchase the nitrate plants. The Alabama Power Company, interested in developing economic power sources to meet the growing demand for electricity among its customers, made an offer for the dam. A large shipbuilding company submitted another offer.[7] In the meantime, Senator Norris was building support in Congress for his point of view. In all, between 1921 and 1933 he introduced nine bills aimed at bringing about Federal ownership and operation of the Muscle Shoals properties. Six of the bills failed in Congress. President Coolidge refused to sign one, and it died by pocket veto.[8] President Hoover vetoed another because he said it "would launch the Federal government upon a policy of ownership and operation of power utilities upon a basis of competition instead of by the proper Government function of regulation for the protection of all the people." He went on to say, "I hesitate to contemplate the future of our institutions, of our Government, and of our country if the preoccupation of its officials is to be no longer the promotion of justice and equal opportunity but is to be devoted to barter in the markets," and that "for the Federal government deliberately to go out to build up and expand . . . a power and manufacturing business is to break down the initiative and enterprise of the American people; it is destruction of equality of opportunity amongst our people; it is the negation of the ideals upon which our civilization has been based."[9]

The Boulder Canyon Project Act

Despite President Hoover's strong feelings concerning the Muscle Shoals project, in 1928 he signed into law the Boulder Canyon Project Act and authorized production of hydroelectric power as a means of making the project self-supporting and financially solvent.

The first of a long series of investigations and reports on the possibility of a development in the Boulder Canyon area to help control the Colorado River was initiated in 1902, soon after passage of the first Reclamation Act. Disastrous floods in 1905, 1907, and 1916 gave impetus to the studies. In 1922, the Bureau of Reclamation issued a report recommending that the Federal government undertake construction of a canal and a high dam. While the engineering aspects of the project were nearly unprecedented, the legal aspects were more complicated still. The people who lived in the Colorado River Basin, citizens of Colorado, Wyoming, Utah, Arizona, Nevada, New Mexico, and California, were all dependent upon the river's water. The equitable division of the water came to be a serious problem. In time, it was settled on the basis of a compact drawn up by a special commission of representatives of the governors of the states involved. The chairman of the commission was the representative of the Federal government, Herbert Hoover, then Secretary of Commerce under President Harding. In 1947 the 726-foot dam that was the result of the Boulder Canyon Project Act was renamed Hoover Dam.[10]

The Hoover Dam power plant has an installed capacity of 1,340,000 kilowatts. It is operated and maintained directly by the Bureau of Reclamation, except for the generating machinery, which is operated and maintained indirectly through operating agents: The City of Los Angeles Department of Water and Power and the Southern California Edison Company. The Hoover Dam project itself owns only 23.2 circuit miles of transmission lines. The states of Arizona and Nevada; The City of Los Angeles Department of Water and Power; the Metropolitan Water District of Southern California; the cities of Glendale, Burbank, and Pasadena; and the Southern California Edison Company, the principal contractors for the energy produced at Hoover Dam, provide their own transmission facilities. In effect, the purchasers come to the dam for their power and carry it away themselves.[11]

Construction of the Hoover Dam was approved by Congress in order to control floods, improve navigation, regulate the flow of the Colorado River, provide for storage and delivery of the river waters for reclamation of public lands and for other beneficial purposes. While power production was no longer entirely incidental to the accomplishment of these purposes, it was given a secondary position and the law was written so that all citizens of Arizona, Nevada, and California, without excluding any group, would have access to the power.[12]

The TVA Act

Passage of the TVA Act in 1933 brought a radical step in a new direction.* Although power was not mentioned

* Tennessee Valley Authority Act of 1933, Public Law No. 17, 73d Cong., 1st Sess., H.R. 5081, 16 USCA 831. The intent of some of the proponents of the act was apparently not clearly stated in the language of the bill proposed to Congress. In his message to the Congress requesting passage of "legislation to create a Tennessee Valley Authority—a corporation clothed with the power of government but possessed of the flexibility and initiative of a private enterprise," President Roosevelt said:

The continued idleness of a great national investment in the Tennessee Valley leads me to ask the Congress for legislation necessary to enlist this project in the service of the people.

It is clear that the Muscle Shoals development is but a small part of the potential public usefulness of the entire Tennessee River. Such use, if envisioned in its entirety, transcends mere power development: it enters the wide fields of flood control, soil erosion, afforestation, elimination from agricultural use of marginal lands, and distribution and diversification of industry. In short, this power development of war days leads logically

in the preamble to the act as one of the purposes for
establishing TVA, the heart of the act was substantially

---

to national planning for a complete river watershed involving many
States and the future lives and welfare of millions. It touches and gives
life to all forms of human concerns.

I, therefore, suggest to the Congress legislation to create a Tennessee
Valley Authority—a corporation clothed with the power of government
but possessed of the flexibility and initiative of a private enterprise. It
should be charged with the broadest duty of planning for the proper use,
conservation, and development of the natural resources of the Tennessee
River drainage basin and its adjoining territory for the general social
and economic welfare of the Nation. This authority should also be clothed
with the necessary power to carry these plans into effect. Its duty should
be the rehabilitation of the Muscle Shoals development and the coordination of it with the wider plan.

Many hard lessons have taught us the human waste that results from
lack of planning. Here and there a few wise cities and counties have
looked ahead and planned. But our Nation has "just grown." It is time
to extend planning to a wider field, in this instance comprehending in
one great project many States directly concerned with the basin of one
of our greatest rivers.

This in a true sense is a return to the spirit and vision of the pioneer.
If we are successful here we can march on, step by step, in a like development of other great natural territorial units within our borders. [House
of Representatives, Document No. 15, 73d Cong., 1st Sess., Apr. 10, 1933.]
This statement, too, was open to interpretation. One view of it
was expressed by David E. Lilienthal, one of the original members
of the TVA Board and later its Chairman, in his private journal:

During the past year, I have had an opportunity of visiting several times
with Mr. Justice Brandeis, once at his summer home at Chatham on
Cape Cod about a year ago, and the other times at his home in Washington. One point which he has made consistently in these conferences has
special timeliness right now. He pointed out that we can't have a democracy and at the same time have great fortunes, nor great disparities in
wealth and power derived from wealth. Accordingly he would tax great
wealth out of existence through income and inheritance taxes. This would
produce tremendous revenues for the government, which he would use
for a program of social service which would have the effect of rendering
useful service and still providing employment.

The importance of this latter part of his thesis is emphasized by his
insistence that we are through increasing our productive machinery as a
part of private business. In support of this point, he referred to the
experience in the razor blade industry, with which he is familiar as a
former counsel for the Gillette people of Boston. He had just heard that
the Gillette people had purchased the plant and property of certain other
razor blade companies, not for the purpose of using those plants to pro-

the same as the previous TVA bills proposed by Senator Norris. In fact, having discovered that under the Constitution the TVA could not be built with power as the primary function, Senator Norris had consciously omitted reference to it. He described his attitude frankly in 1936 during Senate hearings concerning another proposed valley authority, this one to take the whole Mississippi Valley as its province. Senator Norris said: ". . . I will say to you that I think in view of the decisions . . . by

---

duce razor blades, but for the avowed purpose of scrapping them, since the existing facilities owned by the Gillette people and operated by them were adequate to supply all the needs for razor blades which it might have. The same with many other industries where existing facilities were more than adequate for any possible need, and duplication of facilities was maintained for private competitive reasons.

Accordingly, he said, we must look around for enterprises which private business cannot go into because there is no profit in them and because of the public nature of the enterprises, which will render service to the community and at the same time furnish necessary employment to the millions of men who will otherwise be permanently unemployed because of the technological developments of which the razor blade instance is an illustration.

When I asked him concretely what he had in mind, he referred as an instance to the control of soil erosion. He had some figures on the enormous extent to which the rich topsoil of the country was being washed off and carried out to sea by surface waters, with the consequent irreparable loss in value to the country's agriculture, a process which if indefinitely continued might eventually threaten the country's capacity to produce food. Here, he said, is a project calling for billions of dollars of expenditure which no private agency could possibly undertake and which would call for the employment of millions of men, as with forestation, reforestation, slum clearance, and other similar enterprises.

All of this (which he talked to me first about on January 4, 1933) is particularly interesting in view of President Roosevelt's comments at the time he announced the Tennessee Valley project. The President had there in mind the employment of men to improve the economic and social conditions of that valley, irrespective of whether the improvement would pay in dollars and cents. He apparently had in mind two things—the necessity for employing men rather than keeping them on some form of dole for which no useful work was performed, and second, the necessity of enriching the community life of that part of the country. This sounds very much like Brandeis' ideas applied to a particular area.. [David E. Lilienthal, *The Journals of David E. Lilienthal*, vol. I, *The TVA Years 1939-1945*, Harper & Row, Publishers, New York, 1964, pp. 35-36.]

the Supreme Court—I think the constitutionality of this kind of legislation hangs on navigation; so it is important . . . to make navigation important."[13]

When, in 1935, the constitutionality of the TVA Act was being questioned before the United States Supreme Court on the grounds that it was in reality a power authority, Commissioner Stanley Reed, representing TVA, told the Court:

"If we assume that this Act was primarily for navigation, then it would be valid. If we determine that this Act, while stating that it is for navigation, national defense, and flood control, is actually for the purpose of developing power and selling it commercially, the Act would be invalid." [14]

The investor-owned electric power companies serving the Tennessee Valley Region in 1933 did not oppose the proposed development of the valley, but they were deeply concerned that a corporation "clothed with the power of government," as the proposal put it, and armed with subsidies, could enter the power business in the area. The companies offered to purchase power produced by TVA and distribute it to consumers.* But this was

---

* Mr. Wendell L. Willkie, President of the Commonwealth and Southern Corp., said (in hearings before the U.S. Congress, House of Representatives, Tennessee Valley Authority, Committee on Military Affairs, 73d Cong., 1st Sess., 1933, p. 107):

I want to say, Mr. Chairman, that no one has read or referred with more gratification than we have of this magnificent proposed development of the Tennessee Valley. As the responsible executive officers representing this investment in the Tennessee Valley, the largest investment in that valley, we view with a great deal of anticipation the proposed program of the President of the United States with reference to that valley. And we do not come here either as opposition or protestant witnesses against that proposition.

Under cross examination, Mr. E. A. Yates, Vice President of Commonwealth and Southern, added the following testimony on the same point:

Mr. Hill: Mr. Yates, as I understood Mr. Willkie, he said that you all

not to be.   Despite assurances that the TVA Act of 1933
was primarily a navigation and flood control project, with
power production only an incidental activity, passage of
the bill brought quick confirmation of its true aim.
Within a year, Dr. Arthur E. Morgan, the first Chairman
of TVA, stated unequivocally to the Senate Appropriations Committee that power production was the major
purpose of the dams of the Authority. [15]

The TVA preference clause.   The first five TVA bills
which Senator Norris had introduced had spoken forth-
rightly about generation of electricity but had contemplated fair and equitable distribution of the power
among all types of consumers.   The sixth bill had included a different idea, which was to be repeated in the
seventh and eighth.   This new idea was embodied in
the TVA Act of 1933.   It gave preference to states, counties, municipalities, and cooperatives purchasing power
for distribution and included a provision specifying that
any contracts signed with electric companies for sale of
TVA power could be canceled on 5 years' notice if the
power was needed by a preference customer.   In other
words, power enterprises financed with government subsidized capital and excused from paying Federal income
taxes were given preference in the purchase of energy
from power generating enterprises enjoying these same
special privileges.   The idea no longer was to ensure
widespread use of power produced at Federal projects
but to give preferential treatment to government-owned

---

did not oppose the President's plan or program for the development of
the Tennessee River. Is that correct?

Mr. Yates: That is true; yes, sir.

Mr. Hill: As I understand it, the only thing to which you dissent is
the construction of transmission lines. Is that true?

Mr. Yates: That is right. [*Ibid.*, p. 118. See also U. S. Congress, House
of Representatives, Tennessee Valley Authority, hearings before Committee on Military Affairs, 74th Cong., 1st Sess., 1935, p. 253.]

and government-financed agencies. The preference clause was wholly different from the original idea of preference included in the Reclamation Act of 1906. With the new concept of preference the TVA Act became a vehicle to promote government ownership of utilities.

The idea of giving preferences in the purchase of electric energy generated at Federal projects has complicated the problem of government operation of electric power facilities for more than half a century. The Reclamation Act of 1902 had made no reference to power, but it was understood that electricity could be produced from the storage of water behind irrigation dams and that it could be used to run project pumps. The Reclamation Act of 1906 spelled out plainly that any excess power produced at these projects could be sold, with preference being given to municipal uses. It was the use which concerned Congress at the time, not the users.[16]

Language similar to that of the 1906 Act was included in legislation passed in 1911,[17] and the principle was further set forth in an opinion of the Acting Attorney General in 1913. In his opinion, however, the Acting Attorney General emphasized that

The duty to prefer municipal purposes in the making of leases is secondary and incidental. If, where a surplus of power became available, opportunities should occur to dispose of it for municipal uses, and the terms offered in return were at least as advantageous to the project as the terms offered in behalf of other uses, it would be the duty of the Secretary to make the lease for the municipal uses, but not so if, in his judgment, the contract would prove more profitable if made in the other way.[18]

That is, the Secretary of the Interior was not obligated to sell all surplus power at Federal projects to preference customers only. In fact, in 1908 the Secretary allowed a group of citizens to operate three small power plants at a reclamation project in Utah and this practice has been continued ever since. By 1963, there had been close to thirty hydroelectric projects undertaken in which the Federal government built the dam and leased the power privileges.[19]

The Federal Power Act of 1920 contained a preference clause which moved in a direction away from the previous positions but which seems to express much of the same philosophy as the Acting Attorney General's opinion of 1913. It says:

[That] in issuing preliminary permits hereunder or licenses where no preliminary permit has been issued and in issuing licenses under section 808 of this title the Commission shall give preference to applications therefor by States and municipalities, provided the plans for the same are deemed by the Commission equally well adapted, or shall within a reasonable time to be fixed by the Commission be made equally well adapted, to conserve and utilize in the public interest the water resources of the region; and as between other applicants, the Commission may give preference to the applicant the plans of which it finds and determines are best adapted to develop, conserve, and utilize in the public interest the water resources of the region, if it be satisfied as to the ability of the applicant to carry out such plans.[20]

That is, the welfare of the people was paramount and if development of a site by an investor-owned group was considered to be more beneficial to the public at large, that group would be granted a license. A governmental body was to have preference only in the event its proposal was at least equal to that of the nongovernmental group.

The TVA Act went much further. It extended preference to states, counties, municipalities, and cooperative organizations of citizens or farmers "not organized or doing business for profit." * It provided that contracts

* This concept of preference had been expounded by H. S. Raushenbush in 1929 in a symposium *The Socialism of Our Times.*

with investor-owned companies could be canceled on 5 years' notice if the TVA Board of Directors decided that the power was needed for a state, county, or municipality. It provided that if any power were to be sold to an individual or a corporation, they would have to agree to a retail rate schedule fixed by the TVA Board. It directed the TVA Board of Directors to promote the use of electricity in its area, to make studies and carry on experiments for this purpose, and to build transmission lines to farms and small villages. In addition, the act stated that electricity produced should be used primarily for the benefit of the people of the section, particularly residential and rural customers, with sales to industry being in a secondary category.*

He wrote: "We cannot hope to take over the whole eight billion dollar (electric utility) industry successfully, even if it were generally thought advisable to do so at the moment. There would be danger of sabotage. But by putting in a preference that power from these developments shall be furnished by state and municipal plants, we can move toward a system of linked-up plants such as the Ontario Hydroelectric Commission. While the long time aim of the liberal and radical groups is the abolition of the profit system for private use, our present strategy should be to make and take every opportunity to prove that there is something better than the profit system. Within the next ten years we are going to have a chance such as we have not had for the last forty." (H. S. Raushenbush, *The Socialism of Our Times*, The Vanguard Press, New York, 1929, as quoted in *Encroaching Socialism*.)

* Public Law No. 17, 73d Cong., (H.R. 5081) approved May 18, 1933. The TVA rate policy was a matter of controversy, even among the three members of the TVA Board, for a number of years. The two major points of view were recorded in hearings of the Joint Committee on the Investigation of the TVA, 75th Cong., 3d Sess., 1938. On the one hand was Dr. A. E. Morgan, Chairman of the TVA Board, who felt that TVA rates for electric power could be used only as a yardstick if all proper costs were included. Over his objections, however, the several functions of TVA had been divided among the three members of the board and power matters placed in the hands of David E. Lilienthal, a former Chicago lawyer

and member of the Wisconsin Public Utilities Commission. Lilienthal's chief assistant at TVA was Llewellyn Evans, an electrical engineer, who had been employed by the Tacoma, Washington, municipal power agency. In designing TVA rates, Lilienthal called on E. H. Zinder, a member of the staff of the Wisconsin Commission, who later was to be employed by the Rural Electrification Administration and then by the Federal Power Commission, for advice. Zinder wrote Lilienthal a memorandum pointing out that "Three possible principles may be followed by the Authority in determining its rates that lead in three distinct directions. They are: (1) Cost of service basis, (2) value of service basis, and (3) social basis." After describing cost of service basis and value of service basis, both of which are regularly considered in the electric utility business, he described the third basis in these words: "The social basis would disregard cost entirely. It would follow the value of the service where necessary to get the business but go below the additional cost of service where the margin is available from other classes of business in order to spread the use of electricity as much as possible among the small and particularly rural users. It is outright discrimination based upon social values, and therefore might be rationalized as reasonable." He went on to point out that "The social basis would be the one most open to attack by private industries and utilities particularly, as well as by many municipalities who may not be in the subsidized class. It would charge small villages and hamlets far removed from the source of power the same average rate per kilowatt-hour as large cities and industrial customers located near the plant. It would spread rural transmission lines into thin, poor, rural territory where the farmer might be barely able to afford to wire his home for lights only and pay a small nominal cost for the service used. This policy is recommended to the Authority as the one leading to the final results believed to be desired." (Report of the Joint Committee Investigating the Tennessee Valley Authority, Apr. 3, 1939, Sen. Doc. 56, 76th Cong., 1st Sess., pp. 194, 288–290.)

Apparently, Lilienthal followed this advice. Without the consent of the other members of the TVA Board, and without the knowledge of the Chairman, he announced a rate schedule to the press based on the rates of Tacoma, Washington, and using the Zinder "social basis" as justification. The resulting rates, Lilienthal once said, were "a lucky guess." Dr. A. E. Morgan objected vigorously to the idea that rates devised in this way could be described as a "yardstick." As a result of this and other differences of opinion with the other members of the Board, Dr. Morgan eventually was removed from the TVA Board by President Roosevelt.

In 1935 the act was amended to give TVA's managers even more sweeping powers in encouraging government ownership and operation of electric power facilities. They were authorized to acquire existing electric facilities used in serving farms and small villages and to help preference customers acquire distribution systems by awarding them 5-year loans or by selling them the distribution systems TVA had already acquired.[21] They were also able to make contracts for the sale of power that prohibited TVA customers from manufacturing supplemental power or from purchasing power from any other source.* TVA was also able to limit the use of power revenues of its customers so that, except for payments made in lieu of taxes, they could not be diverted to nonpower uses.[22] Thus, it was able to keep its customers completely dependent and to force almost every investor-owned electric utility company in the area out of business.

During the 10-year period from 1934 to 1944 there was a rash of proposals for other valley authorities on the TVA model. In addition to the Mississippi Valley Authority, bills were introduced for an Arkansas Valley Authority, a Missouri Valley Authority, a Columbia River Valley Authority, a Merrimack Valley Authority, and others. There were even bills, introduced by Senator Norris and Congressman John Rankin, to create seven valley authorities that would cover the entire country.[23]

* Power contract between TVA and city of Columbia, dated May 15, 1949: "Municipality shall in no event obtain, by generation, purchase, or otherwise, power from any source, other than the Authority's electric system, without the consent of Authority, unless Authority has refused to supply Municipality such additional quantities of power as may have been applied for as provided herein, and then only to the extent of its requirements in excess of the power available from Authority." (*Annual Report of the Tennessee Valley Authority, 1950*, p. A39.)

Arkansas Valley Authority

The first bill proposing creation of an Arkansas Valley Authority was introduced in the House of Representatives by John E. Miller of Arkansas in 1934.[24] It failed to pass. In 1935 Representative Miller proposed a more comprehensive bill calling for Federal development of the Arkansas, White, Red, and Ouachita River Valleys.[25] During the following years variations of this proposal were presented almost annually.

In 1939 Representative Clyde T. Ellis of Arkansas, who was to become the first general manager of the National Rural Electric Cooperative Association, introduced a bill calling for development of the White River and for the creation of a government corporation to operate it.[26] He made a somewhat similar proposal the following year.[27] Then, in December of 1940 he went to Knoxville, Tennessee, and met with officials of TVA to draft a revised version of the bill.[28] In 1941, Ellis presented his new bill, modeled closely on the TVA and including the Arkansas, St. Francis, Red, and White Rivers. This bill called for flood control and navigation improvement on the rivers, but there was no question about the intent of the bill.[29] In describing it, Ellis said that it provided

. . . for a three-member board (The Arkansas Valley Authority) to administer a well-rounded program of total water control, including irrigation, flood control, navigation, drainage, production and distribution of power, reforestation, wildlife propagation, and erosion and dust control within these basins, subject only to the rights of the affected States. The falling water would be harnessed, insofar as it would not conflict with flood control, navigation, and irrigation, to produce hydroelectric power. Steam plant production of power to facilitate the hydro, using our cheap gas, oil, and coal, is also provided.[30]

At the time, the Denver *Post* quoted Ellis as saying that the Arkansas Valley Authority legislation had been "drafted at the direction of President Roosevelt." He went on to say that the agency would establish a "yardstick" electric power rate for its 308,165-mile area, an area seven times larger than the Tennessee Valley.*

The reason he introduced the bill, Ellis said, was that "in the Arkansas Valley Authority area there is no surplus power for future expansion; an imminent shortage impends; and in terms of new war industries which the government would like to locate in the Arkansas Valley Authority area, many of them using electrolytic processes, we just do not have any power." [31]

Of course, there was no power shortage in the Arkansas Valley region. The investor-owned companies had ample reserve capacity and had plans for building more.

Congress did not approve the idea of establishing an

* Denver *Post*, Jan. 10, 1941. President Roosevelt's interest in the bill was also expressed in a letter to Ellis saying:

"Dear Mr. Ellis: In reply to your letter of September 23 in regard to the Arkansas Valley Authority bills, I want to assure you of my continued interest in the enactment of this legislation.

"The value of such authorities in assuring defense power supply has been amply demonstrated during the past 2 years. I am glad that the White and Red Rivers projects, which in effect will form the nucleus of this Arkansas Valley regional program, are going ahead. Recent studies of the power requirements of the defense program indicate that they should be expedited.

"I am also convinced that such authorities, based on full utilization of the resources of our river basins, can play a vital role in the eventual adjustment to a peacetime economy which the post-war world will require.

"You are, of course, aware of the difficult problems involved in reconciling varying points of view toward this type of legislation. For this reason I am sure that you will appreciate the importance of the careful work which the Bureau of the Budget is doing in reaching a solution which will assure the expediting of these river-basin programs on the soundest possible basis. It would please me very much to see the enactment of the Arkansas Valley Authority at this session. Sincerely yours, Franklin D. Roosevelt." [Congressional Record, 77th Cong., 1st Sess., Vol. 87, Part 13. Oct. 9, 1941, p. A4582.]

Arkansas Valley Authority. Investor-owned companies still supply the area, and there has never been a power shortage.

In January, 1942, Leland Olds, then Chairman of the Federal Power Commission, explained what had been meant by a "power shortage" in the Arkansas Valley. Speaking before a meeting of members of rural electric cooperatives, he said: "Now just a final word as to whether the contention that there is enough power for the defense requirements of the region will hold water. I can assure you that there is never enough power and can never be enough power to meet the requirements of modern war." [32]

Of course, Mr. Olds was not referring to an existing power shortage but was assuming that the war would create an unusual increase in demand for electric power which would require government financing. Not everyone took the same view. Charles W. Kellogg, then president of the Edison Electric Institute, and from June, 1940, to June, 1941, a dollar-a-year power consultant with the Office of Production Management, reasoned that war would not accelerate an increase in the over-all demand for electricity. There would be a shift in industry from the production of civilian goods, such as automobiles, to production of war materials, such as tanks, but the use of energy would be limited by the availability of materials and manpower. He did foresee an increase in output of electric energy in certain industrial areas because factories would be working more hours per day, but he said this would increase the load factors of the power suppliers without corresponding increase in peak demand. More energy would be produced from the existing power-producing capacity because the demand would be steadier. [33]

Kellogg pointed out that England had been concerned

about its ability to meet wartime power needs at the beginning of the war and had hurriedly imposed rationing of electricity on residential and commercial uses. However, it soon became apparent that rationing was not necessary and was soon abandoned. Commenting on the reasons for this situation, *The Electrical Review* of London of April 19, 1940, said:

In 1914 electricity was comparatively little used, so that productive effort had to be turned to the construction of local generating plants, and this often delayed munitions making. Now, owing to its general availability, supply can be obtained generally with little trouble from extensive systems, and the additional load occasioned by meeting the requirements of our armed forces is a relatively small proportion of the whole.[34]

As Kellogg noted, another part of the reason for the English ability to meet wartime power needs was that a power grid had been established on the basis of American experience with interconnection.[35] Mr. Kellogg's view proved to be correct.

Of course, there was a need for governmental control of manufacture of turbines and electric generating equipment. The needs of ships and other wartime uses had to come first. Those in charge of allocating materials had to decide what materials could be allocated to power production, but there was no need for government financing of power facilities once the materials allocations had been made.

Congressman Ellis made one more try at introducing his Arkansas Valley Authority proposal in 1942, this time in a form drafted by the Bureau of the Budget. In presenting the revised bill, Ellis reported that many major cogs of the proposed Authority were already in existence or on the way. They included, he said:

First. The giant Norfork Dam under construction on the White River in Arkansas has been authorized for power in addition to flood control.

Second. The huge Grand River Dam in Oklahoma has been completed, except for its flood-control features, and is producing power.

Third. The Nimrod Dam on the Fourche La Fave in Arkansas has been completed for flood control only, but power can and will be installed.

Fourth. The Fort Gibson and fifth, Markham Ferry Dams on the Grand in Oklahoma have been authorized for both flood control and power, and initial appropriations made for the beginning of their construction.

Sixth. The gigantic Bull Shoals and, seventh, Table Rock Dams on the White in Arkansas and Missouri and, eighth, the Narrows on the Little Missouri in Arkansas have all been authorized for both flood control and power.

Ninth and tenth. Two extensive REA transmission cooperatives, Kamo and Ark-La, in Kansas, Arkansas, Missouri, Oklahoma and Louisiana have been incorporated in the area and are constructing far-flung lines, partially to serve war projects.

Eleventh. Ark-La has ordered construction of a 45,000 kilowatt-gas-fueled generating plant in the sour gas fields of South Arkansas.

Twelfth. The Defense Plant Corporation has ordered construction of a 120,000 kilowatt gas-fueled generating plant on Lake Catherine in Arkansas to supply an aluminum plant.

Thirteenth. REA cooperatives have constructed many thousands of miles of small transmission lines in the area.[36]

This bill also failed to pass the Congress. However, it is interesting to note here the manner in which Ellis suggested tying the REA in with a vast government power project modeled after TVA but covering a much larger area.

In April, 1942, Ellis declared himself a candidate for the Senate from the state of Arkansas. The primary plank in his platform was the Arkansas Valley Authority idea. Mr. Ellis was not elected.[37]

The Mississippi Valley Authority

In 1936 Senator Norris submitted an ambitious proposal "to provide for the control of flood waters in the Mississippi Valley, to improve navigation on the Mississippi River and its tributaries, to provide for the irrigation of arid and semiarid lands, and for other purposes." [38] By that point, few people could mistake what Senator Norris meant by "other purposes."

The bill defined the Mississippi Valley area as "all that section of the United States the waters of which, if undiverted, ultimately flow into the Mississippi River." This meant, roughly, three-quarters of the country. Despite the fact that electric power was not mentioned in the preamble of the bill, the body of the proposal included authorization to sell electric power from dams that might be built and also authorization for construction of steam electric stations.[39] Congress looked on this idea with disfavor, just as it had on the Arkansas Valley proposal.

The seven TVAs

In 1937, President Roosevelt sent a message to Congress suggesting the formation of seven regional authorities, along the lines of the TVA. One was to be for the Atlantic Seaboard, a second for the Great Lakes and Ohio Valley, a third for the drainage basin of the Tennessee and Cumberland Rivers, a fourth for the drainage basin of the Missouri River and the Red River of the North, a fifth embracing the drainage basins of the Arkansas, Red, and Rio Grande Rivers, a sixth for the basins of the Colorado River and rivers flowing into the Pacific south of the California-Oregon line, and a seventh for the Columbia River Basin. The activities of all these bodies was to be coordinated by a National Planning Board "to ensure conformity to national policy." *

Senator Norris introduced a bill proposing the formation of these seven TVAs into the Senate,[40] and a companion bill was presented to the House of Representatives by Congressman John Rankin of Mississippi,[41] the self-styled "chairman of the public power bloc" in Congress.[42] Extensive hearings were held, and a little support for the idea was found.

In later years Congressman Rankin proposed variations of the bill, sometimes suggesting seven authorities and sometimes nine, but Congress never approved them. In 1944, President Roosevelt revived the proposal in a press conference. It attracted brief attention but still found only slight support, and it died a natural death.*

* The New York *Times*, June 4, 1937. The seven TVAs idea apparently originated with President Roosevelt. In a talk with Senator Norris, he took a piece of paper, sketched a map of the United States, and drew on it seven regions. These regions were the authorities proposed in the President's message to Congress. (Lilienthal, *The Journals of David E. Lilienthal*, Vol. I, p. 243.)

* New York *Herald Tribune*, Nov. 15, 1944. One of the difficulties affecting all the regional authority proposals was that two strong points of view were represented in the Administration. One, forcefully advocated by David Lilienthal (see Lilienthal, *op. cit.*,) held that regional authorities should be directed by three-man boards located in the regions and reporting directly to the President. The other view, presented by Harold Ickes and others, held that the authorities should be directed by a single administrator as the Bonneville Power Administration, and that all the administrators should act under a central administration in the Department of the Interior. (See Harold L. Ickes, *The Secret Diary of Harold L. Ickes, The Lowering Clouds, 1939–1941*, Simon and Schuster, New York, p. 400, et seq.) Ickes was anxious that all Federal power activities including the REA be brought under his department. In 1941, he went so far as to have three men from the Interior Department's Power Division, one of whom was H. S. Raushenbush, call on Senator Norris to convince him that this was a wise course. (Lilienthal, *The Journals of David E. Lilienthal*, Vol. I, p. 365.) The attempt was unsuccessful.

Columbia Valley Administration

The week before Christmas, 1940, President Roosevelt, David Lilienthal of the TVA, and Governor Olson of California met in Washington. The purpose of the meeting was to accelerate formation of two regional authorities, one in the Pacific Southwest and the other in the Columbia River Valley. Lilienthal and the TVA staff were assigned the task of drafting a bill that would authorize formation of these agencies.[43] This was done and the bills were introduced, but they were fated to die in committee.

In analyzing the reasons for the failure of these regional proposals, it seemed to Lilienthal that the greatest opposition came from certain agencies of the Federal government which, he thought, had developed considerable political power. Writing in his diary in 1942, he noted that:

The idea of a regional resources development agency runs counter to the vested interest of the existing departments, the Interior Department, the War Department, and the Department of Agriculture. It is almost incredible how powerful these supposed creatures of a democratic government can be in enforcing their vested jurisdictional prerogatives. Like most other jurisdictional or vested interests, they no longer even pretend to defend their position on the ground of merits but simply that their toes are being stepped on.

The political power of such agencies, in the West, as the Bureau of Reclamation of the Department of the Interior, or the AAA in the Department of Agriculture, or the Corps of Engineers in the War Department, is simply astounding. There are large blocs of votes which they control, just as much as the railroad used to control votes, and by some, though not all, of the same methods. The money they use is not expended to line the pockets of Congressmen. But it is public money which they hold out as bait or withhold as punishment in the way of expenditures in a particular Congressional district. This is done boldly and without any apologies whatever. Some of the New Deal politicos in administrative jobs are just as barefaced about the matter of seizing political power through administration of these so-called New Deal laws as the old-line bureaucrats are or as an old-time political hack Tammany alderman could possibly be. . . .

The Columbia River situation is a fair example. That project is designed to control the waters of a single river for multiple public purposes. It has been impossible to get a bill through Congress that coincides with the desires of the people of the region because the Bureau of Reclamation and the Corps of Engineers have more political influence than the people themselves are able to express. This story is told to me time and again by people from that region who have every means of knowing.[44]

In 1949 a new bill was proposed in the Congress providing for a Columbia Valley Administration.[45] In discussing this proposal on the floor of the House, Representative Harris Ellsworth of Oregon said that the proposal

. . . which would turn the sovereign States of the Pacific Northwest into a rigidly controlled unit called a Columbia Valley Authority is too radical a departure toward dictatorship to be tolerated even by the Socialist Party. I have occasionally referred to the scheme as socialistic. I have to take that statement back now. At its meeting in Seattle, May 13, the Socialist Party issued a statement condemning the pending CVA bills: "We realize that CVA is a socialistic venture."

Their formal statement says: "The Socialist Party is alarmed at the present rapid trend toward collectivization without democratic controls. Upon analysis of H. R. 4286, the Mitchell Bill, the Socialist Party finds no adequate safeguards to insure democratic control under this measure. It centralizes power in the President and three of his appointees, thereby in some measure justifying the charge of opponents that CVA will be a step in the direction of the authoritarian state."

I never thought the day would come when I could agree with a Socialist statement, but I do agree with their statement which I have just quoted.[46]

The CVA bills received extensive hearing in committees of the Senate and the House and were opposed by five of seven Western governors.[47] But they were never acted upon by Congress. The majority of the members apparently did not think enough of the idea to bring it to a vote.

Missouri Valley Authority

In 1944 the Federal Administration began an attempt to establish the Missouri Valley Authority, which was to cover all or substantial portions of South Dakota, Nebraska, Missouri, North Dakota, Montana, Wyoming, Iowa, Colorado, and Kansas.[48] To Secretary of the Interior Harold Ickes the idea of such an authority seemed "a major step in the basic reorganization of the government of the United States as we have known it for the last 150 years." [49]

After extended hearings and much public debate, the Senate committees failed to recommend the plan. For a number of years, revised versions of the plan were introduced into Congress, but they met with no success. However, the Federal government has continued to build hydroelectric dams on the Upper Missouri and the REA has made loans to cooperatives to build steam generating plants in the area.

Congress says No

This brief history of the valley authority idea illustrates something of the magnitude of the plans that advocates of government power and members of the Federal Administration had for extending the TVA concept. Some of those who opposed this concept were concerned that multipurpose dams might not be the wisest way to develop the nation's rivers. Some were particularly concerned about the wisdom of having the Federal government enter commercial activity that was being adequately provided for through regular tree-market channels. Others may have felt, as did the prominent socialist Norman Thomas, that the TVA is "the only genuinely socialistic act" in the New Deal.[50] The feeling developed that a small group of people were using the TVA method as part of an effort to bring about government control of the economy without the understanding and support of the citizens of the nation.

The Bonneville Project Act

The amended preference provision of the TVA Act had worked quickly to create a government-financed electric enterprise in the Tennessee Valley region, but before the results of this development could be fully evaluated, the Bonneville Project Act of 1937 was written and a preference clause included that seems to have been intended as a promotional device for government ownership of electric facilities. In no previous act had customers of government-financed power agencies been so clearly and arbitrarily favored over the customers of investor-owned companies in the disposition of Federal power.

As early as 1914 the Department of the Interior, through the Bureau of Reclamation, began investigating the possibilities of developing the Columbia River. From time to time, the War Department had also made surveys of the river and its tributaries, and in 1927 Congress authorized surveys of a number of projects in the area.[51] Thus, in 1933 when the National Industrial Recovery Act authorized the construction of dams and other public works as a measure to meet the needs of the depression, it was possible to prepare a plan for the development of the Columbia in a very short time.[52]

The plan that served as the foundation for development of the river contemplated the construction of ten dams from the Canadian border to the Pacific. They were (1) Grand Coulee, (2) Foster Creek, (3) Chelan, (4) Rocky Reach, (5) Rock Island, (6) Priest Rapids, (7) Umatilla Rapids, (8) John Day Rapids, (9) The Dalles, and (10) Bonneville. On September 30, 1933, construction was started on the first of these, at Bonneville, under the supervision of the Corps of Engineers. The project was formally authorized by Congress in 1935.[53]

In 1934 President Roosevelt had appointed a National Power Policy Committee to develop a plan to unify national policy in power matters. It was not to be merely a fact-finding body, but rather one for the development of national policy.[54]

In announcing appointment of the Committee, President Roosevelt noted that it would, among other activities, shape legislation concerning holding companies and the regulation of electricity in interstate commerce. It would also develop means whereby electricity would "be made more broadly available at cheaper rates to industry, to domestic and particularly, to agricultural customers." It was to operate under the PWA, and Secretary of the Interior Harold Ickles was named Chairman. The other members were Morris L. Cooke, REA Administrator; Robert E. Healy, Securities and Exchange Commission; David F. Lilienthal, TVA; General Edward M. Markham, War Department; Frank R. McNinch, Chairman, FPC; and T. W. Norcross, Forest Service, Department of Agriculture.[55] Before the Committee finished drafting recommendations for the entire nation, it paused to prepare special recommendations concerning the Bonneville Project. The President sent them to Congress with his approval in February, 1937,[56] and after 6 months the Bonneville Project Act was passed.

It stated that the Bonneville "administrator shall at all times, in disposing of electric energy generated at said project, give preference and priority to public bodies and cooperatives." It required that at least 50 percent of the available power be set aside for use of preference customers up to January 1, 1942, and that any portion of the 50 percent that preference customers could not use immediately could be disposed of temporarily to non-preference customers until preference customers could come forward to claim it. The act gave governmental bodies time to organize and obtain the necessary financial support to enter the power business, and it directed the Administrator to build and operate any transmission facilities necessary to transmit power to customers.[57]

The wording of the preference clause was strong, and it was used by John D. Ross, the first Bonneville Power Administrator, in an aggressive fashion. Ross had a vision of a superpower system covering the entire United States that would link the Federal dams along the Columbia River with Hoover Dam, the TVA, and, eventually, the New York State developments along the St. Lawrence River.[58] In 1938 he sketched a direct-current transmission system that would form these projects and existing municipal plants into a national grid (Chart 3·1). "Private power," he said, "has failed completely to foresee . . . the needs of the future."[59] Only government-owned power projects could accomplish this feat, according to Ross. The fact that it was not technologically nor economically feasible for direct current transmission to be used in the manner he described apparently did not enter into his thinking.

The Bonneville Power Administration grew quickly, and it was only the foresight, planning, and tenacious spirit of the investor-owned power companies in the re-

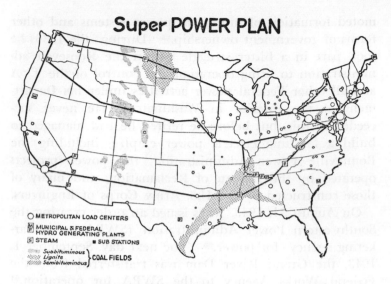

Super POWER PLAN

○ METROPOLITAN LOAD CENTERS
Ⓜ MUNICIPAL & FEDERAL
   HYDRO GENERATING PLANTS
Ⓢ STEAM   ■ SUB STATIONS

Subbituminous
Lignite   } COAL FIELDS
Semibituminous

Chart 3·1

gion which made it possible for the companies to stay in business and to grow in the face of all efforts to end their existence.[60]

Department of the Interior

As it became apparent that Congress was not going to approve establishment of additional valley authorities on the TVA model and that the preference clause as it had been developed in the Bonneville Project Act was too strong to suit most Americans, the Department of the Interior began a series of activities which used a modified preference clause to make valley authorities unnecessary.

Harold Ickes, the Secretary of the Interior, had been a vigorous proponent of government ownership of electric power facilities since the days of the Bull Moose campaign of 1910.[61] As PWA Administrator, he had actively promoted formation of municipal power systems and other forms of government ownership.[62] During the 1930s he took part in a bitter struggle within the Roosevelt administration to bring operation and control of the TVA and all other Federal power activities under his Department of the Interior in Washington. He never succeeded in this, but before he retired he had managed to build a far-flung electric power empire, including the Bonneville Power Administration, the power projects operated by the Bureau of Reclamation, and many of those constructed by the U.S. Army Corps of Engineers.

On August 31, 1943, Ickes issued an order creating the Southwestern Power Administration (SWPA) as a marketing agency for power.[63] The next day, September 1, 1943, the Grand River Dam was transferred from the Federal Works Agency to the SWPA for operation.[64] At the same time, the SWPA was given authority to take over the sale and distribution of electric power from Denison Dam on the Red River between Texas and Oklahoma and from the Norfork Dam on the North Fork of the White River in Northern Arkansas.[65]

In December, 1944, Congress passed the Flood Control Act of 1944 which gave the Secretary of the Interior authority and responsibility for selling electric power generated at governmental hydroelectric plants.[66] This act marked a significant change in the approach being taken by the advocates of government ownership in the power business. Although various multipurpose projects had been authorized by Congress prior to 1944, there had not been any definition of policy for marketing the energy they produced. Through public debate and in congressional committees extensive consideration was given to the question of marketing policy. In hearings on the Flood Control Act of 1944, Senator Overton, chairman of the Flood Control Subcommittee of the Senate Commerce Committee, said:

> I think I can safely say it was the opinion of the majority of the committee, if not all of them—of practically all of the members—that the Federal government should not take advantage of these dams and reservoirs in the generation of power to drive out existing private utilities that had been constructed, quasi-public in their character and under regulation by States, to drive them out of existence after they have been built at such large cost and be destructive of private capital that had been employed very largely, if not exclusively, for general public benefit.[67]

In explaining the intent of language used in the proposed act, the Senate committee stated that it desired an amendment which provided a convenient and practical method of disposing of power at projects under control of the War Department without setting up "a government power trust" which would be unduly competitive with existing utilities. The committee inserted a proviso in the proposed act which authorized the Secretary of the Interior to construct and acquire only such transmission lines or related facilities as might be necessary in order to make the power and energy generated at the projects available in wholesale quantities for sale on fair and reasonable terms and conditions to facilities owned by the Federal government, governmental bodies, cooperatives, and investor-owned utilities. The committee noted that preferences should be granted in the sale of power and energy to governmental bodies and cooperatives when the power is generated at projects financed by the Federal government.[68]

Senator McClellan of Arkansas said that a compromise along these lines would be fair to all parties, but he felt that its real test would lie in the way it was administered. He said:

The amendment . . . I think comes about as near being fair to both the utilities and the government as any provision which has yet been developed or proposed does . . .

In my judgment, if that provision . . . were properly administered, there would be no discrimination. No particular advantage would be given to one over another—for instance, to private enterprise over cooperatives or over public bodies. Certainly the provision is broad enough in its terms to permit the exercise of honest and sound discretion. The real test of this section or provision would be determined by the character of administration which would be applied to it.[69]

Section 5 of the Flood Control Act

Section 5 of the Flood Control Act of 1944 has an important place in the development of government power activities. It states:

Sec. 5. Electric power and energy generated at reservoir projects under the control of the Department of the Army and in the opinion of the Secretary of the Army not required in the operation of such projects shall be delivered to the Secretary of the Interior, who shall transmit and dispose of such power and energy in such manner as to encourage the most widespread use thereof at the lowest possible rates to consumers consistent with sound business principles, the rate schedules to become effective upon confirmation and approval by the Federal Power Commission. Rate schedules shall be drawn having regard to the recovery (upon the basis of the application of such rate schedules to the capacity of the electric facilities of the projects) of the cost of producing and transmitting such electric energy, including the amortization of the capital investment allocated to power over a reasonable period of years. Preference in the sale of such power and energy shall be given to public bodies and cooperatives. The Secretary of the Interior is authorized, from funds to be appropriated by the Congress, to construct or acquire by purchase or other agreement, only such transmission lines and related facilities as may be necessary in order to make the power and energy generated at said projects available in wholesale quantities for sale on fair and reasonable terms and conditions to facilities owned by the Federal Government, public bodies, cooperatives, and privately owned companies. All moneys received from such sales shall be deposited in the Treasury of the United States as miscellaneous receipts.[70]

Because of the crucial place of this chapter in the story of government power, it seems worthwhile to review the language in some detail. The section begins by describing the subject it will deal with: "Electric power and energy generated at reservoir projects. . . ." It refers to no other energy, such as energy generated in steam plants. Moreover, the projects it indicates are projects which unquestionably can be constructed by the Federal government under the Constitution. These include flood control and navigation projects, not projects built solely to produce electric power. The section authorizes the Secretary of the Interior to: "transmit and dispose of such power and energy. . . ."

And the reference is clearly to energy generated at the reservoir projects, not to some other energy, such as might be generated by steam. Later, the section outlines specific limitations placed on the authorization of transmission facilities. These limitations are intended to clarify the policy taken by Congress. "The Secretary of the Interior is authorized . . . to construct or acquire . . . only such transmission lines . . . as may be necessary. . . ."

This would seem to clarify the question of duplicating transmission lines. Certainly, this seems to have been the intent of the draftsmen. If some power company were to agree to build a certain transmission line at its expense, it would not seem necessary for the government to build such a line, and under the Flood Control Act of 1944, it would be improper for the government to do so.

Consider the question of steam generating stations as

they relate to power policy, defined in Section 5. It states:

> The Secretary of the Interior is authorized . . . to construct only such facilities as may be necessary in order to make the power and energy generated at said projects available . . .

Clearly, the act refers to power and energy generated at hydroelectric projects. Authorization is given only to build facilities to make hydroelectric power, not power from steam plants.

The language of the act does not authorize the Department of the Interior to build steam generating stations or to duplicate existing transmission lines. Under the act the Department does not have the right to build transmission lines which companies, financed in the free market, are willing and able to build. The intent of the act seems to have been to circumscribe the activities of the Department of the Interior in the electric power business so that the broad public interest would be served, rather than simply the interests of the advocates of government ownership. It did not give to the Department of the Interior a utility responsibility to assure a continuing power supply to preference customers.

The comprehensive plan

On November 21, 1945, Secretary Ickes appointed Douglas Wright, the Administrator of the Southwestern Power Administration, as marketing agent for all government power from river plants "in the area which is defined as comprising the states of Arkansas and Louisiana, that part of the states of Kansas and Missouri lying south of the Missouri River Basin, and east of the 98th meridian, and that part of the states of Texas and Oklahoma, lying east of the 99th meredian and north of the

San Antonio River Basin." It is an area of about 300,000 square miles, about six times as large as the entire state of Arkansas. It covers an area similar to that approved for the Arkansas Valley Authority which Congress had disapproved.

The order authorized the Administrator to buy or build transmission lines, to assist governmental bodies and cooperatives in buying, operating, and maintaining distribution systems, and to fix rates at which the governmental bodies and cooperatives could resell power purchased from Federal projects. Much of this seemed contrary to the language and intent of the Flood Control Act of 1944.[71]

In February, 1946, Wright appeared before a congressional committee to ask for funds to carry out what he called a "comprehensive plan" for the SWPA region.*

*Interior Department Appropriation Bill for 1947, Hearings before the House of Representatives Subcommittee of the Committee on Appropriations, 79th Cong., 2d Sess., pp. 7, 39. The "comprehensive plan" was strikingly similar to a plan which had been discussed in Washington for a number of years. In 1941, Robert Craig, Deputy Administrator of the REA, told a reporter: "The plan as now conceived would interconnect existing major publicly owned generating plants with new ones to be established, the whole probably to be connected with the TVA system, in order to get and distribute the power now sorely needed for defense in those three states, Louisiana, the TVA region, and other sections of the South and Southeast." The reporter wrote:

Some of it can be done fairly quickly while other phases will require several years. The cost is only a guess, until engineers can go into it to make thorough and complete estimates and investigations. Robert Craig, deputy administrator of the Rural Electrification Administration, said his guess is that it will run somewhere between 50 and 75 million dollars.

The whole thing, Craig says, is now in the "conversational stage," but certain parts of it are far beyond that. The idea is to use existing public power plants, which, of course, are beyond that stage and transmission lines, some of which are planned or under construction, together with new power plants, both hydro and steam, and new transmission lines. There is no good estimate right now as to how great a power pool it will make

He proposed to spend $125 million to build a transmission system largely duplicating the existing lines in the

because the shoe will be cut more or less, to fit the last—it will be enough to fill as much of the foreseen requirements as possible.

In addition to proposed or authorized hydro plants in those states, there are at least two steam plants getting very definite consideration. One of these is a steam plant at Gilmer, Upshur County, Texas. Craig said estimates show that power can be generated there, using natural gas, for approximately four mills per kilowatt hour.

Another steam plant is being proposed for the sour gas fields of Southern Arkansas. The cost there would approximate three mills.

Craig said that these rates are as low or lower than those afforded by many hydro-electric plants and they have the advantage that they can be constructed much more quickly than a hydro plant.

Both of these projects are definitely in the picture for connection in the proposed power network. Others are being given consideration but are not as definitely in the picture as these two.

One such project in Arkansas is a proposed steam plant in Franklin County, near Cass, and near the proposed Cass Lake recreation project. Nearby coal deposits would provide cheap fuel to operate a steam power generation unit.

For the hydroelectric plants, the chief sources of supply would be the Possum Kingdom Dam on the Brazos River in Texas and the Grand River Dam in Northwestern Oklahoma. Both are built and ready to supply power. To these would be added the Norfork Dam on the White River in Arkansas when it is completed and the Whitney Dam on the Brazos in Texas if and when authorized and constructed. Norfork is under construction and Whitney Dam is now pending in Congress for authorization. Legislation approving the latter will probably be passed by Congress this summer.

These are the main sources, but there will probably be others later, particularly on the White River.

As to the interconnections to form the power pool, REA has already approved a loan for construction of a heavy transmission line from the Possum Kingdom Dam to carry power to REA cooperatives. Under the general plan, this would be extended to become a link in the system.

The Kamo project, which calls for construction of a transmission line from Grand River Dam over into Arkansas and up into Missouri, also has been approved for a loan by REA. Under the general plan, it would go over to connect with Norfork Dam and from there, probably, the connection with TVA would be made.

Other lines would be built to connect these with the steam plants at Gilmer and in the sour gas fields, as well as any other public hydro and steam plants that may be constructed.

The idea is to get a source of power to meet defense requirements throughout that whole section. Right now, the power and defense question is a case of which comes first, the chicken or the egg. Defense projects area. He said he would also need to build steam plants in order to provide power when the hydroelectric projects were low on water. The steam plants were to cost another $75 million. In all, the plan proposed Federal expenditures of $200 million to build power facilities to serve people who already had an ample supply. Nothing in the proposal suggested building farm lines where they were needed or suggested an intent to get electricity to people who did not already have it.[72] An examination of maps of the existing transmission system

---

have been held back from that section, to an extent, because of a power shortage and those states find it difficult to get power development because there is no immediate demand for power on the spot. Now it appears that this difficulty is getting ironed out, to get the defense plants and their need for power coordinated.

Craig said that in the case of steam plants that certain standardized types and sizes can be built almost as quickly as the defense production plants, providing they can get priorities on generating equipment. This applies particularly to the proposed steam plants at Gilmer and in Arkansas.

Applying it to an actual example of what he means, Craig said consideration is being given to establishment of a zinc plant and an aluminum plant in Arkansas, but power shortage has been holding them back. He pointed out, however, that if the plants are authorized and at the same time a power plant in the sour gas fields is authorized, and given priority for equipment, both can be finished and ready for operation at about the same time.

He pointed out that this power plant could be started out as a 10,000 kilowatt plant at first and be enlarged later. That would be a standardized plant for which equipment can be turned out comparatively quickly. With a priority order to get equipment, it can be built within a year, he said. That capacity, he said, generates power enough to make 4,380 tons of aluminum a year.

A much larger plant, standardized at 30, 40, or 50 thousand kilowatts could be built in between a year and 16 months. [*Arkansas Democrat,* June 16, 1941.]

Clyde Ellis, in 1942, had described it as being well under way. It was of course the Arkansas Valley Authority in another guise. (Congressional Record, Vol. 88, Part 8, 77th Cong., 2d Sess., 1942, p. A238.) More will be said in Chapter 8 about the role of the REA, an agency authorized to help extend lines to rural customers, in building these large power systems, duplicating existing systems, to serve nonrural customers.

in the area and the lines proposed by SWPA gives an indication of the duplication involved (Chart 3·2).

The investor-owned companies serving the Southwest had made a formal proposal to the Department of the Interior that the peaking power generated at Federal hydroelectric projects be integrated with power produced at their steam plants.[73]   This approach, they pointed out, would increase the value of the government power.   The companies would be purchasing the energy at its full value, and any savings realized from the arrangement would be passed on to the consuming public under government regulation.

The companies informed the committees of Congress which were considering the SWPA request for $200 million of their proposal.[74]   Congress refused to grant SWPA the appropriation it desired and instructed it to make contracts with the companies in the region in order to

Chart 3·2

Transmission Lines Proposed by SWPA in 1946
AND EXISTING LINES IN THE AREA

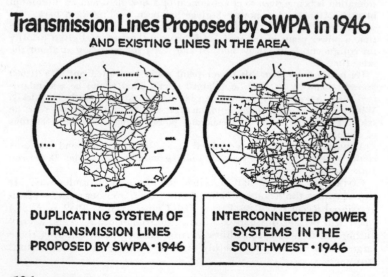

| DUPLICATING SYSTEM OF TRANSMISSION LINES PROPOSED BY SWPA · 1946 | INTERCONNECTED POWER SYSTEMS IN THE SOUTHWEST · 1946 |

avoid duplication and to pass the greatest benefit on to the public.

Another attempt at government ownership had not obtained congressional approval. But within a short time the rural electric cooperatives in the Southwest proposed the formation of a number of super-cooperatives which would generate and transmit energy. Unlike the appropriations for the activities of the Department of the Interior, appropriations for the REA are not reviewed project by project. A blanket authorization is made and the Administrator, without specific congressional approval, decides on how it is to be used. In this way, REA funds were provided to the super-cooperatives to build steam generating stations and transmission lines which then were tied in with SWPA.[75] In this way a system like the SWPA comprehensive plan which Congress turned down could be developed—without specific congressional approval.

Secretary Ickes' marketing policy

Little over a year after passage of the Flood Control Act of 1944, on January 3, 1946, Secretary Ickes issued a memorandum on power policy to all staffs of the Department of the Interior.[76] In it he said that even those laws not directly involving the Department of the Interior should serve to fix the general policy of the Department in administering power programs. By taking this position it becomes possible to circumvent the restrictions on departmental activities spelled out in specific laws. The memorandum stated that:

The Congress over a 40-year period has enacted a large number of laws relating to electrical power activities. Most, but not all, of these acts relate specifically to the Department of the Interior. The others serve equally to fix the general policy that must guide all

Interior Department staffs and officials in their administration of power programs. In recent years the Congress has greatly increased the responsibilities of the Department for the development and disposition of electrical energy. It is, therefore, appropriate to recapitulate the guiding principles which emerge from the individual acts of Congress, and which must govern the administrative actions of this Department in discharging its responsibilities relating to electrical power.

The primary objectives of the acts of Congress (excerpted in the attachment) may be summarized as follows:

1. Federal dams shall, where feasible, include facilities for generating electrical energy. (Reclamation Act of April 16, 1906; Act of July 25, 1912; the Tennessee Valley Authority Act of 1933; the Flood Control Acts of 1938, 1944 and 1945.)

2. Preference in power sales shall be given to public agencies and cooperatives. (Reclamation Act of April 16, 1906; the "Raker Act" of December 19, 1913; Federal Water Power Act of 1920; Boulder Canyon Act of 1928; Tennessee Valley Authority Act of 1933; Rural Electrification Act of 1936; Bonneville Act of 1937; Fort Peck Act of 1938; Reclamation Project Act of 1939; Flood Control Act of 1944.)

3. Power disposal shall be for the particular benefit of domestic and rural consumers. (Tennessee Valley Authority Act of 1933; Rural Electrification Act of 1936; Bonneville Act of 1937; Fort Peck Act of 1938.)

4. Power shall be sold at the lowest possible rates consistent with sound business principles. (Tennessee Valley Authority Act of 1933; Bonneville Act of 1937; Fort Peck Act of 1938; Flood Control Act of 1944.)

5. Power disposal shall be such as to encourage wide-spread use and to prevent monopolization. (Tennessee Valley Authority Act of 1933; Rural Electrification Act of 1936; Bonneville Act of 1937; Fort Peck Act of 1938; Flood Control Act of 1944.)

These basic policies are prescribed by Congress. It is the job of the Department of the Interior to carry them out, and to see that the administration of its power programs will in fact secure these objectives. The following principles are designed to implement the congressional policy. They will guide all staffs and officials of the Department who deal with power.

I PLANNING AND CONSTRUCTION

(a) Hydroelectric generating facilities shall be designed and installed in all projects where feasible. The project shall have its own steam standby and reserve facilities where necessary to independent operation on an economical and efficient basis.

(b) Facilities shall be designed and installed to provide the type of power and service required by public agencies and cooperatives.

(c) Construction shall be economical and efficient.

(d) Government hydroelectric plants within a region shall be integrated by transmission ties.

(e) Transmission outlets to existing and potential wholesale markets shall be adequate to deliver power to every preferred customer within the region upon fair and reasonable terms. They must be owned and controlled by the Government unless privately owned facilities should be made available upon terms which assure full accomplishment of the basic objectives of the congressional power policy and which do not reward the private company simply because of its strategic location or monopolistic position.

(f) Allocations of costs on multiple-purpose projects shall not result in power consumers paying for facilities not fairly to be attributed to the operation of the power system, except as may be necessary to make the project feasible as required by law.

OPERATION AND SALES

(a) Active assistance, from the very beginning of the planning and authorization of a project, shall be given to the organization of public agencies and cooperatives for the distribution of power in each project area. The statutory objectives are not attained by merely waiting for a preferred customer to come forward and offer to purchase the power.

(b) Operations shall be economical and efficient.

(c) Wholesale rate schedules shall be nondiscriminatory and shall be designed to bring power at the lowest possible rates to distributors that are principally serving domestic and rural consumers.

(d) Resale rate and other provisions shall be included in wholesale contracts with distributors to insure that power is furnished to the ultimate consumer at the lowest possible rates, which shall reflect as nearly as may be the cost of the service.

THE FEDERAL GOVERNMENT IN THE POWER BUSINESS *129*

(e) Public agencies and cooperatives shall be encouraged to build diversified loads and markets and neither the operations nor the markets of these agencies or of the Government facilities shall be restricted by contracts or operating agreements which might serve to limit the widespread use of the power from the Federal project.

(f) No contracts shall be made that operate to foreclose public agencies and cooperatives from obtaining power from the Government project. Contracts with these organizations shall recognize their preferential character and assure them full opportunity to secure the benefits of Federal power. Contracts with privately owned companies shall be limited in time and shall contain provisions for the cancellation or modification by the Government as necessary to insure preference to public agencies and cooperatives.

(g) Rates, contracts, and financial data shall be made public.

(h) A diversified development of the industries and resources of the region shall be given active encouragement in order to benefit the load factor and to promote the economic stability of the project as well as to aid in regional development.

(i) Public agencies and cooperatives which are existing or potential customers of the Federal project shall be given every assistance in promoting sound programs and operations.

This list of guiding principles is not intended to be exhaustive but is designed to serve as the primary operating basis for attaining the objectives which Congress has prescribed for Federal power programs. These principles will guide all staffs and reviewing official of the Department of the Interior who are administering power activities. The administration and review of these activities will be continued by the agencies and officials heretofore designated.[77]

The memorandum claims authority to build steam plants. It reflects a desire to have the Federal government assume full utility responsibility. It claims a requirement to provide the type of power and service required by governmental agencies and cooperatives, not simply if facilities are necessary, but in any instance. It claims authority to deliver power to every preference customer in a region. It asserts the right to withdraw from power contracts with investor-owned companies whenever necessary to ensure adequate supplies of energy are available for preference customers, and it undertakes to actively assist in the organization of preference groups.

Congress has never authorized any governmental body to assume public utility responsibility—the responsibility for furnishing all the power requirements of all customers, when and where the power is needed. Each one of these directives goes beyond the intent of Congress and the last is a declaration of intent to develop government ownership in the power business as rapidly as possible.

Bureau of Reclamation

The Bureau of Reclamation was created as part of the Department of the Interior in 1902 to locate, construct, operate, and maintain works for the storage, diversion, and development of waters for the reclamation of arid and semiarid lands in the Western states.[78] Except in the Columbia River Basin where BPA operates, it markets its own power. It also markets surplus power from projects built by the Corps of Engineers in the Missouri Basin and California, and from the International Boundary and Water Commission Dam on the Rio Grande.[79] As of 1966, it had an investment allocated to power of some $1,715,600,000 (Table 3·1).

Development of this vast Federal power system continues. In April, 1961, Kenneth Holum, Assistant Secretary of the Interior, said that "President Kennedy has declared it is his policy, and Secretary Udall has reiterated it on several occasions, to provide leadership directed to the development of a nation wide high-voltage, com-

Table 3·1 Power Capacity by Projects—Bureau of Reclamation

Project	Kilowatts in operation	Kilowatts under construction	Total Fed. investment, millions†	Allocated* to power, millions
Boise	36,500	....	$ 68.6	$ 4.8
Boulder Canyon	1,344,800	....	176.6	148.2
Central Valley	1,013,850	449,200	2,135.3	445.1
Collbran	13,500	....	16.6	10.3
Colorado Big-Thompson	183,950	....	162.7	61.1
Colorado River Front Work and Levee System	7,200	....	37.8	NA
Colorado River Storage	1,008,000	208,000	679.0	505.8
Columbia Basin	1,944,000‡	....	993.8	177.3
Eklutna	30,000	....	33.8	33.8
Grand Valley	3,000	....	8.4	0.2
Hungry Horse	285,000	....	102.1	77.4
Kendrick	68,400	....	32.6	17.7
Minidoka	13,400	....	38.9	2.6
Missouri River Basin	174,200	250,000	111.3	71.2
North Platte	4,800	....	36.6	7.2
Palisades	114,000	....	59.8	10.5
Parker-Davis	345,000	....	150.3	109.3
Provo River	4,950	....	37.9	1.1
Rio Grande	24,300	....	31.1	10.0
Riverton	1,600	....	30.4	0.5
Rogue River Basin	16,000	....	28.1	9.2
Seedskadee	....	10,000	48.7	3.4
Shoshone	10,600	....	25.2	4.4
Weber Basin	5,700	....	105.4	NA
Yakima	23,250	....	65.3	4.5
Total	6,676,000	917,200	$5,216.3	$1,715.6

* Some allocations tentative.   † Includes irrigation costs where part of project includes power; excludes costs of dams and irrigation works if no power installation is involved.

mon carrier transmission grid." [80] And in an interview the following month he said, "I think there will be many opportunities for the Department of the Interior to work with rural electric cooperatives and REA as an agency of the Federal government, in accomplishing transmission interties between the regional systems of the Federal government in the Department of the Interior." [81]

Southeastern Power Administration (SEPA)

Through the Bonneville Power Authority, the SWPA, and the Bureau of Reclamation, the Department of the Interior held control of Federal power projects in the western portion of the nation. In March, 1950, Oscar Chapman, then Secretary of Interior, established the Southeastern Power Administration (SEPA) to market surplus energy generated at projects under the control of the Army Corps of Engineers in the states of Alabama, Florida, Georgia, Kentucky, Mississippi, North Carolina, South Carolina, Tennessee, Virginia, and West Virginia. [82] Presently, it is planning power sales in Indiana and Illinois as well. [83]

SEPA does not own nor operate any transmission facilities. The power it sells is delivered to the TVA, to preference customers, and to investor-owned companies either at the project sites or by contractual arrangement over facilities of the investor-owned companies. [84]

In 1961 the Comptroller General of the United States reported to Congress that the Federal Power Commission had disapproved the rates and charges in an SEPA agreement with TVA for the sale of power generated at three projects. The Comptroller General noted that the Flood Control Act of 1944 imposes a responsibility on the Secretary of the Interior to obtain FPC confirmation and approval of rate schedules for power generated at Corps of

Engineers projects.[85] In this instance, on May 20, 1958, the FPC had held that the rates, based on the incremental allocation of costs and an interest charge of only 2 percent on the unamortized investment, would not return project costs as required by the Flood Control Act of 1944.[86] The Department of the Interior, however, took the position that it had used a proper basis for determining costs and that since Congress had not objected to the terms of the agreement it was justified in ignoring the FPC ruling. The Comptroller General recommended that the President direct the Secretary of the Interior to submit a revised schedule of rates to the FPC.[87]

In November, 1964, the Comptroller General reported to Congress that SEPA was still selling hydroelectric power from the three projects to TVA at the disapproved rates. About $12.6 million in additional revenues would have been collected over the previous 15 years if rates conforming to the criteria contemplated by the FPC had been in effect, the report stated. [88]

In December, 1964, the FPC announced that it was approving a revised rate schedule, based on an interest rate of 2.5 percent.[89]

Corps of Engineers

In the southeast, the Corps of Engineers has thirteen multiple-purpose projects with hydroelectric facilities in operation. These projects have an installed generating capacity of 1,677,600 kilowatts.[90] The Corps also has made expenditures for advance engineering and design on additional multiple-purpose projects with hydroelectric facilities in the area.[91]

The Corps of Engineers has responsibilities in navigation, flood control, hydro power, water supply, water quality control, recreation, fish and wildlife preservation, shore protection, and related purposes.[92] It operates throughout the entire United States and has an investment allocated to power of some $4,228,300,000. The Corps markets power only from the St. Mary's project in Michigan. Elsewhere, surplus electric energy it produces is marketed by agencies of the Department of the Interior, such as BPA, SWPA, SEPA, and the Bureau of Reclamation.[93] (Table 3·2)

Transmission lines

In 1963, Secretary of the Interior Stewart Udall asserted authority to grant or deny right of way across public lands for non-Federal transmission lines.[94] The Department of Agriculture took the same position for Federal forests.[95] On the basis of this policy, the Federal government can bar investor-owned companies from building many power lines and has assumed the right to order companies with lines built across public lands to deliver surplus power to preference customers.[96] (Chart 3·3)

Chart 3·3

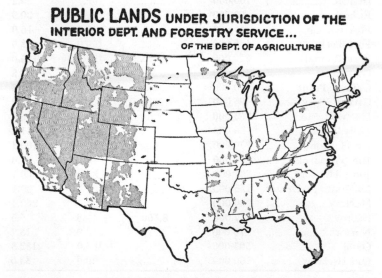

PUBLIC LANDS UNDER JURISDICTION OF THE INTERIOR DEPT. AND FORESTRY SERVICE...
OF THE DEPT. OF AGRICULTURE

Table 3·2 Corps of Engineers Projects, 1966

Project	Kw existing	Kw under construction	Est. Fed. investment, millions	Allocated to power,* millions
Albeni Falls	42,600	....	$ 31.1	$ 30.8
Allatoona	74,000	....	32.1	24.2
Beaver	112,000	....	44.2	31.1
Big Bend	409,500	58,500	104.4	102.7
Big Cliff	18,000	....	†	†
Blakely Mountain	75,000	....	33.6	25.0
Bonneville	518,400	....	84.3	57.8
Buford	86,000	....	44.5	35.9
Bull Shoals	340,000	....	88.4	63.3
Center Hill	135,000	....	44.8	32.0
Cheatham	36,000	....	30.5	17.0
Chief Joseph	1,024,000	....	144.3	140.0
Clark Hill	280,000	....	79.1	70.3
Cougar	25,000	....	54.7	10.4
Dale Hollow	54,000	....	26.2	16.6
Dardanelle	124,000	....	79.0	36.3
Denison	70,000	....	75.6	19.8
Detroit	100,000	....	62.7	39.2
Eufaula	90,000	....	119.6	30.9
Fort Gibson	45,000	....	42.5	16.9
Fort Peck	165,000	....	159.0	83.5
Fort Randall	320,000	....	197.0	125.0
Garrison	400,000	....	291.0	148.8
Gavins Point	100,000	....	48.9	30.6
Greers Ferry	96,000	....	46.7	30.2
Hartwell	264,000	....	89.2	82.6
Hills Creek	30,000	....	45.8	11.2
Ice Harbor	270,000	....	125.3	100.4
Jim Woodruff	30,000	....	46.5	23.0
John H. Kerr	204,000	....	87.4	69.1
Lookout Pt.-Dexter	135,000	....	87.9	39.1
McNary	980,000	....	294.7	260.4
Narrows	17,000	8,500	15.8	5.5
Norfork	70,000	....	29.0	13.7
Oahe	595,000	....	338.0	182.3
Old Hickory	100,000	....	49.9	33.6

Table 3·2   Corps of Engineers Projects, 1966 (continued)

Project	Kw existing	Kw under construction	Est. Fed. investment, millions	Allocated to power,* millions
Philpott	14,000		$ 13.6	$ 6.9
St. Mary's	18,400	52,000	12.7	12.7
Sam Rayburn			58.0	20.9
Table Rock	200,000		66.0	53.5
Tenkiller Ferry	34,000		23.6	11.8
The Dalles	1,119,000		247.9	237.9
Walter F. George	130,000		84.5	47.8
Whitney	30,000		41.9	8.1
Wolf Creek	270,000		79.5	59.2
Barkley	130,000		142.0	44.0
Broken Bow		100,000	39.6	22.1
Carters		250,000	67.6	57.6
Cordell Hull		100,000	57.5	27.6
DeGray		68,000	54.3	21.7
Dworshak		400,000	231.0	209.8
Green Peter-Foster		100,000	82.3	35.5
J. Percy Priest		28,000	48.8	8.1
John Day		2,160,000	448.0	336.2
Kaysinger Bluff		152,000	173.0	35.6
Keystone		70,000	123.0	30.7
Laurel River		61,000	22.7	16.6
Little Goose		405,000	152.0	106.1
Lower Granite		405,000	187.0	146.1
Lower Monumental		405,000	187.0	144.9
Millers Ferry		75,000	53.2	32.3
Ozark		100,000	63.2	35.8
Robert Kerr		110,000	96.5	41.6
Stockton		45,200	57.4	14.8
Webbers Falls		60,000	83.8	23.2
Clarence Cannon		54,000	70.6	15.8
Libby		420,000	352.0	268.0
Jones Bluff		68,000	52.6	30.5
West Point		72,000	64.2	25.7
Total	9,379,900	5,827,200	$6,710.6	$4,228.3

* Some allocations tentative.   † Included with Detroit.

Thus, the Department of the Interior can control the construction and use of transmission systems in many parts of the country.

In addition, the Department has pieced new sections of transmission lines to its own growing system almost every year. The question of development of a Federal transmission grid has never been considered by Congress, but bit by bit the Department of the Interior is moving toward its construction. One year there was a relatively modest request for funds to build a line in Idaho.[97] Another year there was a request to construct a line from BPA to Southern California.* In the years to come, other stretches of line may be built. Piecemeal a Federal system interconnecting the Federal power projects and municipal and state agencies is being developed.

Alaska Power Administration

In June, 1967, Secretary of the Interior Udall announced establishment of still another power agency—the Alaska Power Administration. In discussing the role of this new agency, Secretary Udall said, "We are firmly convinced an available supply of abundant low-cost power is essential to the future development of Alaska." He suggested the possibility of hydroelectric developments on the Susitna River, Bradley Lake, Lake Grace, Takatz Creek, and in addition, thermal power developments using fossil fuels and nuclear energy—all to be combined with transmission facilities. In short, he appeared to be

---

* This line, of course, is under construction and is known as the Pacific Northwest-Pacific Southwest Intertie. See Committee Print, Department of the Interior of the U.S., *Report to the Appropriations Committees of the Congress of the United States Recommending a Plan of Construction and Ownership of EHV Electric Interties Between the Pacific Northwest and Pacific Southwest.*

proposing a complete utility system be constructed by the Department of Interior in Alaska.[98]

As the years go on, the combination of hydroelectric projects of the Corps of Engineers and the Bureau of Reclamation, the dams and steam plants of TVA, the transmission lines of the Department of the Interior and the REA-financed cooperatives, along with steam generating plants being financed by the REA and such other Federal incursions into power production as the Hanford, Washington, atomic plant, begins to resemble more and more closely the plan suggested by John D. Ross in 1938 and even the national power system outlined by Dr. Carl E. Thompson and the Public Ownership League in 1924.

REFERENCES

1. U.S. Department of the Interior, Bureau of Reclamation, *Bureau of Reclamation Project Feasibilities and Authorizations,* 1957, p. 78.
2. *Ibid.,* pp. 15–16.
3. *A History of Navigation on the Tennessee River System,* House Document 254, 75th Cong., 1st Sess., 1937, pp. 115–139.
4. J. S. Ransmeier, *The Tennessee Valley Authority,* Vanderbilt University Press, Nashville, Tenn., 1942, pp. 41–44.
5. *Ibid.,* p. 44; J. King, *The Conservation Fight,* Public Affairs Press, Washington, D.C., 1959, pp. 98, 108–109.
6. *Ibid.,* p. 143.
7. *Ibid.,* pp. 101–103.
8. *Ibid.,* p. 174.
9. *Congressional Record,* 71st Cong., 3d Sess., Vol. 74, Part 7, Mar. 3, 1931, pp. 7046–7048.
10. U.S. Department of the Interior, *The Story of Hoover Dam,* U.S. Government Printing Office, Washington, 1961, pp. vi–vii, 13, 17.
11. *Ibid.,* pp. 54, 68.
12. Boulder Canyon Project Act, approved Dec. 21, 1928, Public Law 642, 70th Cong., 2d Sess.
13. *Hearings before a Subcommittee of the Committee on Agriculture and Forestry, U.S. Senate, on S. 3524,* 74th Cong., 2d Sess., Part 1, Apr. 8, 1936, p. 169.

14. *George Ashwander et al., Petitioners v. Tennessee Valley Authority, et al., Respondents,* before the U.S. Supreme Court, Washington, Dec. 20, 1935. Argument of Hon. Stanley S. Reed.

15. *Hearings before the Subcommittee of the Committee on Appropriations, U.S. Senate, on H.R. 9830, Deficiency and Emergency Appropriation Bill, 1934 and 1935,* 73d Cong., 2d Sess., pp. 262–263.

16. U.S. Department of the Interior, Bureau of Reclamation, *op. cit.,* pp. 15–16. Public Law 412, 74th Cong., H.R. 8632, 16 USCA, 831i, approved Aug. 31, 1935.

17. U.S. Department of the Interior, *Federal Reclamation Laws Annotated,* Vol. I, Mar. 2, 1861, to Aug. 14, 1946, pp. 96, 145.

18. 30 Op. Attorney General 197, quoted in *The Anatomy of Preference,* National Association of Electric Companies, 1956, p. 8.

19. R. A. Tudor, "Partnership with Government in Power Production," *Civil Engineering,* October, 1955; *Hearings before Subcommittee on Flood Control of the Committee on Public Works, House of Representatives,* 88th Cong., 1st Sess., Part I, Mar. 1, 1963, p. 215.

20. Federal Water Power Act, Section 7, approved June 10, 1920. Public Law 280, 66th Cong., H.R. 3184, 16 USCA 800.

21. Public Law 412, 74th Cong., H.R. 8632, 16 USCA 831i and 16 USCA 831k-1, approved Aug. 31, 1935.

22. See TVA Contract with City of Memphis, Jan. 1, 1963, *Annual Report of the Tennessee Valley Authority,* 1963, pp. A37, A41.

23. S. 2555 and H.R. 7863, 75th Cong., 1st Sess., 1937.

24. *Public Utilities Fortnightly,* Mar. 29, 1934, Vol. 13, pp. 421–422.

25. *Congressional Record Index, H.R. 3609,* 74th Cong., 1st Sess., Vol. 79, Part 14, Jan. 3, 1935, to Aug. 26, 1935, p. 772.

26. *Congressional Record, H.R. 2784,* 76th Cong., 1st Sess., Vol. 84, Part I, Jan. 18, 1939, p. 462.

27. *Congressional Record, H.R. 10410,* 76th Cong., 3d Sess., Vol. 86, Part 10, Aug. 27, 1940, p. 11079.

28. Knoxville, Tennessee *Journal,* Dec. 18, 1940.

29. *Congressional Record, H.R. 1823,* 77th Cong., 1st Sess., Vol. 87, Part I, Jan. 10, 1941, p. 122.

30. *Congressional Record,* 77th Cong., 1st Sess., Vol. 87, Part I, Jan. 24, 1941, p. 292.

31. Kansas City *Star,* Jan. 10, 1941.

32. *Congressional Record,* 77th Cong., 2nd Sess., Vol. 88, Part 8, Jan. 12, 1942, p. A100.

33. C. W. Kellogg, "The Utilities Are Prepared," *EEI Bulletin,* June, 1940.

34. *Ibid.*
35. *Ibid.*
36. *Congressional Record,* 77th Cong., 2d Sess., Vol. 88, Part 8, Jan. 26, 1942, pp. A236–A238.
37. Administration of the Rural Electrification Act, *Hearings before a Subcommittee of the Committee on Agriculture and Forestry, U.S. Senate, on S. Res. 197,* 78th Cong., 2d Sess., Part 4, p. 1047 et seq., 1944.
38. S. 3524, 74th Cong., 2d Sess., Jan. 9, 1936.
39. *Ibid.*
40. S. 2555, 75th Cong., 1st Sess., 1937.
41. H.R. 7863, 75th Cong., 1st Sess., 1937.
42. *Congressional Record,* 78th Cong., 1st Sess., Vol. 89, Part 9, Jan. 28, 1943, pp. A355–A356.
43. David Lilienthal, *The Journals of David E. Lilienthal, The TVA Years, 1939–1945,* Harper & Row, Publishers, New York, 1964, pp. 244–246 et seq.
44. *Ibid.,* pp. 493–494.
45. *Congressional Record,* 81st Cong., 1st Sess., Vol. 95, Part 4, Apr. 19, 1949, S 1645, p. 4724 and H.R. 4286, p. 4699.
46. *Ibid.,* Part 5, May 31, 1949, p. 7035.
47. Columbia Valley Administration, *Hearings before the Committee on Public Works, U.S. Senate, on S1595, S1631, S1632, S1645,* 81st Cong., 1st Sess., Part 1, 1949; *Hearings before the Committee on Public Works, House of Representatives, on H.R. 4286, H.R. 4287,* 81st Cong., 1st Sess., 1949.
48. *Congressional Record,* 78th Cong., 2d Sess., Vol. 90, Part 5, Aug. 18, 1944, p. 7083.
49. *Hearings before a Subcommittee of the Committee on Commerce, U.S. Senate, on S555,* 79th Cong., 1st Sess., Part 3, Apr. 18, 1945.
50. Chattanooga, Tennessee *Times,* Feb. 15, 1934.
51. Rivers and Harbors Act of 1927, House Document 308.
52. *First Annual Report of the Bonneville Administrator,* House Document 86, 76th Cong., 1st Sess., Jan. 4, 1939, pp. 1–2.
53. *Ibid.*
54. White House Release, July 16, 1934.
55. *Ibid.*
56. President's letter and *Progress Report of National Power Policy Committee on the Bonneville Project,* Senate Document 21, 75th Cong., 1st Sess., Feb., 1937.
57. Bonneville Project Act, 1937, Public Law 329, 75th Cong., H.R. 7642, 16 USCA 832c, Aug. 20, 1937.
58. "Electric Power of the Future," a speech by J. D. Ross before the Engineers' Club of Seattle, Wash., July 28, 1938.

59. *Ibid.*, p. 6.
60. For a summary of the companies' activities, see J. E. Corrette, *EEI BULLETIN,* July, 1964.
61. Harold L. Ickes, *The Secret Diary of Harold L. Ickes, The First Thousand Days,* Simon and Schuster, Inc., New York.
62. *Ibid.*
63. Order No. 1865, Department of the Interior Release, Sept. 1, 1943.
64. *Ibid.*
65. *Ibid.*
66. Flood Control Act of 1944, Public Law 534, 78th Cong., H.R. 4485, 16 USCA 825s.
67. *Hearings before a Subcommittee of the Committee on Commerce, U.S. Senate, on H.R. 4485,* 78th Cong., 2d Sess., June 5, 1944, p. 380.
68. *Senate Report 1030,* 78th Cong., p. 3.
69. *Congressional Record,* 78th Cong., 2d Sess., Vol. 90, Part 6, Nov. 22, 1944, p. 8330.
70. Flood Control Act of 1944, Public Law 534, 78th Cong., H.R. 4485, 16 USCA 825s.
71. Department of the Interior Release, Order No. 2135, Nov. 21, 1945.
72. Interior Department Appropriations Bill for 1947, pp. 44, 80, 129; *Hearings before the House of Representatives, Subcommittee of the Committee on Appropriations,* 79th Cong., 2d Sess., pp. 7, 39.
73. *Ibid.*, pp. 50–51.
74. *Ibid.*, p. 51.
75. U.S. Department of Agriculture, Rural Electrification Administration Release, Nov. 25, 1950.
76. Reprinted in *Hearings of the Interior and Insular Affairs Committee, House of Representatives,* 83d Cong., 1st Sess., pp. 7–9.
77. *Ibid.*
78. *U.S. Department of the Interior, Bureau of Reclamation Project Feasibilities and Authorizations,* 1957, p. 3.
79. *Annual Report of the Secretary of the Interior,* 1962, p. 143.
80. Kenneth Holum, Address before the Annual Convention of the American Public Power Association, San Antonio, Texas, Apr. 25, 1961, p. 5.
81. National Rural Electric Cooperative Association, *Rural Electrification,* May, 1961, p. 16.
82. Comptroller General of the U.S., *Audit of Southeastern Power System and Related Activities, Fiscal Years 1959 & 1960,* October, 1961, p. 2.

83. Indianapolis, Indiana *Times,* June 2, 1964.
84. Comptroller General of the U.S., *op. cit.,* p. 2.
85. *Ibid.,* pp. 5–6. (The projects were Wolf Creek, Center Hill, and Dale Hollow.)
86. *Ibid.,* p. 5, and FPC Release No. 13589, Dec. 23, 1964.
87. Comptroller General of the U.S., *op. cit.,* pp. 5–6.
88. Comptroller General of the U.S., *Sale of Hydroelectric Power by the Department of the Interior . . . at Rates Not Approved by the FPC,* November, 1964, p. 2.
89. FPC Release No. 13589, Dec. 23, 1964.
90. U.S. Department of the Interior Release, June 29, 1964.
91. Comptroller General of the U.S., *Audit of Southeastern Power System and Related Activities, Fiscal Years 1959 & 1960,* October, 1961, p. 2.
92. *Annual Report of the Chief of Engineers, U.S. Army, on Civil Works Activities,* Vol. 1, p. 1, 1963.
93. *Annual Report of the Secretary of the Interior,* 1962, pp. 143, 248.
94. Joint Release, Office of the Secretary of the Interior and Office of the Secretary of Agriculture, Mar. 24, 1963.
95. *Ibid.*
96. *Ibid.*
97. U.S. Department of the Interior, BPA Release, Sept. 3, 1963.
98. U.S. Department of the Interior Release, June 18, 1967.

Chapter 4

How far has government
power gone?

Government ownership in the electric power business has followed a multitude of paths. One way or another, it has grown considerably during the past three decades.

Compare the Federal hydroelectric projects in 1933 (Chart 4·1) with the Federal hydroelectric projects in 1965 (Chart 4·2). Compare the Federally owned steam plants in 1933 (Chart 4·3) with the Federally owned steam plants in 1965 (Chart 4·4). Compare the REA-financed generating plants in 1941 (Chart 4·5) with the REA-financed generating plants in 1965 (Chart 4·6). Then add the municipal systems and other non-Federal governmental power systems (Chart 4·7). Then see the approximate power-marketing areas of Federal agencies and the TVA (Chart 4·8) and look to see the Federal power transmission lines (Chart 4·9), so many of which have been constructed needlessly, often overlapping existing investor-owned power lines. Then recall how the generating capacity of these government power systems has grown in the 30 years from 1935 to 1965 (Chart 4·10) and that one out of four Americans now receives electric-

FEDERAL HYDROELECTRIC POWER PLANTS
1933

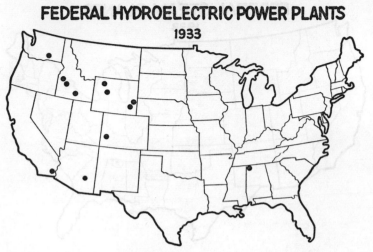

Chart 4·1

Chart 4·2

FEDERAL HYDROELECTRIC POWER PLANTS
1965

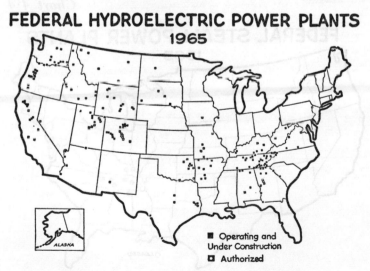

ALASKA

■ Operating and
Under Construction
◻ Authorized

HOW FAR HAS GOVERNMENT POWER GONE? *145*

FEDERAL STEAM PLANTS
1933

Chart 4·3

Chart 4·4

FEDERAL STEAM POWER PLANTS
1965

○ *LEASED*

146 GOVERNMENT IN THE POWER BUSINESS

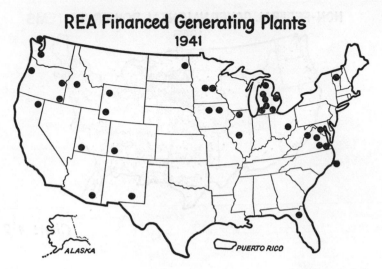

REA Financed Generating Plants
1941

Chart 4·5

Chart 4·6

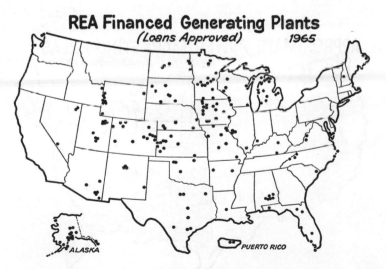

REA Financed Generating Plants
(Loans Approved)   1965

NON-FEDERAL GOVERNMENTAL POWER SYSTEMS
1965

Chart 4·7

Chart 4·8

APPROXIMATE POWER MARKETING AREAS
FEDERAL AGENCIES • 1965

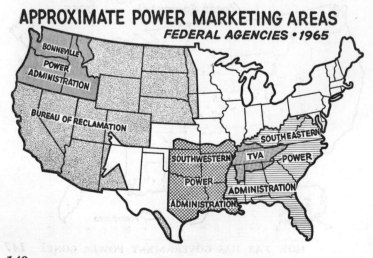

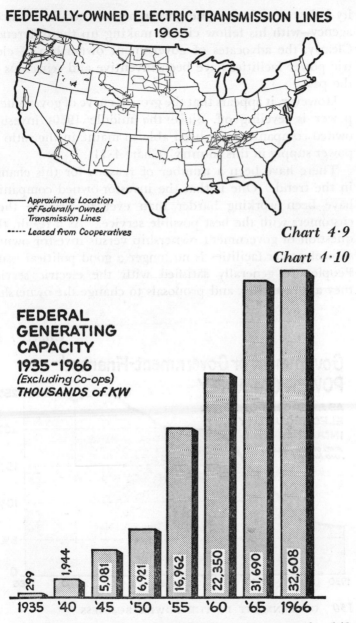

FEDERALLY-OWNED ELECTRIC TRANSMISSION LINES
1965

—— Approximate Location
of Federally-Owned
Transmission Lines

----- Leased from Cooperatives

Chart 4·9

Chart 1·10

**FEDERAL
GENERATING
CAPACITY
1935-1966**
(Excluding Co-ops)
THOUSANDS of KW

299 | 1,944 | 5,081 | 6,921 | 16,962 | 22,350 | 31,690 | 32,608

| 1935 | '40 | '45 | '50 | '55 | '60 | '65 | 1966 |

HOW FAR HAS GOVERNMENT POWER GONE? **149**

ity below cost from some government-owned or financed agency—with his fellow citizen making up the difference. Clearly, the advocates of government ownership of electric power facilities have been inventive and tenacious in the past.

However, it appears that the growth curve of government power is leveling off. Since the middle 1950s investor-owned companies have been able to maintain the ratio of power supply in this country (Chart 4·11).

There have been a number of reasons for this change in the trend. One is that the investor-owned companies have been working harder than ever to provide their customers with the best possible service. As a result, the question of government ownership versus investor ownership of power facilities is no longer a good political issue. People are generally satisfied with the electric service they are receiving, and proposals to change the ownership

Chart 4·11

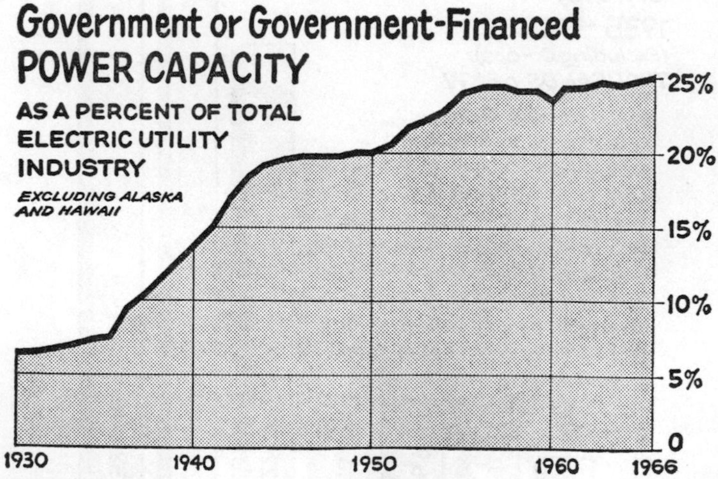
Government or Government-Financed
POWER CAPACITY
AS A PERCENT OF TOTAL
ELECTRIC UTILITY
INDUSTRY
EXCLUDING ALASKA
AND HAWAII
25%
20%
15%
10%
5%
0
1930
1940
1950
1960
1966

of electric suppliers are no longer good vote-getters. This change in attitude toward the power industry and the way it came about make up one of the most interesting chapters in the history of the electric utility industry in the United States of America. It will be discussed more fully in Chapter 10.

Chapter **5**

Is there a need
for government power?

The purpose of the electric utility industry is to provide an ample supply of electric energy, reliably and economically. This is a big job, particularly in a nation that uses more electricity than any other country in the world.

In a society such as the United States it would seem that use of tax financing for power facilities would be a last resort—taken only if the free market could not provide necessary funds. If the system developed under free-market financing and government regulation were not effective, we might look for another approach. Thus, discussion of government power requires an examination of the record of the alternative—the investor-owned electric light and power industry which now supplies electric energy to some 79 percent of the electricity customers in the nation.[1] (Chart 5·1)

Development of the industry

Under the free-market system as it exists in the United States, competition is generally relied upon to keep prices fair and reasonable. Direct government ownership has

152 GOVERNMENT IN THE POWER BUSINESS

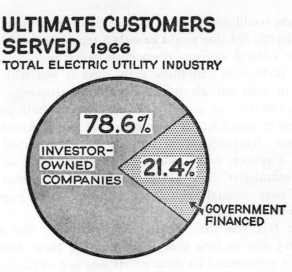

ULTIMATE CUSTOMERS
SERVED 1966
TOTAL ELECTRIC UTILITY INDUSTRY

78.6%
INVESTOR-
OWNED
COMPANIES

21.4%

GOVERNMENT
FINANCED

Chart 5·1

not usually been considered necessary or desirable. The electric utility business in the United States was begun in this tradition. Companies were formed and operated wherever investors decided electricity could be sold.

Competition for customers was vigorous. In Chicago, for example, there were at one time some 25 or 30 separate utility enterprises vying for customers. They operated at varying voltages with unstandardized equipment. Their distribution lines often duplicated each other, with one company serving a customer while a second company served the house next door.[2]

The costs of setting up a central electric station, with its expensive generating equipment and distribution systems, were high. In 1896, more than half the central stations in existence operated only during the hours after dark, and there was even some question on the part of certain early utility men whether the central station business could continue to exist. Some pessimists feared that electric lighting might be only a temporary fad.[3]

The central stations themselves were small and relatively inefficient. In those early days it was still impossible to transmit electricity over long distances. As a result, the stations were located as close to their potential markets as possible. This means that the fuel needed to produce electricity often had to be transported many miles, a process which added to the cost. It also meant that central stations could be located only in cities where there were enough people to support their expensive, part-time operations.

The fact was that, during its first years, the electric industry was so new that the operating men themselves did not understand its nature. It was not until the 1890s that central station managers began to realize that if electricity was to be anything other than a luxury, the rates to consumers would have to be rearranged. A pricing system had to be worked out which would encourage use of electric energy and charge the customer who made use of the company's investment most steadily during the year the lowest possible price.

Without the electric motor the infant electric utility industry could not have existed. The motor made it possible for companies to expand from the part-time operation of producing energy for lighting to the full-time operation of producing energy for lighting and power. By 1893 an efficient dynamo had been developed, an economic method of transferring energy from the point of use had been worked out, and reliable motors were being manufactured. The door was open to an enormous potential market. The immediate interest of the public, of investors, and of the electric utility men turned out to be the field of urban transportation. The development of streetcar lines put the electric companies into the power business.

Other developments helped the electric industry to more solid footing. The reduction of energy consumed by incandescent lamps from $6\frac{1}{2}$ watts per candle in 1882 to $3\frac{1}{10}$ watts per candle in 1890 made the use of electricity more economical for consumers. A distribution system was developed that radically reduced the amount of copper needed and thus substantially lowered the cost of building distribution lines. Possibly most important, the development of the alternating-current system made long-distance transmission possible. Central stations no longer had to be located in the areas where electricity was being used. They could be near fuel facilities and water transportation in low-land-cost areas, and the stations could be larger, permitting further economies. As a result, costs could be lowered enough so that somewhat less densely populated areas could be served profitably and rates could be adjusted to encourage greater use of electricity.[4]

After 1900 one of the most notable tendencies in the industry was toward the consolidation of small, individually owned stations into larger systems. This tendency, made possible by increasing knowledge of higher voltage transmission, combined with the extensive installation of generating and consuming equipment of higher and higher efficiency, brought cheaper and better service to the public.

One typical case was that of the Boston Edison Company, which covered an area of one-eighth of a square mile in 1885. By 1907 it was servicing an area of almost 509 square miles. The Central Illinois Public Service Company was serving eighty-seven communities by the end of 1912. Originally, these communities had been supplied electricity by forty-nine separate generating plants. The unification of service brought a reduction in the cost of producing electricity of 4.21 cents per kilowatt-hour.[5]

Consolidation of this kind took capital. In the beginning, the typical central station was owned by one man. Corporate ownership, with its greater facility for attracting capital, came slowly. By 1902, however, 73 percent of the 2,805 investor-owned central stations were owned by corporations, and the percentage increased year by year.[6]

By 1910 electric utility men were able to see a pattern in the growth of their industry. Like any new business, the companies had first served the market that was immediately available and promised the surest return: the thickly populated centers. Experience in producing and selling electricity, coupled with technical advances, then made it possible for the companies to serve smaller population centers. Although in 1900 there was still heated debate about whether a company could profitably serve a manufacturing town of 100,000 many companies were moving into the smaller areas. With further technical advances it became possible to bring electricity to towns and villages. This step-by-step process has brought electricity to almost every factory, home, and farm in the land.

The nature of the industry and the state of the art of producing electricity are such that progress to this goal has demanded steady and systematic activity. No shortcuts have been possible. For the good of its customers, its investors, and the nation, the industry has had to be built on the soundest possible base.

Today, there are some 350 investor-owned electric light and power companies. Through a process of evolution, these companies have grown during the years to the efficient organizations they are today. Small companies have been merged into larger ones. Weak companies have joined with stronger. Always, the aim has been to achieve that size and that financial condition which, with the technology available, would assure customers an ample, reliable, and economical supply of electric energy.

Planning for the future

The use of electricity has been expanding rapidly. In recent years production has been growing at an average rate of 7.17 percent per year compounded. This is about twice the average rate of growth per year compounded of the whole economy as measured by the gross national product (Chart 5·2).

The vast power networks which have been developed in this country include over four times the miles of transmission lines of the Soviet Union—although Russia's land area is about three times the size.[7] (Chart 5·3)

Chart 5·2

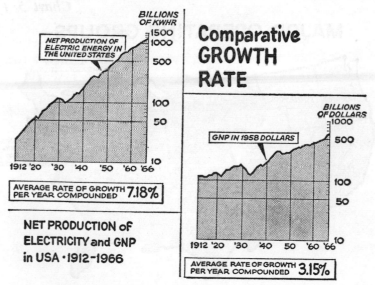

Comparative GROWTH RATE

BILLIONS OF KWHR

NET PRODUCTION OF ELECTRIC ENERGY IN THE UNITED STATES

1912 '20 '30 '40 '50 '60 '66

AVERAGE RATE OF GROWTH PER YEAR COMPOUNDED 7.18%

NET PRODUCTION of ELECTRICITY and GNP in USA · 1912–1966

BILLIONS OF DOLLARS

GNP IN 1958 DOLLARS

1912 '20 '30 '40 50 '60 '66

AVERAGE RATE OF GROWTH PER YEAR COMPOUNDED 3.15%

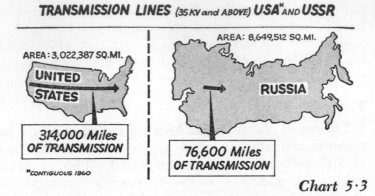

AREA: 3,022,387 SQ.MI.

UNITED STATES

314,000 Miles OF TRANSMISSION

CONTIGUOUS 1960

AREA: 8,649,512 SQ.MI.

RUSSIA

76,600 Miles OF TRANSMISSION

Chart 5·3

Most of the United States now receives electric service from a series of giant interconnected systems and power pools, made up of a number of companies. About 97 percent of the electric generating capacity in this country is provided from these groups. They serve all but about 3 percent of the electric needs of the nation.[8] (Chart 5·4)

Chart 5·4

MAJOR OPERATING GROUPS

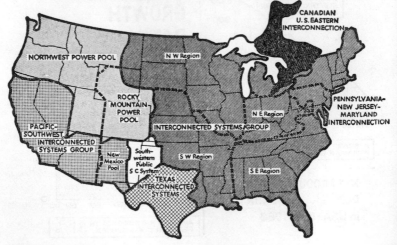

The largest of the groups extends from the Rocky Mountains to the Atlantic and from Canada to the Gulf of Mexico. In 1965 the United States' portion of this group had an estimated generating capability of 167 million kilowatts.[9] That is, all the generating capability in this great system was operating in synchronism—the electric energy throughout the system pulsing together. In terms of horsepower, it is as though 224 million horses were running in step.

Value of interconnections

When a power system is dependent on hydroelectricity and lacks sufficient steam power, a drought can create serious difficulties. This happened in 1941 in the Southeast. When the shortage took place, many industries in the Tennessee Valley region were producing war material and were dependent upon electric power. The situation seemed desperate. TVA was dependent upon hydroelectric power—unlike the investor-owned companies in the area. Consideration was given to tying generators on the ocean liner *Normandie* and on an aircraft carrier docked at Mobile into the system to supply the needed energy.[10] To forestall shutdowns of essential war industries, more than a score of investor-owned power companies operating in the states surrounding Tennessee began sending electricity into TVA. Some of this power came from as far west as Texas and as far north as Pennsylvania and Ohio. According to Leland Olds, then Chairman of the Federal Power Commission, TVA received 349 million kilowatt-hours of electricity under net transactions from neighboring investor-owned companies during the 26-week period from May 25 through November 22, 1941.[11] (Table 5·1)

It is sometimes said that the large Oak Ridge nuclear development could not have been supplied with its huge

Table 5·1   Extracts from Summary of Energy Transactions between
TVA and Other Utility Systems during 26-week Period
May 25 to Nov. 22, 1941, Inclusive

Company	Net transactions, kwhr	
	Receipt by TVA	Delivered by TVA
Commonwealth & Southern Corporation	—	153,400,800
Arkansas Power & Light Company	61,387,200	—
Kentucky Utilities Company	78,019,200	—
Kentucky-Tennessee Light & Power Co.	11,222,400	—
Appalachian Electric Power Co.	114,592,800	—
Carolina Power & Light Co.	68,040,000	—
Connected utilities small plants	15,640,800	—
Total	348,902,400	153,400,800

requirements for electric energy during and after World
War II except through some government-financed project
such as TVA.   The fact is that many areas of the country
could have supplied the power needed by the Oak Ridge
project and also continued to provide the energy needed
by their other customers as well. (Table 5·2)

The amount of power available at a given location is
not limited by the reserve margin of the particular company serving the area involved.   Through their interconnections, companies can obtain power from other companies.   Thus, the power potential of an area is limited
only by the aggregate reserves of the systems which are
interconnected.[12]   Apparently, the decision to locate the
Oak Ridge plant in Tennessee was made in 1942.   In
that year the total electric utility industry in the nation
had a 25 percent margin of reserve.[13]

Actually, the Oak Ridge project had its own 238,000-
kilowatt steam power plant and was buying only its
additional requirements through TVA.   Throughout the

Table 5·2 Availability of Electricity in the Various Regions of the U.S., 1941-1942

Region	Capability, kw	Actual non-coincident peak loads, kw	Margin of reserve	
			Kilowatts	Percent
1941:				
New England	3,050,000	2,485,000	565,000	22.7
Middle Atlantic .	9,110,000	7,310,000	1,800,000	24.6
Central industrial	13,490,000	11,440,000	2,050,000	17.9
West central	2,260,000	1,660,000	600,000	36.1
Southern	7,745,000	6,380,000	1,365,000	21.4
Rocky Mountain .	1,540,000	1,305,000	235,000	18.0
Pacific	4,955,000	4,070,000	885,000	21.7
U.S. total	42,150,000	34,650,000	7,500,000	21.6
1942:				
New England	3,205,000	2,365,000	840,000	35.5
Middle Atlantic ...	9,440,000	7,170,000	2,270,000	31.7
Central industrial	14,170,000	11,635,000	2,535,000	21.8
West central	2,330,000	1,630,000	700,000	42.9
Southern	8,515,000	6,935,000	1,580,000	22.8
Rocky Mountain ..	1,555,000	1,245,000	310,000	24.9
Pacific	5,635,000	4,870,000	765,000	15.7
U.S. total	44,850,000	35,850,000	9,000,000	25.1

summer, fall, and winter of 1941 and into the spring and early summer of 1942, TVA was purchasing power from neighboring electric utility systems. It did not begin delivering power to Oak Ridge until 1943. That year the total electric utility industry had an 18.8 percent margin of reserve. By June, 1945, just before the first atomic bomb was dropped on Hiroshima, TVA was supplying 274,000 kilowatts for Oak Ridge. The industry had a 26.5 percent reserve in 1945, which amounted to some 10,500,000 kilowatts.[14] Today, some projects operated

IS THERE A NEED FOR GOVERNMENT POWER? *161*

by the Atomic Energy Commission are receiving electric service from power facilities financed wholly in the free market.

Isolated operation

Lately we have been hearing that on-site, isolated generating plants that provide space heating, cooling, and all other electrical services by making use of waste heat can have a potential peak efficiency approaching 80 percent in converting raw fuel into energy whereas the efficiency of a good conventional steam turbine in a power system is almost 40 percent. Actually the 80 percent figure is a theoretical one which might possibly represent efficiency during some single month of the year. The record shows that, on the average, the over-all efficiency of such isolated plants is closer to 35 percent because the isolated plant must be designed to adequately supply the building's electrical requirements, including sufficient reserve regardless of the heating and cooling needs.

But that is not the main point. Efficiency of conversion is important. But in generating electricity, whether in a large power system or in an isolated plant, the costs related to the kilowatt-hours used—such as the fuel costs —account for only about 15 percent of the total cost of furnishing electricity. That is, only 15 cents out of a dollar of costs are controlled by or affected by the efficiency of conversion from raw fuel to electric energy. About 60 percent of the costs, or 60 cents out of the dollar, is related to the fixed costs such as the return on investment, depreciation, and taxes. The remaining 25 cents out of the dollar represent other costs such as salaries, wages, and materials and supplies.

A large interconnected power system has primary advantages over an isolated plant, all of which relate to the fixed costs affecting the 60 cents out of a dollar of total costs. These are:

1. The interconnected power system has a lower per-cent reserve requirement.

2. The interconnected power system uses very large generating units, and the price per kilowatt of capacity of a big unit is less than the price per kilowatt of a small unit.

3. The interconnected power system results in greater utilization of diversity.

These three factors enable the interconnected power system to supply electric capacity with fixed charges that are some 30 percent less than those of the isolated plant. In addition, the interconnected power system has greater reliability and closer frequency control.

This 30 percent saving in fixed costs applies to the 60 cents out of a dollar of total costs, thus representing a saving of some 18 percent in the total cost of power (30 percent of 60 cents). The theoretical 80 percent efficiency which would reduce production expense by about one-half applies to only 15 cents out of a dollar of the cost of making electricity. The saving represented is only 7.5 percent of the total cost. The savings in fixed charges are about $2\frac{1}{2}$ times the savings represented by doubling the efficiency of conversion—even if this were within the realm of feasibility.

Picture what would happen today if two isolated, on-site generating plants were built near each other. The first thing any good engineer would do would be to interconnect them.

This would make possible the interconnection of an area within a town and would provide greater operating economy within the area. Next, the two plants operating together would interconnect with other plants in the community, and soon the entire town would be interconnected. Further interconnections would occur between neighboring towns; then states and regions would be interconnected and we would be right back where we are today.

The fact is that the trend is away from use of isolated generation in industry (Chart 5·5).

It is away from isolated municipal systems (Chart 5·6).

There is no indication that we are going to turn and climb back up the hill.

The industry record

In this country, power plant and transmission capability have always been kept well ahead of demand. Even during World War II when urgent war needs and restrictions of materials and supplies created many difficulties, the electric utility industry was able to meet all the demands made on it. In recognition of this record, J. A. Krug, Director of the Office of War Utilities, said in 1943: "Power has never been 'too little or too late.' There is today no shortage of power. This is in sharp contrast

Chart 5·5

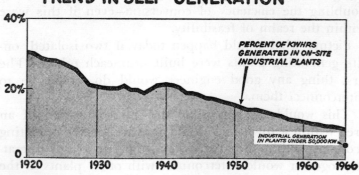

TREND IN SELF-GENERATION

PERCENT OF KWHRS
GENERATED IN ON-SITE
INDUSTRIAL PLANTS

INDUSTRIAL GENERATION
IN PLANTS UNDER 50,000 KW

40%

20%

0

1920   1930   1940   1950   1960   1966

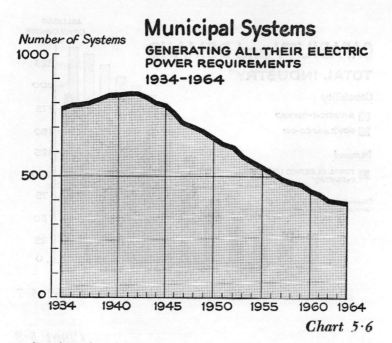

Municipal Systems
GENERATING ALL THEIR ELECTRIC
POWER REQUIREMENTS
1934-1964

Number of Systems

1000

500

0

1934   1940   1945   1950   1955   1960 1964

Chart 5·6

to the situation as to many other vital necessities. I do
not know of a single instance in which the operation of a
war plant has been delayed by lack of electric power
supply." [15]

At the end of 1966, the generating capability of the
total electric utility industry in the contiguous United
States was 248 million kilowatts—providing an estimated
annual gross margin of reserve of about 17 percent at the
time of the annual regional peak loads.[16] (Chart 5·7)

The investor-owned companies have been spending, on
the average, about $3.4 billion a year for new plant and
equipment, or 9 percent of all new construction for all
American business (Chart 5·8). This annual spending,
on the average the largest of any industry in America, is
an important contributor to the expansion of the Ameri-

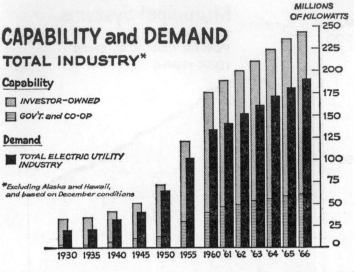

CAPABILITY and DEMAND

TOTAL INDUSTRY*

Capability

INVESTOR-OWNED

GOV'T. and CO-OP

Demand

TOTAL ELECTRIC UTILITY INDUSTRY

*Excluding Alaska and Hawaii, and based on December conditions

MILLIONS OF KILOWATTS

1930 1935 1940 1945 1950 1955 1960 '61 '62 '63 '64 '65 '66

Chart 5·7

Chart 5·8

CONSTRUCTION EXPENDITURES

INVESTOR-OWNED ELECTRIC UTILITIES

AVERAGE NEW PLANT and EQUIPMENT SPENDING 1956-1965

$3.4 BILLION PER YEAR

THE EQUIVALENT OF

9% of New Construction for All American Business

can economy and the creation of new jobs (Chart 5·9). In fact, the total net capital investment of the investor-owned electric utility industry is the largest of all industries in the nation and represents about 12 percent of all the capital presently invested in United States business (Chart 5·10).

On the average, in recent years, the electric power companies have been one of the leading industries in tax payments (Chart 5·11).

Making use of business management operating under government regulation, the United States has developed the most advanced power system in the world, with about as much electric power capacity as the next five countries in the world combined (Chart 5·12). In terms of production of electricity per capita, the best measure available of the over-all effectiveness of a power system, this country produces three times that of the Soviet Union, and

Chart 5·9

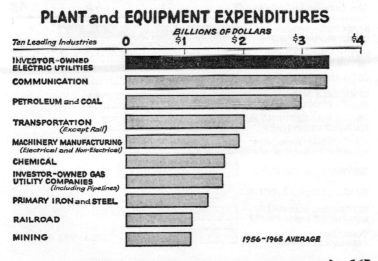

PLANT and EQUIPMENT EXPENDITURES

BILLIONS OF DOLLARS

Ten Leading Industries   0 $1 $2 $3 $4

INVESTOR-OWNED ELECTRIC UTILITIES

COMMUNICATION

PETROLEUM and COAL

TRANSPORTATION *(Except Rail)*

MACHINERY MANUFACTURING *(Electrical and Non-Electrical)*

CHEMICAL

INVESTOR-OWNED GAS UTILITY COMPANIES *(Including Pipelines)*

PRIMARY IRON and STEEL

RAILROAD

MINING   *1956-1965 AVERAGE*

IS THERE A NEED FOR GOVERNMENT POWER?   **167**

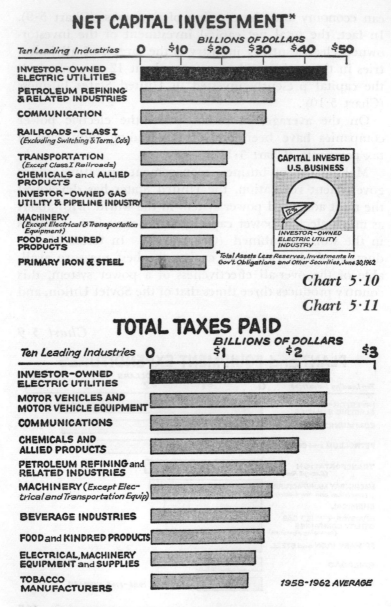

NET CAPITAL INVESTMENT*

BILLIONS OF DOLLARS

Ten Leading Industries 0 $10 $20 $30 $40 $50

INVESTOR-OWNED ELECTRIC UTILITIES

PETROLEUM REFINING & RELATED INDUSTRIES

COMMUNICATION

RAILROADS - CLASS I
(Excluding Switching & Term. Co's)

TRANSPORTATION
(Except Class I Railroads)

CHEMICALS and ALLIED PRODUCTS

INVESTOR - OWNED GAS UTILITY & PIPELINE INDUSTRY

MACHINERY
(Except Electrical & Transportation Equipment)

FOOD and KINDRED PRODUCTS

PRIMARY IRON & STEEL

CAPITAL INVESTED
U.S. BUSINESS

12%

INVESTOR-OWNED
ELECTRIC UTILITY
INDUSTRY

Total Assets Less Reserves, Investments in Gov't. Obligations and Other Securities, June 30, 1962

Chart 5·10

Chart 5·11

TOTAL TAXES PAID

BILLIONS OF DOLLARS

Ten Leading Industries 0 $1 $2 $3

INVESTOR-OWNED ELECTRIC UTILITIES

MOTOR VEHICLES AND MOTOR VEHICLE EQUIPMENT

COMMUNICATIONS

CHEMICALS AND ALLIED PRODUCTS

PETROLEUM REFINING and RELATED INDUSTRIES

MACHINERY *(Except Electrical and Transportation Equip)*

BEVERAGE INDUSTRIES

FOOD and KINDRED PRODUCTS

ELECTRICAL, MACHINERY EQUIPMENT and SUPPLIES

TOBACCO MANUFACTURERS

1958-1962 AVERAGE

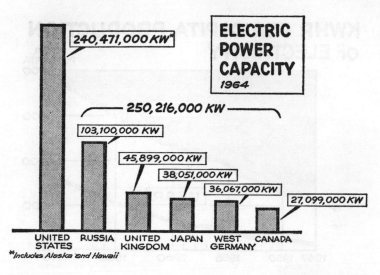

ELECTRIC POWER CAPACITY
1964

240,471,000 KW*

250,216,000 KW

103,100,000 KW

45,899,000 KW

38,051,000 KW

36,067,000 KW

27,099,000 KW

UNITED STATES   RUSSIA   UNITED KINGDOM   JAPAN   WEST GERMANY   CANADA

Includes Alaska and Hawaii

Chart 5·12

studies indicate that the curves will not cross at any point in the foreseeable future.[17] (Chart 5·13)

Improved efficiency in construction and operation, the promotional nature of electric rates, the industry's encouragement of greater use of electricity, diversity in power use, and, of course, good government regulation all have been important in lowering the average price of electricity. These factors have combined so that today the average price per kilowatt-hour used in the home is almost half what it was 25 years ago, even though the cost of living has more than doubled (Chart 5·14).

Over the years, the over-all average revenue for a kilowatt-hour has been declining (Chart 5·15).

Despite the multitude of services electricity performs, its place in the family budget is small. According to Federal government statistics, only a little over 1 percent of disposable personal income goes for electricity—less

KWHR PER CAPITA PRODUCTION of ELECTRICITY

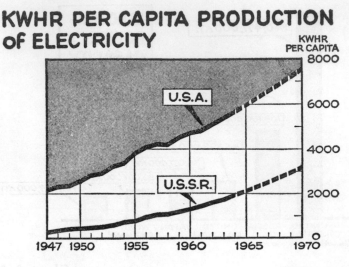

KWHR PER CAPITA

U.S.A.

U.S.S.R.

8000

6000

4000

2000

0

1947 1950   1955   1960   1965   1970

Chart 5·13

Chart 5·14

Electric Utility Industry PRICE RECORD
1913-1966

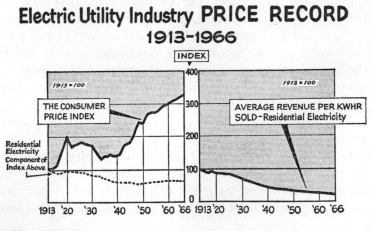

INDEX

1913 = 100

THE CONSUMER PRICE INDEX

Residential Electricity Component of Index Above

1913 = 100

AVERAGE REVENUE PER KWHR SOLD – Residential Electricity

400

300

200

100

0

1913 '20   '30   '40   '50   '60 '66   1913 '20   '30   '40   '50   '60 '66

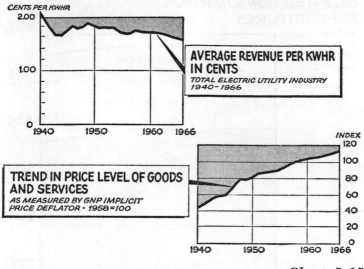

Chart 5·15

than what is spent on cigarettes and other tobacco products.[18] (Chart 5·16)

The low cost of electricity is illustrated even more dramatically in industry, where electric energy powers most of our machinery. In the latest year for which statistics are available, only about seven-eighths of one percent of the product value for all United States manufacturing industries went for electricity.[19]

A study made by the Edison Electric Institute applying the Gompertz curve, which is often used in studying economic and business trends, indicates that this nation is just entering a period of sustained growth in the use of electric energy that should continue well into the twenty-first century, not really leveling off until around the year 2200. At that point, per capita use should be about 100,000 kilowatt-hours (Chart 5·17).

Based on Census Bureau estimates, population growth

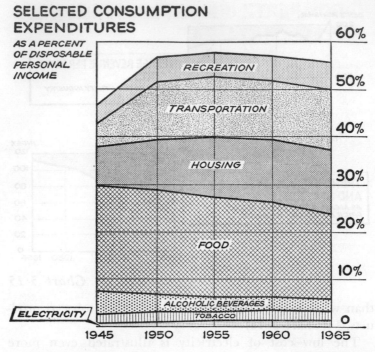

SELECTED CONSUMPTION
EXPENDITURES

AS A PERCENT
OF DISPOSABLE
PERSONAL
INCOME

60%

50%

40%

30%

20%

10%

0

RECREATION

TRANSPORTATION

HOUSING

FOOD

ALCOHOLIC BEVERAGES

TOBACCO

ELECTRICITY

1945   1950   1955   1960   1965

Chart 5·16

in this country probably will follow a pattern that will
reach 1 billion people in about the year 2400. This is a
density of about 280 persons per square mile, or a little
greater than that of the state of Pennsylvania today
(Chart 5·18).

Total kilowatt-hours, then, can be expected to continue
to increase by geometric progression past the end of this
century and to continue to increase by at least constant
amounts through the next century (Chart 5·19).

The approximately 350 investor-owned electric light
and power companies are working together to meet the
power needs of the future. They begin planning lo-

GOMPERTZ CURVE Fitted to KWHRS Per Capita · U.S.A.

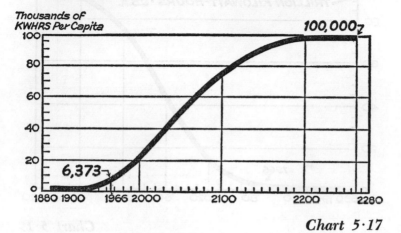

Thousands of KWHRS Per Capita

100,000

6,373

Chart 5·17

Chart 5·18

POPULATION in the United States

GOMPERTZ CURVE APPLIED TO U.S. CENSUS DATA AND ESTIMATES TO 1985

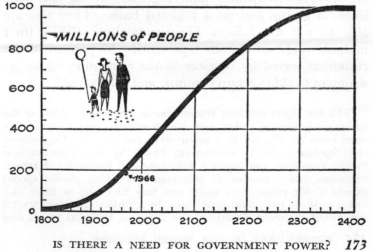

MILLIONS of PEOPLE

1966

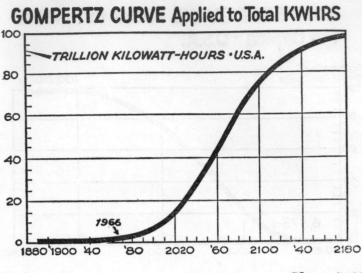

GOMPERTZ CURVE Applied to Total KWHRS

TRILLION KILOWATT-HOURS • U.S.A.

1966

Chart 5·19

cally, to meet local needs. The next step is company-wide planning, where the needs of the districts are balanced and coordinated. But the process does not stop there. The companies plan together, across corporate lines, in groups and on a regional basis. They also are able to use the Edison Electric Institute (EEI), their national trade association representing 97 percent of the customers served by investor-owned companies, as an instrument to aid in group planning and discussion.*

*EEI has eighty standing committees in which some 2,500 of the nation's top electric utility men and women work together. The committees are divided into seven divisions: General; Engineering and Operating; Sales; Accounting; Power Systems Coordination; Public, Employee, and Investor Relations; and Research. A typical committee has a number of subcommittees which pursue special aspects of the committee's work, and may have one or more task forces to study individual problems. In addition, there are several committees reporting directly to the Board of Directors which deal

In 1964 EEI member companies were conducting over 1,800 research projects, including research in atomic power. Electric utility companies became interested in atomic power as soon as the achievement of nuclear fission become known to the public. In 1954, Congress for the first time opened the door for American industry to engage in development and construction of its own atomic power plants. Some companies grouped together to share the cost of these projects. Others worked independently. Within 12 years, 130 electric companies, in cooperation with the Atomic Energy Commission and equipment manufacturers, were participating in forty-seven projects aimed at making atomic energy a practical, economic source of electric power. Ten atomic power plants were in actual operation, contributing to the electricity supply of consumers in New York, Pennsylvania,

with matters of special importance to the industry or internal affairs of the EEI.

The committees of the Institute provide a valuable forum in which industry engineers, accountants, economists, lawyers, sales-financial people, and others can meet together, exchange ideas and experience, and discuss common problems. Through this group process it is possible to maintain flexibility and local initiative and, at the same time, coordinate activities in areas of common interest. For example, the EEI Research Division acts as a clearinghouse for information on research activities within the industry so that duplication of effort can be avoided whenever possible. As part of this activity, it conducts a survey of the research being done for the electric utility companies by equipment manufacturers and by the companies themselves, including research projects which the companies have decided to carry out through the EEI. For 1964, the survey found that 148 of the EEI member companies, the EEI, and fourteen equipment manufacturers reported a total expenditure of $152.7 million. This represents only a portion of the great mass of research expenditures that benefit electric consumers. Research on appliances and other utilization devices and in fields from which by-product benefits may be available to the industry have not been measured.

Illinois, Michigan, the New England states, California, and the Southeast.

Research programs such as these help ensure a continuing abundance of electric power in this country. As a guide to the future, EEI makes continuing studies of growth in electric power use in the years to come. From time to time, the results of the studies are published—not as goals to be met, but as the considered judgment of many people in the industry on what will actually occur.

The latest EEI forecast of the future of the electric utility industry, made in 1959, was made on the basis of components of the gross national product that show definite correlations to the electric utility industry data. For example, reasonably good correlations were found between disposable personal income and domestic kilowatt-hour sales, between personal consumption expenditures for services and kilowatt-hour sales to small light and power customers, and between the Federal Reserve Board Index of Industrial Production and sales to large light and power customers. This forecast was compared with the plans of the companies and showed a high degree of compatibility. When two such different approaches to forecasting bring such similar results, it is possible to be reasonably confident of their reliability. Each year the forecast is checked against the actual record of the industry. Thus far, there has been no need to revise it. In fact, the forecast for 1966 proved to be accurate within 1 percent.

The EEI studies indicate that by the year 2000 total power output in the country will probably be in a range of 6 trillion to 10 trillion kilowatt-hours a year, depending on the rate of growth of the economy and the rate at which new energy uses are introduced (Chart 5·20).

Of course, any prediction for a period 4 decades

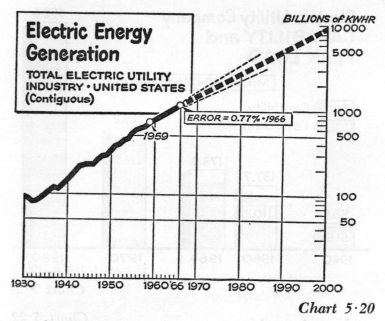

Chart 5·20

away has to be viewed with caution. As points nearer in time are studied the prediction can become more reliable.

By 1980, electric companies expect to have nearly quadrupled their 1960 power-producing capability, reaching a total of 492.6 million kilowatts that year (Chart 5·21).

To expand their power supply systems, the companies will nearly quadruple their 1960 investment by 1980 (Chart 5·22). Between 1960 and 1970 some $8 billion will be spent for transmission alone (Chart 5·23).

Where will all the money come from? About 50 percent of the capital requirements between 1960 and 1980 will be generated internally, and the remaining 50 percent—some $66.5 billion—will be provided through the free market (Chart 5·24).

About 4 million men and women, drawn from every walk of life, are direct shareowners in power companies.

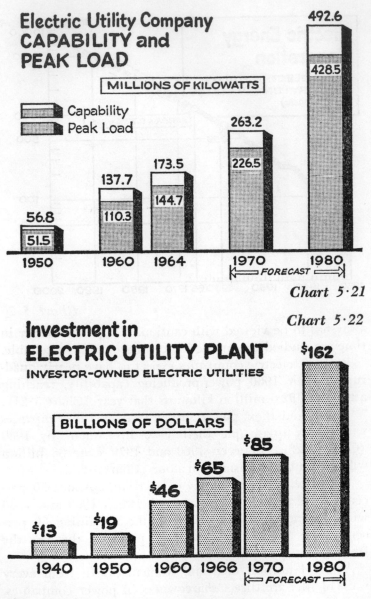

Electric Utility Company CAPABILITY and PEAK LOAD

MILLIONS OF KILOWATTS

Capability
Peak Load

492.6
428.5

263.2
226.5

173.5
144.7

137.7
110.3

56.8
51.5

1950   1960   1964   1970   1980
FORECAST

Chart 5·21

Chart 5·22

Investment in ELECTRIC UTILITY PLANT

INVESTOR-OWNED ELECTRIC UTILITIES

BILLIONS OF DOLLARS

$162

$85

$65

$46

$19

$13

1940   1950   1960   1966   1970   1980
FORECAST

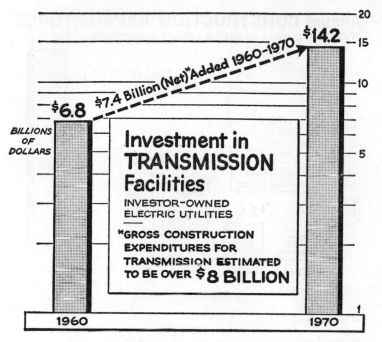

$20

$14.2 —15

$7.4 Billion (Net)* Added 1960-1970 —10

$6.8

BILLIONS
OF
DOLLARS

Investment in
TRANSMISSION
Facilities

INVESTOR-OWNED
ELECTRIC UTILITIES

*GROSS CONSTRUCTION
EXPENDITURES FOR
TRANSMISSION ESTIMATED
TO BE OVER $8 BILLION

—5

1960   1970

Chart 5·23

In addition, investments made by insurance companies, mutual savings banks, pension funds, and the like give nearly every American an indirect financial stake in the industry. As the total economy grows, there is no question but that the sums needed to build the power facilities of the future can continue to be raised in the free market.[20]

Public opinion surveys indicate that only about one-third of the American people believe there is any reason for government to be in the power business. Almost two-thirds of the public feel that their local power company is well-equipped to meet all local needs for electricity. At the same time, some people think that power

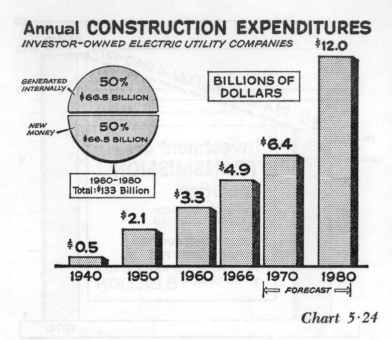

Annual CONSTRUCTION EXPENDITURES
INVESTOR-OWNED ELECTRIC UTILITY COMPANIES **$12.0**

GENERATED INTERNALLY — 50% $66.5 BILLION

NEW MONEY — 50% $66.5 BILLION

BILLIONS OF DOLLARS

1960–1980 Total: $133 Billion

$6.4
$4.9
$3.3
$2.1
$0.5

1940 1950 1960 1966 1970 1980
⟵ FORECAST ⟶

Chart 5·24

companies in other areas may need help from the government. In a 1965 survey people were asked if there was a need for government to produce or sell electricity in their part of the country. Only about 13 percent said Yes. But twice as many of these same people, 28 percent, said that government power was needed in other parts of the country.[21]

Investor-owned power companies have always been able to provide the public with an ample supply of electricity. Their power plant and transmission capability has always remained ahead of demand. Not knowing the facts, some people have been awed by the task of supplying electric power in the quantities needed throughout the country and have concluded that companies cannot do it alone. When the facts about the over-all power supply

180 GOVERNMENT IN THE POWER BUSINESS

situation are explained, most people agree there is nothing to indicate that the portion of the nation's power needs now being financed through government by the nation's taxpayers cannot be served entirely through the free market in the traditional American manner.

Incidental to river development

During the early years of this century there was widespread interest in hydroelectric development. Water power was equated with cheap power, and there was a rush to develop the available dam sites. These locations soon became relatively scarce, and in later years it became more difficult and much more costly to produce power at the remaining sites. This is one reason, of course, that an increasing percentage of our electric power is produced in steam generating stations.

Because of the interest of governmental bodies in such aspects of river development as navigation and flood control, it is natural that the suggestion be made that government provide capital for further hydroelectric developments. In fact, some people believe that hydroelectric developments, such as those along the Tennessee River or the Columbia River, are so large and require so much capital that only government can undertake them. The facts do not bear this out.

Almost 17 percent of the electric energy of the electric utility industry in this country is produced in hydroelectric stations.[22] (Chart 5·25) Some of these stations are relatively small, and some are very large. Many are operated by investor-owned companies. In fact, about 36 percent of the electric utility industry's hydroelectric capacity is owned by investor-owned companies under licenses from the Federal Power Commission.[23] (Chart 5·26)

A large part of the present government power program

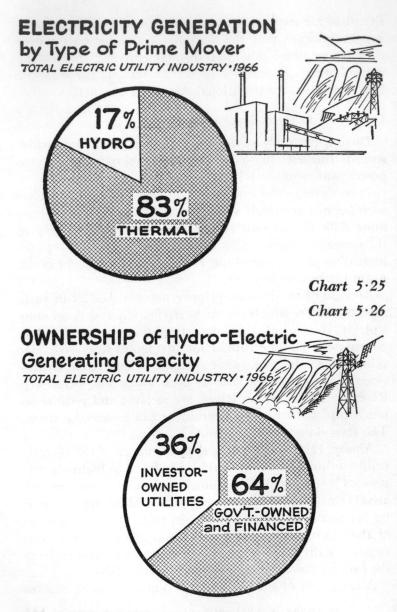

ELECTRICITY GENERATION
by Type of Prime Mover
TOTAL ELECTRIC UTILITY INDUSTRY · 1966

17%
HYDRO

83%
THERMAL

Chart 5·25

Chart 5·26

OWNERSHIP of Hydro-Electric
Generating Capacity
TOTAL ELECTRIC UTILITY INDUSTRY · 1966

36%
INVESTOR-OWNED UTILITIES

64%
GOV'T.-OWNED and FINANCED

182   GOVERNMENT IN THE POWER BUSINESS

has been brought about as part of river development projects. Most people agree that government can serve a useful purpose in providing flood control, in providing for irrigation, in preventing soil erosion, and in acting in other ways to conserve resources. Such activities may require the building of dams, and people often equate dams with hydroelectric development. What most people do not understand is that all dams are not alike. Those built primarily for flood control and those built for power development are markedly different.

Normally, a flood control dam is relatively low, requires few attendants, and is relatively simple to construct. The dam is provided with sluices or holes near the bottom. These are of a size that will let through as much water as can be accommodated by the channel below (Chart 5·27).

As a rule, the reservoir on the up-stream side of the dam is empty. The normal stream flows through the sluices. When flood water arrives, the dam holds it back, creating

Chart 5·27

CROSS SECTION OF
A FLOOD CONTROL DAM

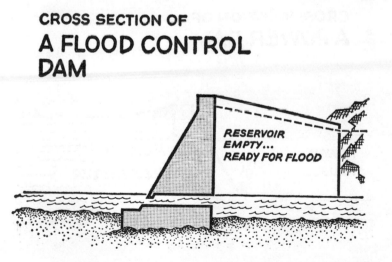

RESERVOIR EMPTY... READY FOR FLOOD

a temporary reservoir. The reservoir then gradually empties through the sluices and is ready to hold back the next flood.

But an empty reservoir cannot generate power. Electricity at a hydroelectric dam is produced from falling water, and the higher the fall the greater the amount of power. As a result, power dams are usually built as high as the river banks and reservoir space will permit within the economics based on stream flow and the object of the dam is to keep the reservoir as full as possible (Chart 5·28).

Sometimes effective flood control and generation of dependable hydroelectricity work at cross purposes. Dr. Arthur E. Morgan, the first Chairman of the Tennessee Valley Authority, testified before Congress in 1937 that

My chief fear in combining flood control and power is that in later years, in times of dry weather, power interests begin to encroach

Chart 5·28

CROSS SECTION OF
A POWER DAM

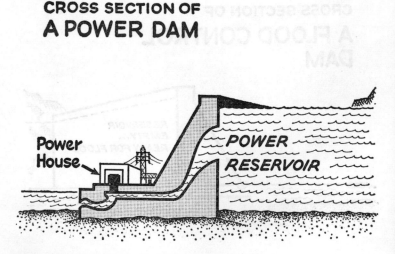

upon flood-control storage, and then if there should be a big flood, the storage space might be in use for navigation and power when it should have been kept empty.[24]

Dr. Morgan first came to national attention as engineer for a series of flood control dams in Ohio along the Miami River. These dams carry a plaque stating: "THE DAMS OF THE MIAMI CONSERVANCY DISTRICT ARE FOR FLOOD PREVENTION PURPOSES. THEIR USE FOR POWER DEVELOPMENT OR FOR STORAGE WOULD BE A MENACE TO THE CITIES BELOW." [25]

Of course, it is possible to combine flood control dams and power dams. This is done, in effect, by building one dam on top of the other (Chart 5·29). The only sure way of accomplishing effective flood control in a multiple-purpose dam of this type would be to provide for uncontrollable sluices. As soon as gates are installed, the human element enters. The Grand River Dam in Oklahoma is a case in point. The dam was designed by the Army Engineers so that a substantial part of the reservoir would

Chart 5·29

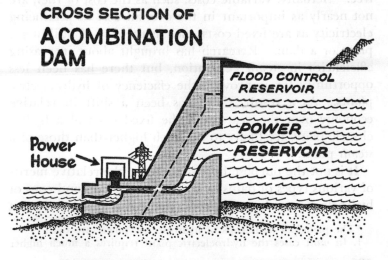

CROSS SECTION OF
A COMBINATION
DAM

FLOOD CONTROL RESERVOIR

POWER RESERVOIR

Power House

be reserved for flood control. However, the dam was being operated primarily for hydroelectric production and a need was felt to generate all the power possible. The sluice gates remained closed and the dam was operated with a practically full reservoir. When the flood of 1943 came the gates were opened—but not soon enough. The farms below the dam had the worst flood in history, worse than if no dam had been there at all.[26]

Multiple-purpose dams, such as those operated by the Tennessee Valley Authority and other government agencies, are expensive to construct, require large reservoirs that keep acres of land permanently under water, and do not provide the most effective form of flood control. Why, then, are they built? Probably the chief reason is that most people, in addition to thinking that all dams are alike, believe that hydroelectric power is cheaper than power produced in steam plants. This seems a reasonable assumption on the surface: Fuel for a steam plant must be purchased while the water at a hydroelectric station is free. Actually, variable costs, such as the cost of fuel, are not nearly as important in the over-all cost of producing electricity as are fixed costs, such as the cost of building a plant or a dam. Research has brought about increasing efficiencies in steam generation, but there has been less opportunity for improving the efficiency of hydroelectric plants. As a result, there has been a shift in relative economy over the years, and the fixed costs of a hydroelectric plant are likely to be much higher than those of a steam plant.

It is not the purpose here to examine the relative merits of various types of dams or to analyze the pros and cons of hydroelectric and steam production,* but simply to point

*The principal handicaps of hydroelectric power are that:
1. In most cases the hydroelectric plant requires a much higher

out that misunderstandings relating to river development and water power have led some people to the idea that government should be in the business of producing electric energy at government-owned dams.

The paying partner theory

The sale of electric power produces revenue. People who understand the value of such activities as flood control

---

investment per kilowatt of capacity. In both steam plants and hydro plants there must be a turbine and a generator. But the hydro plants call for an expensive dam, and the company usually has to buy considerable land for the reservoir.

2. The hydroelectric plant must be built at a suitable site on the river. The site may be some distance from the point where the power is needed. This calls for a higher investment in transmission facilities. Usually the steam plant can be located nearer the load centers.

3. Frequently the hydro plant depends on stream flow which is sometimes intermittent. In many cases the hydroelectric plant cannot be used around the clock every day in the year. It must be supplemented by steam power.

4. The steam plant offers greater opportunities for improvement in design. Witness the fact that in the early days of the industry it took about 8 pounds of coal to make a kilowatt-hour in a steam plant. Also, the investment cost per kilowatt in the steam plant has been fairly steady.

5. Frequently the hydro dam is built to carry out some other purpose, such as flood control, in which case the two functions may work at cross purposes. In 1940 this trend in favor of steam plant generation was noted by Mr. Gano Dunn, president of J. G. White Engineering Corporation, when he was serving as power consultant to the Advisory Commission of the Council of National Defense. He summed up his viewpoint as follows (Report No. 1953, accompanying Senate Joint Resolution 285), as printed in Congressional Record, 76th Congress, 3d Sess., vol. 86, Part 9, July 29, 1940, pp. 9667–9669: "And today, in 1940, a new plant can develop a kilowatt-hour for nine-tenths of a pound of coal. In that scaling down from eight pounds of coal per kilowatt-hour to 0.9 pounds of coal per kilowatt-hour, steam power passed water power, and now is much the cheaper power when costs are calculated on the same basis for each form of power."

and irrigation have sometimes suggested that incidental power produced at dams constructed for these purposes be sold to help pay the cost of the dams. In this way, they say, the sale of electric power will help pay for useful governmental activities.

The belief that revenue derived from the sale of power will help pay the cost of river development is widespread. Chapter 7 contains a summary of an economic study showing that where government builds a dam it derives the greatest amount of income by licensing a company financed in the free market to build the power facilities—not from producing and selling incidental electricity. By selling the available falling water to the company and then taxing the company as it does any enterprise, keeping the price of power to consumers under government regulation, government gains more income and benefits the nation as a whole.

The yardstick concept

For many years, both in this country and abroad, it has been understood that certain kinds of business requiring the investment of large amounts of capital have an obligation to provide service to anyone who applies for it, and to do so at reasonable rates. In these industries, such as the telephone, water, gas and electric, where fixed costs are relatively high, direct competition in the sense that one grocery store competes with another grocery store across the street is not in the public interest. Government regulation can provide the public with safeguards ordinarily obtained through this kind of competition. Of course, there is keen competition of other kinds in many of these industries. For example, coal, oil, gas, and electric utility companies all compete in the heating market, and gas and electric utilities compete vigorously to serve refrigerators, washers, dryers, and other appliances as well. The same conditions exist for government agencies acting in these businesses as for investor-owned companies, except that government power has no independent government regulation.

If the cost of capital for a power company is on the order of 6 percent per year (although in some situations it is higher) and taxes each year are at the rate of about 5 percent of the investment, these two fixed costs add up to about 11 percent on the investment. A $4.45 investment is required to produce $1 of annual revenue in the power business; 11 percent of $4.45 is 49 cents, or approximately half of every dollar of revenue the company receives annually. Where there are two power suppliers in a community, the duplication of facilities results in higher costs for electric service, which is against the public interest. To avoid these higher costs many communities franchise only one electric power supplier to serve their area, although they have the right to issue franchises to as many as they like.

Under the American economic system, most industries look to the law of supply and demand to regulate prices. When there is only one supplier in an area, some substitute must be found for this technique. In the power business the substitute is provided by government regulation.

Government regulation of public utilities is usually embodied in a state public utility commission. The task of the regulatory agency is not to guarantee a set return on the investment in power facilities. Its purpose is to see to it that the public interest is properly served and that the return on the investment is not excessive, yet is sufficient to ensure continued flow of capital into the industry. The company management is responsible for operating the property in a way that will maintain good earnings at a reasonable price—the price being regulated by the independent government body.

It is sometimes thought that regulated industries are guaranteed a return on their investment. This is not so. The regulatory body prevents a company from earning an excessive return. But during the Depression years most utility companies were earning far less than what is generally considered a fair return. The regulatory bodies did not raise all rates to produce a fair return. In fact, it is doubtful that increased rates during those years would have produced increased revenues.

Electric companies which operate across state lines and those which are licensed by the Federal government to develop water power on navigable streams and for other reasons must comply with regulations of the Federal Power Commission. In addition, the Securities and Exchange Commission has regulatory powers over electric companies which are part of holding company systems.

From time to time, groups of people who have not understood the effectiveness of these regulatory agencies have suggested that some kind of yardstick is needed to measure whether or not companies are charging the proper costs for the power they sell. Although this idea is given little credence today, it still persists to a degree.

The American trust in competition enters into this attitude. People feel that most competition is good and that, therefore, competition between government-owned power suppliers and investor-owned companies should be good, too. But the real competition in the electric utility business is with suppliers of other forms of energy and between managements of electric companies themselves, which are constantly striving to outdo each other in performance and in lowering prices. The subsidies provided government power suppliers make them an unrealistic and ineffective yardstick.

During the early 1930s the yardstick idea was discussed frequently. In 1933, in a discussion of the TVA Act on the floor of the House of Representatives, Representative Montet of Louisiana explained that the purpose of the legislation was to establish a yardstick,[27] and a year later David E. Lilienthal, then one of the three directors of TVA, said that

The first duty of the Tennessee Valley Authority in its power program is to set up what the President has called a "yardstick" by which to measure the fairness of electric rates. It has an additional function. It is a reminder that unless that business is carried on by private corporations with a due sense of responsibility to the paramount public interest, that the public, at any time may assume the function of providing itself with this necessity [sic] of community life.[28]

The sponsors of TVA understood, however, that an important element was being omitted from their "yardstick." Some years later, when Congress was considering a bill to place taxes on TVA, Senator George Norris, author of the TVA Act, said: "A proposal from a great association of Tennessee says, in effect, 'Let the TVA property be subject to taxation the same as everybody else's property. . . .' If we go to that extreme, Senators can see that the TVA would be out of business in 3 months." [29]

Any difference in price between government power and investor-owned power can be traced to subsidies in the cost of capital and to taxes. As General Herbert D. Vogel, then Chairman of TVA said in 1956, ". . . insofar as we fall short on that [i.e., paying Federal income tax], this is not a yardstick. And I don't kid myself, and I think no one should kid himself, that a yardstick is involved in this." [30]

The natural tendency for people to compare prices as they are without regard to costs not included in the lower prices keeps the yardstick idea alive. This imposes upon the investor-owned power companies of the nation a responsibility to call the attention of their customers to the fact that the customers of government power agencies pay only part of the cost of their electric service. Of course, some people are willing to accept government power projects in their areas with full knowledge that the power they will purchase will not be paying its full share of taxes or reflect the full cost of capital. They are willing to accept the benefits being brought to them at the expense of the nation's taxpayers. Possibly if more of these people had full knowledge of the economic facts and the long-range implications of their actions, they would not act as they do.

Politics

It is natural that elected officials will want to cultivate the good will of their constituents. They want to make their constituents happy. They want to do well in representing the interests of the voters in their districts. Wisely or not, people in every country seem to make demands upon their national governments for special benefits for their own communities or regions. In this country, some elected officials feel they should make special efforts to see that Federal funds are appropriated and put to use in their districts.

Under such conditions it is almost inevitable that government expenditures for resource development and other activities become involved in politics. As this phenomenon seems to be characteristic of a free society, the best that can be expected is that accurate economic facts be understood by as many people as possible.

Advocates of government planning

There are people in all societies who believe that their well-being will be achieved best through a system of government planning. The record does not seem to bear out their point of view, for standards of living in free societies such as America are higher than those of government-planned economies, such as the Soviet Union, yet the ideal of a perfectly planned economy appeals to some people nonetheless.

Government ownership of electric power is an essential part of the program of those who advocate complete government control of the economy. In their view, all natural resources, all banks, all railroads, all communications facilities, and all the basic means of production should come under strict government control. The majority of the American people, however, do not have this view. They are strongly opposed to communism and to socialism. Because of this opposition, the activities of the advocates of the government-planned society have not been a large factor in the entry of government into the electric utility business. But these activities have had a certain influence that should not be overlooked.*

Other factors

There are many other factors which affect government ownership of electric power facilities. Even the Federal Power Commission (FPC) has sometimes acted in ways that have tended to contribute to the problem. For instance, when the FPC approves below-cost electric rates of

---

* See "Encroaching Socialism," prepared by *Public Service Magazine* of St. Paul, Minn., for an interesting account of the activities of this group.

Federal agencies, when it publishes comparisons between average bills of customers of investor-owned companies and those of government-financed power suppliers without pointing out the subsidies being supplied to the government power agencies, or when it applies standards in evaluating power projects that favor government operation, the FPC is encouraging extension of government in the power business.

The chief reasons given today in support of government power programs are that, (1) such programs are needed, (2) a yardstick is needed to measure the fairness of electric rates, (3) government power helps pay for other governmental functions, and (4) government power helps in regional economic development. In this chapter we have given primary attention to the first two, the supposed need and the yardstick. Let us now analyze three major Federal power activities—the TVA, the BPA, and the REA—in order to understand the relationship of taxes and the cost of money in these projects and to see whether their electric power programs really do increase the government's revenue.

REFERENCES

1. EEI.
2. Edwin Vennard, *The Electric Power Business*, McGraw-Hill Book Company, New York, 1962, p. 75.
3. T. C. Martin, "The Daylight Work of Central Stations," *NELA Proceedings*, 1897, pp. 423–425.
4. Samuel Insull, "Twenty-five Years of Central Station Commercial Development," *NELA Proceedings*, 1910, p. 211 et seq.
5. U.S. Bureau of the Census, *Central Electric Light and Power Stations*, 1907, p. 96.
   U.S. Bureau of the Census, *Central Electric Light and Power Stations*, 1912, p. 112.
6. U.S. Bureau of the Census, *Central Electric Light and Power Stations*, 1907, p. 17.

7. U.S. Bureau of the Census, *Statistical Abstract of the United States,* 1965, Table 4, p. 9; Table 1274, p. 911; EEI, *A Report on Electric Power Developments in the USSR—1963,* Table IV, p. 141; EEI, *Historical Statistics,* Table 48, p. 40.

8. FPC, *National Power Survey,* 1964, Vol. 1, p. 14.

9. EEI.

10. David Lilienthal, *The Journals of David E. Lilienthal, The TVA Years, 1939–1945,* Harper & Row, Publishers, New York, 1964, p. 317.

11. *Preliminary Hearings before the Subcommittee of the Committee on Appropriations, House of Representatives, on the Agriculture Department Appropriations Bill for 1943,* 77th Cong., 1st Sess., p. 170.

12. *Hearings before the Subcommittee on Flood Control of the Committee on Public Works, House of Representatives, on H.R. 3236, H.R. 4266,* 85th Cong., 1st Sess., 1957, p. 224.

13. *Ibid.*

14. W. H. Sammis, *Testimony before the Subcommittee on Flood Control of the Committee on Public Works on H.R 3236, H.R. 4266,* 85th Cong., 1st Sess., pp. 224, 227.

15. J. A. Krug, address in Chattanooga, Tenn., Feb. 16, 1943, Office of War Information Release NB-555, p. 2.

16. EEI, *41st Semi-annual Electric Power Survey—April 1967,* Pub. 67-30.

17. FPC, *World Power Data,* 1964, p. 5.

18. U.S. Department of Commerce, *The National Income and Product Accounts of the U.S.,* 1929–1965, pp. 44–47.

19. U.S. Department of Commerce, *Annual Survey of Manufactures,* 1962 (computed by EEI).

20. EEI, *I Want to Know About the Electric Utility Industry,* 1967, p. 28.

21. Opinion Research Corporation, 1965.

22. EEI, *Statistical Yearbook of the Electric Utility Industry for 1966,* Table 10S.

23. *Ibid.,* Table 2S.

24. *Hearings before the Subcommittee of the Committee on Appropriations, House of Representatives, on the Second Deficiency Appropriation Bill for 1937,* 75th Cong., 1st Sess., p. 345.

25. Edwin Vennard, *Dangers of the TVA Method of River Control,* 1945, p. 30.

26. *Ibid.,* pp. 28–29.

27. *Congressional Record,* 73d Cong., 1st Sess., Vol. 77, Part 3, Apr. 24, 1933, p. 2277.

28. David Lilienthal, Speech before the League of Women Voters, Boston, Mass., Apr. 24, 1934, Release of TVA, Apr. 25, 1934, p. 2.
29. *Congressional Record*, 76th Cong., 1st Sess., Vol. 84, Part 4, Apr. 13, 1939, p. 4214.
30. *Hearings before the House of Representatives Subcommittee on Appropriations on Second Supplemental Appropriation Bill,* 84th Cong., 2d Sess., 1956, p. 652.

Chapter **6**

The Tennessee Valley Authority

TVA has been a controversial issue for more than 30 years. To some, it is a great and successful government project which has tamed a river and brought benefits to the people of the area and the nation, while to others it is an experiment in socialism that should never be repeated. Most people today think of it as primarily a water project, combining navigation, flood control, and hydroelectricity. Because TVA has come to represent government power to many people, and because it is widely misunderstood, it will be helpful to review how TVA began, what it is today, and what its accomplishments actually have been.

The beginnings

The controversy grew in intensity during the 1920s. In an attempt to bring a dispassionate and unbiased view to the subject, the U.S. Army Corps of Engineers was asked to report on the various ways the Tennessee River might be developed.[1] In an exhaustive study sent to the House of Representatives on March 24, 1930, the Chief of Engineers concluded that irrigation was not needed in the Tennessee Basin but that flood control was needed and navigation could be improved. He pointed out that electric power was being developed along the Tennessee River in accordance with the Federal Water Power Act, which provided for comprehensive development of navigable waterways for navigation, power, and other beneficial uses.[2] At the time there were twenty-three hydroelectric developments within the Tennessee River Basin. In addition, the Tennessee Electric Power Co. was developing sites on the Tocoa River, one project was being constructed on the Pigeon River, the Aluminum Company of America was building new power plants along the Little Tennessee River, and the Federal Power Commission was considering applications for preliminary permits for development of a number of other sites in the area.[3] With these considerations in mind, the Chief of Engineers proposed a plan for a series of low dams which would aid in flood control and improve navigation but that would not be suitable for power production. However, he suggested that provision be made so that any two or more of the low dams could be replaced by a high dam, which would be constructed by an investor-owned company, municipality, or state with the Federal government responsible only for the cost of the locks and other facilities necessary for navigation.[4] The total cost to the government of this approach was estimated at about $30 million.[5]

As created by Congress in 1933, TVA began a different course. A series of high dams were built and steam plants were added. The total investment in TVA, as of June 30, 1964, was $3.13 billion, of which $2.59 billion was invested in electric power.[6]

Although TVA was labeled primarily a navigation and flood control project, with electric power to be an incidental by-product, the steam plant capacity of TVA grew in a fashion that even some of its strongest proponents did not envision. The constitutionality of this shift in direction has been open to considerable question. In 1935, for example, John Lord O'Brian, Special Counsel for TVA, was arguing the constitutionality of Wilson Dam, the first of the series of dams built by TVA. During his presentation before the U.S. Supreme Court, Justice McReynolds asked:

MR. JUSTICE MCREYNOLDS Is there a steam plant in connection with this project?

MR. O'BRIAN Yes, your Honor. That was mentioned earlier. There is a large steam plant which was built at Muscle Shoals before the dam was built.

MR. JUSTICE MCREYNOLDS For what purpose?

MR. O'BRIAN For the purpose of equipping the war munitions plant immediately as quickly as possible, with power.

MR. JUSTICE MCREYNOLDS Is that used to generate electricity?

MR. O'BRIAN No sir; it has never been used. It stands there idle. Much is made in my opponents' brief of the danger of the Government selling power from the steam plant. That steam plant is not in this case. It never has been used. It has been maintained. It has been leased to the Alabama Power Co., which has used it as a stand-by facility with which to meet breakdowns in its service. There is nothing in this record to show that the Authority ever intends to use it for the purpose of generating power for sale, and I disavow any such intention at this time.

MR. JUSTICE BUTLER I know; but you assert the power, do you not?

MR. O'BRIAN No; I do not.

MR. JUSTICE BUTLER Do you say that to aid in disposing of the electricity incidentally produced from this navigation dam, the Congress has no power under the Constitution to build stand-by plants to supply their customers, to keep the current going?

MR. O'BRIAN If you mean breakdown facilities, yes; it could. It would have to. Any regulated system would have that.

MR. JUSTICE BUTLER And then to meet great demands upon the peak?

MR. O'BRIAN No; I do not think that could be done in this case.[7]

The Court found that the one dam under discussion, Wilson Dam, had been constructed for constitutional purposes, that is, for national defense and navigation. The power generated incident to the operation of this dam, the Court said, could be sold. No opinion was expressed concerning any other part of the TVA activity.*

In a later case the Court held that, although investor-owned power companies might suffer by the competition of the TVA power program, only states or local government units could raise the constitutional questions involved. As a result, the principal constitutional issue—whether TVA should operate as an electric power system with steam plants as well as hydroelectric facilities—has never been resolved.[8]

By 1964, 83 percent of TVA's investment was in power facilities.[9] (Chart 6·1) In 1964, over 77 percent of TVA's energy was produced in steam-electric plants [10] (Chart 6·2). TVA has turned into a large power system furnishing electric utility service, and in the way it is built and run it is like any large electric company (Chart 6·3).

TVA today

In 1964, TVA's total power capability was 13.8 million kilowatts, or about 25 percent of the total government and cooperative power capability. It is the largest of the

*The Court, speaking through Chief Justice Hughes, said: "We limit our decision to the case before us as we have defined it . . . We express no opinion as to the validity of such an effort, as to the status of any other dam or power development in the Tennessee Valley, whether connected with or apart from Wilson Dam, or as to the validity of the Tennessee Valley Authority Act or of the claims made in the pronouncements and program of the Authority apart from the questions we have discussed in relation to the particular provisions of the contract of Jan. 4, 1934, affecting the Alabama Power Company." (297 U.S. 288:56 Supreme Court 466; 80 Law Ed. 688.)

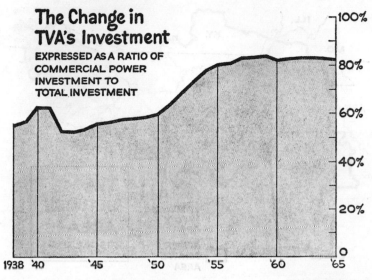

The Change in TVA's Investment

EXPRESSED AS A RATIO OF COMMERCIAL POWER INVESTMENT TO TOTAL INVESTMENT

Chart 6·1

Chart 6·2

TVA Steam and Hydro Electric Generation
PERCENT OF TOTAL GENERATION
(Including Alcoa Dams and Cumberland Basin)

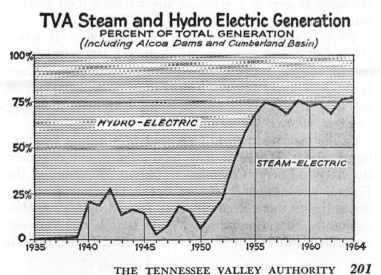

HYDRO-ELECTRIC

STEAM-ELECTRIC

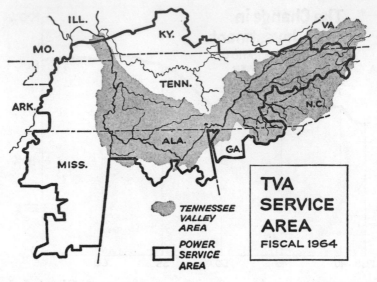

TENNESSEE
VALLEY
AREA

POWER
SERVICE
AREA

TVA
SERVICE
AREA
FISCAL 1964

Chart 6·3

government-financed power suppliers, and its 13.8 million kilowatts is over 6 percent of the nation's total electric utility industry's capability.[11]

TVA is a wholesale supplier of electricity. It serves about 200 customers. Among them are 105 municipally owned electric systems, 50 rural electrical cooperatives. It also sells power directly to more than 22 industrial plants and a small number of Federal defense agencies with very large or unusual power requirements.

In the fiscal year 1964, TVA sold 24.4 billion kilowatt-hours, about 36 percent of its total sales, to one customer, the Atomic Energy Commission (AEC), an agency of the Federal government.[12] (Chart 6·4) This one customer not only uses more electricity than is used by Maine, Massachusetts, New Hampshire, Rhode Island, and Vermont combined, but uses it at a very high load factor, since it

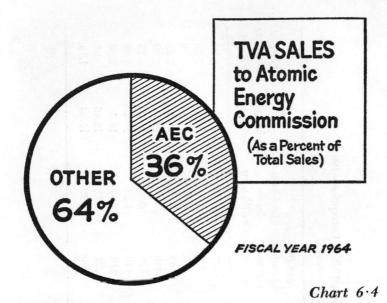

TVA SALES
to Atomic
Energy
Commission
(As a Percent of
Total Sales)

AEC
36%

OTHER
64%

FISCAL YEAR 1964

Chart 6·4

uses electric power around the clock, every day, every night of the year. Of course, investor-owned companies also serve the Atomic Energy Commission, and because of the unusual size and nature of the load, the companies have formed separate corporations in order to serve the business.[13]

In order for the TVA power business to be analyzed and compared with investor-owned companies, two adjustments have to be made. First, the AEC business must be removed from TVA, and second, the wholesale business of TVA must be combined with its municipal distributors. TVA then is quite similar to a large investor-owned company. Its total power capability is then estimated to be about 10.6 million kilowatts, or about 5 percent of the nation's total.

Table 6·1 shows the largest electric utility enterprises ranked according to total assets (net) and also shows elec-

Table 6·1 Largest U.S. Electric Utility Enterprises—1964
(Total Net Asset Basis)

	Total assets, net, billions	Electric operating revenues, millions	Maximum demand, million kw	Kwhr sold, billions	Electric customers, millions
Consolidated Edison Co. of N.Y., Inc.	$3.24	$647	5.51	23.8	2.90
Pacific Gas and Electric Co.	3.09	520	6.16	30.6	2.25
Tennessee Valley Authority*	1.99	275	9.43	44.1	.98
Commonwealth Edison Co.	1.94	565	6.10	29.1	2.23
Southern California Edison Co.	1.86	450	5.46	28.0	2.09
The Southern Co. System	1.80	413	6.52	31.2	1.75
American Electric Power Co. System	1.75	419	6.24	36.2	1.48
Public Service Electric and Gas Co.	1.69	319	3.67	16.3	1.50
Consumers Power Co.	1.20	222	2.38	12.46	.93
Philadelphia Electric Co.	1.20	260	3.29	15.60	1.13

* Excluding AEC, including municipal distributors.

tric operating revenues, kilowatts of demand, kilowatt-hour sales, and customers. TVA, as adjusted, is also shown in the table. It can be seen from this table that, as adjusted, TVA is comparable to other large electric power systems.

TVA and the price of electricity

Much of the controversy about TVA stems from its pricing policy. TVA's rates are low compared with those of most investor-owned companies, and the low rates result in a greater use of electricity in the Tennessee Valley. TVA claims that the low rates permit use of mass-production methods with lower costs, that the venture is profitable to the government, and that it can serve as a yardstick for the rates of the other power companies.

In the power business, generally speaking, the cost of making and delivering additional units of electricity has been less than the average cost of all units. Because of this, from the early days of the industry—before the turn of the century—rates have been designed with a sliding-scale feature so that the average unit price to the customer goes down as he uses more electricity. This has brought down the average revenue per kilowatt-hour sold despite the fact that inflation has brought about increases across the board in the cost of labor, materials, and supplies.*

The promotional electric rates were designed to encourage increased use of service. But one basic economic fact had to be kept in mind in the setting of rates: the service should not be sold below cost. While the cost of making one more kilowatt-hour is likely to be less than the average

*For a more detailed discussion of electric utility rate making and the relationship between the use of energy and the price, see Edwin Vennard, *The Electric Utility Business*, McGraw-Hill Book Company, New York, 1962.

cost per kilowatt-hour, the lowest step in the rate should not be below the cost of making the added kilowatt-hour.

Money from Congress

When Congress established TVA in 1933, TVA was not required to pay any interest on the funds it received from the government or to pay any Federal income taxes. Whatever the reason or reasons behind this decision, TVA did not pay any interest on funds appropriated for it from 1933 through 1959.[14]

The gross appropriations by Congress for the TVA power business amounted to $1.4 billion through 1961, and for 26 years TVA paid no interest on this money.[15] During this period when Congress was appropriating funds for TVA, total Federal spending was greater than income and the government had to borrow money. If the interest rate the government paid for borrowed money had been applied to the funds appropriated to TVA, the unpaid interest on these funds would have been $561,978,243 from 1934 through 1964—even after deducting $157,055,000 which TVA returned to the Treasury. That is, it cost the Federal government $561,978,243 in interest charges from 1934 through 1964 to borrow the money it gave to TVA. (TVA paid interest of only $9,665,972 on $65 million worth of bonds sold to the Treasury and the Reconstruction Finance Corporation. These bonds have since been redeemed.)

TVA has made payments to the general fund, and through 1964 these payments amounted to $225,059,000. In addition, payments totaling $65,072,000 have been made in redemption of bonds sold in the fiscal period 1939 to 1941. During the fiscal year 1964, payments to the U.S. Treasury totaled $50,206,000, comprising $40,206,000 of interest and $10,000,000 of annual repayment as provided under Public Law 86-137.[16] This is sometimes referred to as a return on the government investment, but it falls short of meeting the government's out-of-pocket cost of money and does not begin to compensate for the $1.4 billion Congress has invested in the project.

Taxes

Two of the main sources of revenue for the Federal government are personal income taxes and taxes on the income of corporations. Naturally, the tax paid by a corporation is included in the price of the goods or service it sells. The corporation has no income except from the sale of its product or service. In this sense, investor-owned electric companies, like other corporations, are tax collectors for the government's account. The tax bill paid by the power companies amounted to 23 cents for each $1 of electric revenue in 1964.[17]

TVA makes certain payments in lieu of taxes to state and local governments. Also, the distributors make similar payments to their local governments. However, these combined payments in 1964 amounted to only 0.95 percent of the gross plant investment of TVA (excluding AEC) and its municipal distributors. On the average, electric companies pay 2.33 percent of their gross plant investment in state and local taxes yearly. This is about $2\frac{1}{2}$ times the rate paid by TVA.[18]

In addition, companies pay, on the average, 2.64 percent of their gross plant in Federal income taxes.[19] TVA and its municipal distributors pay no Federal income taxes.

Adjustment for cost of money and taxes

The effect of these two items on TVA's revenue can be easily calculated. According to Federal Power Commission (FPC) statistics, the nation's investor-owned electric utilities earn, on the average, about 5 percent on gross plant. Such earnings are required for free-market financing. Also, according to FPC statistics, the total taxes of investor-owned companies are equivalent to 5.0 percent of gross plant. If TVA had been required in 1964 to earn a 5 percent return on its gross plant account and pay in taxes the equivalent of 5.0 percent of its gross plant account, it would have been necessary to increase TVA's gross operating revenue by about 50 percent that year. This fact means that its rates would have needed to be raised about 50 percent to produce this revenue.[20]

If all of TVA's rates were raised by about 50 percent and compared with the rates of the investor-owned companies operating under similar conditions, the rates would be about the same. This is to be expected, for TVA has not found a new way to make and distribute electricity. It uses the same kind of generators, transmission system, and distribution systems; it follows the same procedures in accounting, meter reading, and engineering; it employs the same kind of people.

When advocates say that government power serves as competition for the electric companies, the situation is like a 100-yard dash in which one of the runners is permitted to start on the 35-yard line. This favored runner may win the race but he can hardly claim to be a faster runner because of his victory. This is not competition in the sense in which the word is usually used.

Relationship between rates and use of service

The price of a commodity or service has a bearing on the amount of it that can be sold. Companies can encourage people to use more electricity by reducing the price, and investor-owned electric companies have followed this practice since the beginning of the business. However, this does not mean that earnings or efficiency can be improved by making a rate below the cost of service. By largely ignoring two of the principal items of expense, cost of money and taxes, TVA is selling electricity below cost.

For example, in its schedule of residential rates TVA has a price of 4 mills per kilowatt-hour. A part of the electricity used for house heating and water heating falls on this price block. This rate is less than half the actual price of furnishing space-heating and water-heating service, no matter whether the enterprise is financed by government or through the free market.

The rates are so designed as to place a floor between $6\frac{3}{4}$ and $7\frac{1}{2}$ mills on the average rate, regardless of use. This is below cost.

That the 4-mill block in the rate is far too low can be gathered from this fact: TVA charges 3.90 mills per kilowatt-hour for the energy it sells to AEC—nearly the same price at which it sells a block of energy for retail house heating. In 1964, TVA sold 24.4 billion kilowatt-hours to AEC, and AEC's load factor is higher than 97 percent, compared with a much lower load factor for residential house heating. The effect is that AEC—and the American taxpayer—pay a rate that is subsidizing electric house heating in the TVA area.

TVA reports that 28 percent of its residential customers are heating their homes electrically. Reports also show saturations of 67 percent for electric water heaters and 82 percent for electric ranges.[21] This is understandable because the energy is sold for approximately two-thirds of the fair market price.

If TVA's sale of electricity for home use is adjusted by reducing the house heating, electric ranges, and water heating to the national average (which is about what it would be if TVA were not selling the service below cost), the use of energy per customer in TVA's territory is found to be about the same as the average for the nation.

Industrial sales

The same subsidies found in TVA's residential service also apply to TVA's sales of energy to big industries. Electric energy is a vital ingredient of industrial growth, and some industries, such as aluminum plants, require large amounts of electric power in relation to the value of their product. In these industries the cost of electricity may be more than 10 percent of the cost of the finished product. For this reason a number of plants have gone to the TVA area. There the electricity can be bought at something like two-thirds the fair market price. If it were not for the below-cost rates of TVA, some of these industries would probably have located in other parts of the country. One might well ask why the taxpayers of New York State, for example, should be taxed to subsidize industrial electric rates of TVA so that TVA can attract industries from New York to Tennessee.

Advocates of TVA try to turn this question aside by replying that TVA buys generators and equipment from suppliers all over the country; but so do the investor-owned electric companies and so would investor-owned companies if they still operated in Tennessee. And TVA would still be buying generators and equipment if it were paying the market price of money and a full share of taxes.

Advocates of TVA also argue that the very low rates encourage people to use many appliances which are made by manufacturers from other states. This too seems like a strange argument. It is like saying, "Give me $50 so that I can buy a bicycle from you. We both benefit. I get the bicycle and you get the business."

TVA as a yardstick

TVA rates, insofar as they improperly take into account cost of money and taxes, are not a proper measure of the rates of investor-owned companies. If the yardstick idea were to have validity, the same rules that apply to investor-owned companies should apply to TVA; TVA should pay the market cost of money and taxes equivalent to those of the investor-owned companies.*

In 1956 General Herbert D. Vogel, then Chairman of the TVA, had this to say on the subject: "I cannot ignore the very real advantages accruing to any system which operates for minimum earning rather than a normal profit and which is not required by law to pay interest on its obligations or income taxes to the Federal government. In all fairness, it must be admitted that these result in consumer advantages not enjoyed by the customers of private power companies. Any talk about establishing a measure for the cost of power without reference to these factors is, of course, absurd." [22]

Since the Federal government uses investor-owned companies as a means of collecting taxes from people, why does it not also use TVA for this purpose? Why should the people served by TVA not pay Federal income taxes in their electricity bill as do other citizens?

Analysis of TVA expenses

TVA has given wide publicity to its claims that its operating expenses, on a kilowatt-hour basis, are lower than those of investor-owned companies. Many reasons are given for these claims, the principal one being that

* See the discussion of this subject in Chapter 5, and in *Congressional Record*, 76th Cong., 1st Sess., Vol. 84, Part 4, Apr. 13, 1939, p. 4211.

TVA uses the mass production technique of increased volume and relies upon this to decrease its unit costs.

Naturally, sales volume has a bearing on expense and all economists know that the aim of any business enterprise should be to increase the volume as a means of lowering or holding down unit costs. This is a basic economic principle in the power business. It was not discovered or originated by TVA.* A careful analysis of TVA's expenses shows that TVA has not found any new and less costly way of making and distributing electricity.

Table 6·2 is one of the tables that has been presented by TVA and its supporters to support their argument.

Similarly, a TVA publication stated:

Operating costs are unusually low on the combined TVA-distributor system. The cost of production last year averaged 2.0 mills for each kilowatt-hour sold. This was less than half the average for the nation's privately owned utilities. Other items of operating expense—transmission, distribution, customers' accounting, sales promotion, and administrative and general—follow a similar pattern, averaging only 40 to 50 percent of the national averages.[23]

Table 6·2 and the preceding statement err in four major respects:

1. The kilowatt-hour is not the proper unit to use in comparing all expenses. For example, customer account-

* For example, the idea of "mass production" of electricity and its relation to low rates, increased use, and company growth was discussed by Samuel Insull in a speech in 1910 titled "Massing of Energy Production: An Economic Necessity." During the course of this talk, he said, "Our experience [at Commonwealth Edison Co. in Chicago] is that the lower we set the price per unit of energy, if we will get at our customers and educate them to the uses of electricity, the greater is that use, within certain limitations. It follows that our bills, and consequently our profits, are greater." (Samuel Insull, *Central Station Electric Service*, Chicago, 1915, p. 140.)

**Table 6·2   Cost of Producing and Marketing Electric Power
(Mills per Kilowatt-Hour of Energy Sold)**

	TVA area, fiscal year 1958	Privately owned* utilities in U.S., calendar year 1957	TVA area costs as approximate percentage of privately owned* utilities
Operating expenses:			
Production	2.00	4.52	40
Transmission and distribution	.51	1.57	30
Customer acctg. and collection	.13	.51	30
Sales promotion and research	.05	.27	20
Administration and general	.32	1.05	30
Depreciation	1.16	1.66	70
Total	4.17	9.58	50

Excluding Service to Atomic Energy Commission (AEC)

Operating expenses:			
Production	1.66	4.67	40
Transmission and distribution	.96	1.69	60
Customer acctg. and collection	.25	.55	50
Sales promotion and research	.09	.29	30
Administration and general	.51	1.13	50
Depreciation	1.74	1.76	100
Total	5.21	10.09	50

* Investor-owned electric utilities.

ing and collecting expense does not vary with kilowatt-hours but rather with the number of customers.

2. It is not proper to compare TVA with the whole investor-owned electric utility industry. The comparison should be with investor-owned companies operating under similar conditions—that is, serving a southern area with low-cost coal supplies and labor.

3. It is an obvious error to use comparisons including AEC. TVA sold about 24.4 billion kilowatt-hours in 1964 to AEC. The table shows customer accounting and collecting expense as 0.13 mills per kilowatt-hour; at this rate this expense would amount to almost $3,200,000 for the one customer AEC. Obviously, it doesn't take over $3,-200,000 a year to read the meter, make out a bill, collect the money, and enter the account for one customer.

4. As TVA sells electricity below cost, its customers use more kilowatt-hours. (If TVA gave it away, people would use still more.) Dividing this greater number of kilowatt-hours into the operating expense, which does not increase proportionately, gives a lower cost for each kilowatt-hour, but it is an error to conclude that this proves any greater efficiency of operation.

A proper comparison

There are two comparable investor-owned companies operating under conditions somewhat similar to TVA. These are The Southern Company and the Middle South Utilities Company, both neighbors of TVA. Table 6·3 shows how they compare.

Most of TVA's steam plants have been built since World War II and hence are newer than some of the plants of investor-owned companies. It is erroneous to compare their efficiency with all investor-owned stations. Table 6·4 shows the twenty-five most efficient power plants in the

Table 6·3 Comparison of TVA, Middle South Utilities Company, and The Southern Company

Year ended Dec. 31, 1964	TVA System*	Middle South Utilities Co.	The Southern Company
Customers served	977,440	993,055	1,749,139
Kilowatt-hours sold (thousands)	44,097,884	15,436,629	31,191,956
Gross revenue	$275,173,000	$245,294,000	$412,539,000
Capacity, kw	10,300,000	3,461,337	6,509,255
% steam generation	65.3%†	99.3%	82.3%
% hydro generation	34.7%†	0.7%	17.7%
Load factor	57.8%	53.3%	60.0%

* Service to AEC removed and wholesale business of TVA combined with retail business of its municipal distributors. Fiscal year ended June 30, 1964.

† For TVA as a whole, including AEC, the fiscal-year 1964 figures are steam generation 77%, hydro generation 23%.

United States during 1964 with their heat rates in Btu per kilowatt-hour.

This is not intended to prove that TVA is inefficient but merely to point out the fallacy in the TVA statements implying far greater efficiency than the investor-owned companies.

Proper allocation of costs

The various items of electric utility expense are, in the main, functions of three factors: (1) sales (in kilowatt-hours or dollars), (2) customers, and (3) size of plant required (in kilowatts or dollar value). Generally, expenses are more nearly related to one of these factors than to the others. For example, as previously indicated for AEC, customer accounting and collecting expense is more

Table 6·4   The 25 Most Efficient Steam-Electric Stations for 1964
Based on Heat Rate, Btu per kwhr (Listed in Order of Efficiency)

Plant name	System	Heat rate, Btu per kwhr
Brayton Point	New England Power Co.	8776
Eddystone	Philadelphia Electric Co.	8824
Dickerson	Potomac Electric Power Co.	8878
Mercer	Public Service Electric & Gas Co.	8878
Campbell, J. H.	Consumers Power Co.	8892
Portland	Metropolitan Edison Co.	8955
Karn, Dan E.	Consumers Power Co.	8965
Big Sandy	Kentucky Power Co.	8971
Breed	Indiana & Michigan Electric Co.	8996
Allen, G. G.	Duke Power Co.	9067
St. Clair	Detroit Edison Co.	9100
Kanawha River	Appalachian Power Co.	9105
Clinch River	Appalachian Power Co.	9112
South Oak Creek	Wisconsin Electric Power Co.	9136
Bay Shore	Toledo Edison Co.	9161
Gallatin	Tennessee Valley Authority	9170
Gaston	Southern Electric Generating Co.	9172
Philip Sporn	Ohio Power Co.	9188
Milliken	New York State Electric & Gas Corp.	9194
Canadays	South Carolina Electric & Gas Co.	9198
Tanners Creek	Indiana & Michigan Electric Co.	9204
McMeekin, Silas	South Carolina Electric & Gas Co.	9208
River Rouge	Detroit Edison Co.	9220
Widows Creek "B"	Tennessee Valley Authority	9220
Brunner Island	Pennsylvania Power & Light Co.	9225

closely related to the number of customers than to kilo-watt-hour sales, and a more nearly true picture is presented if the comparison is made on the proper basis. Table 6·5 shows the proper comparisons of operating expenses.

As might be expected, there is little difference in the various expense items of TVA as compared with investor-owned companies.

Table 6·5 Comparison of Operating Expenses of TVA, Middle South Utilities Company, and The Southern Company

Year ended Dec. 31, 1964	TVA Systems*	Middle South Utilities Co.	The Southern Company
Sales-related:			
Production cost, hydro—mill per kwhr	0.71	†	0.52
Customer-related:			
Distribution expense per customer (annual)	$16.08	$17.16	$10.63
Customer accounting & collecting expense per customer (annual)	6.33	6.19	6.37
Sales promotion expense per customer (annual)	3.15	5.82	4.46
Related to size of plant, demand, or investment:			
Transmission expense—percent of investment in transmission facilities	2.12%	1.93%	1.47%
Depreciation—percent of gross investment	2.55%	3.02%‡	2.71%
Other:			
Administrative and general expense—		Not	
Percent of other operating expenses	10.8%	Available	12.9%

* Fiscal year ended June 30, 1964.
† Less than 1 percent of total generation.
‡ Including gas and transit utilities.

Has TVA raised living standards?

Living standards in the TVA territory and in the South generally have been lagging behind the rest of the country. When TVA was formed some people thought it would bring about a more rapid improvement. Naturally, spending $2 billion in one area should have an effect on its economy, and advocates of the TVA idea claim that TVA has raised living standards in the region it serves.

Investor-owned power companies as a group made investments in new facilities at a rate of $4.0 billion in 1965. In terms of capital formation, this is equal to about two new TVA power systems every year. In the South, growth has been above the national average, with the result that capital expenditures for power facilities in that area have been above the national average, both in TVA territory and in the non-TVA territory regions.

In terms of population, Tennessee gained 24 percent from 1946 to 1964 while ten other Southeastern states gained 35 percent. In personal income per capita, Tennessee gained 116 percent from 1946 to 1964 while the others gained 125 percent. In total personal income Tennessee also lagged behind the others, gaining 167 percent as against 205 percent for the ten other Southeastern states.

In total bank deposits, Tennessee gained 151 percent from 1946 to 1964 while the other states gained 155 percent (Chart 6·5).

Among the other ten Southeastern states, Tennessee ranks fifth in population, sixth in personal income per capita, fifth in total personal income, fourth in small light and power customers, fifth in business concerns in operation, seventh in value of farm products sold, third in employment in manufacturing, sixth in value of construction contracts awarded, and fifth in individual income and employment taxes paid.[24]

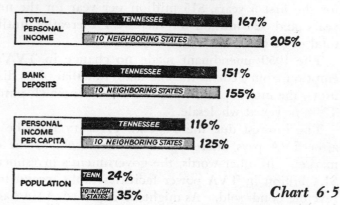

PERCENT GAIN IN SELECTED
ECONOMIC INDICATORS 1946-1964

	TENNESSEE	10 NEIGHBORING STATES
TOTAL PERSONAL INCOME	167%	205%
BANK DEPOSITS	151%	155%
PERSONAL INCOME PER CAPITA	116%	125%
POPULATION	TENN. 24%	10 NEIGH. STATES 35%

Chart 6·5

These facts hardly seem to furnish a sound basis for
claims that the state's economy has been improved above
those of its neighbors.

Revenue bond financing

Prior to 1959 most of TVA's financing, with the excep-
tion of a $65 million bond issue sold to the Reconstruction
Finance Corporation (RFC), came from appropriations
by Congress. The government got the money to finance
TVA either from tax revenues or by selling government
bonds. Some small amount came from cash receipts taken
in by TVA itself. In the power business, owing to the
large investment per dollar of gross revenue, earnings
alone are not enough to finance new property extensions.

In 1959, the TVA Act of 1933 was amended to permit
the TVA to sell its own bonds in the open market and to
require the TVA to pay interest to the Federal government on appropriated capital. Interest would be at the
computed average interest rate payable by the Federal
Treasury upon its marketable public obligations. The
1959 amendment also requires TVA to repay $1 billion

to the U.S. Treasury in annual installments. These annual installments are to range from $10 million per year for the first 5 years, $15 million per year for the next 5 years, and $20 million for each year thereafter until the total of $1 billion has been repaid.[25]

The 1959 amendmant made no change in TVA's exemption from Federal income taxes nor that of its distributors, the municipalities and cooperatives which purchase TVA power at wholesale.

The interest due the Federal Treasury is to be paid after TVA pays interest on the bonds sold in the open market. In other words, the government's investment of $1.4 billion in TVA power facilities ranks second to the revenue bonds sold. As might be expected, TVA has had no trouble selling its bonds in the free market.

The 1959 amendment does not change two basic facts about TVA:

1. TVA is not required to pay the government the going rate of return that people want for the use of their money when used in the power business.

2. TVA's taxes, on the basis of percent of gross plant for the combined operations, continue to be less than one-fifth of the equivalent total taxes paid by investor-owned companies.

The new financing does not change the fact that if TVA had to earn 5 percent on its total gross plant account and taxes equivalent to those paid by investor-owned companies, it would still have to raise its rates about 50 percent. In other words, the nation's taxpayers continue to subsidize the below-cost rates of TVA.

What should be done with TVA?

TVA is now a large, full-fledged electric utility business serving a large section of the country. It should be treated as any other public utility.

For economic reasons, all public utilities are sole suppliers in the areas they serve. In place of direct competition there is government regulation. All investor-owned companies are under some regulation, but TVA is not. The reason TVA's rates are a source of controversy is that there is no independent body to oversee the rates in order to balance the interests of the supplier and the user.

The first step in solving the TVA problem should be to put it under appropriate government regulation. This would not be hard to do. Here is a possible way:

1. The power business could be separated from the other functions of the TVA such as flood control, navigation, soil conservation, malaria abatement, fertilizer production, and the like. The power business of TVA could then be set up as a separate government corporation. The other functions of TVA could be handled by appropriate departments of government.

2. The electric service provided the Atomic Energy Commission could be separated from the regular TVA business. Then TVA power operations would not be distorted by the AEC load.

3. The electric power portion of TVA could be put under the jurisdiction of the appropriate government regulatory bodies by an amendment to the TVA Act. These regulatory agencies could be asked to fix TVA's rates to earn the market price of money on the total power investment and pay taxes on the basis of percent of plant account equivalent to the taxes paid by investor-owned companies.

If this were done, the American taxpayers, who are the owners of TVA, would get a fair return on their investment and the people of Tennessee and the TVA area would be able to pay, in their electricity bills, the same taxes as most other Americans pay in their electricity bills (Table 6·6).

Table 6·6 Tennessee Valley Authority June 30, 1964

Project	Capacity, kw, 1964 Hydro	Steam	Federal power investment	Direct power facilities	Allocated to power	Total nonpower allocations	Other nonpower plant	Total completed works	Capacity under construction kw
Multipurpose dams:									
Kentucky, Ky.	160,000		$48,318,175	$19,441,830	$28,876,345	65,886,213		$114,204,388	
Pickwick, Tenn.	216,000		27,943,096	22,228,432	5,714,664	14,155,218		42,098,314	
Wilson, Ala.	598,000		54,182,991	45,608,130	8,574,861	39,481,759		93,664,750	
Wheeler, Ala.	356,400		50,110,748	40,408,811	9,701,937	34,748,038		84,858,786	
Guntersville, Ala.	97,200		20,217,756	12,355,099	7,862,657	13,711,272		33,929,028	
Hales Bar, Tenn.	99,700		20,708,340	14,888,059	5,820,281	10,689,725		31,398,065	
Chickamauga, Tenn.	108,000		20,921,440	12,979,608	7,941,832	15,963,136		36,884,576	
Watts Bar, Tenn.	150,000		19,280,174	12,899,001	6,381,173	18,316,299		32,596,473	
Fort Loudoun, Tenn.	128,000		21,288,931	12,289,744	8,999,187	17,924,918		39,213,849	
Norris, Tenn.	100,800		12,982,937	4,952,828	8,030,109	17,911,666		30,894,603	
Hiwassee, N. C.	117,100		13,755,329	8,769,681	4,985,698	8,241,011		21,996,340	
Cherokee, Tenn.	120,000		18,465,934	9,545,218	8,920,716	15,786,084		34,252,018	
Chatuge, N. C.	10,000		4,595,408	1,829,489	2,765,919	4,356,603		8,952,011	
Nottely, Ga.	15,000		4,196,339	2,133,551	2,062,788	3,471,611		7,667,950	
Fontana, N. C.	202,500		86,402,876	13,074,014	23,328,862	39,839,048		76,241,924	
South Holston, Tenn.	35,000		13,753,197	5,077,561	8,675,636	16,930,639		30,683,886	
Watauga, Tenn.	50,000		16,785,052	8,218,834	8,566,218	14,874,539		31,659,591	
Douglas, Tenn.	112,000		22,188,947	11,219,747	10,969,200	22,204,942		44,393,889	
Boone, Tenn.	75,000		15,700,479	10,021,086	5,679,393	7,952,972		23,653,451	
Melton Hill, Tenn.									72,000
Nickajack, Tenn.									97,200

Single-purpose dams:					
Apalachia, N. C.	75,000	$22,327,494	$22,327,494	$22,327,494	
Fort Patrick Henry, Tenn.	86,000	11,582,634	11,582,634	11,582,634	
Great Falls, Tenn.	31,860	4,590,954	4,590,954	4,590,954	
Ocoee No. 3, Tenn.	27,000	8,004,821	8,004,821	8,004,821	
Ocoee No. 2, Tenn.	21,000	2,635,763	2,635,763	2,635,763	
Blue Ridge, Ga.	20,000	4,941,302	4,941,302	4,941,302	
Ocoee No. 1, Tenn.	18,000	2,647,179	2,647,179	2,647,179	
Wilbur, Tenn.	10,700	2,277,523	2,277,523	2,277,523	
Nolichucky, Tenn.	10,640	1,549,231	1,549,231	1,549,231	
Steam plants:					
Widows Creek, Ala.	1,175,000	$156,708,567	$156,708,567	$156,708,567	500,000
Kingston, Tenn.	1,440,000	189,082,880	189,082,880	189,082,880	
Shawnee, Ky.	1,350,000	206,669,120	206,669,120	206,669,120	
Paradise, Ky.	1,300,000	170,025,899	170,025,899	170,025,899	
Johnsonville, Tenn.	1,275,000	161,709,528	161,709,528	161,709,528	
Colbert, Ala.	720,000	94,876,512	94,876,512	94,876,512	500,000
Gallatin, Tenn.	1,050,000	132,304,532	132,304,532	132,304,532	
John Sevier, Tenn.	720,000	100,331,997	100,331,997	100,331,997	
Watts Bar, Tenn.	240,000	19,130,982	19,130,982	19,130,982	
Wilson, Ala.	64,000	910,494	910,494	910,494	
Bull Run, Tenn.					900,000
Alcoa Dams	423,715				
Cumberland Basin Projects	595,000				130,000
		$562,560,388*	$562,560,388*	$562,560,388	
		88,481,874†	88,481,874†	137,539,801	
		$99,057,927	$99,057,927	99,057,927	
Totals	4,019,615	$2,335,147,823	$2,161,290,347	$173,857,476	$377,445,693 / $2,811,651,443 / 2,199,200
	9,384,000				
Total hydro and steam	13,353,615				

* Transmission.
† General and other.

REFERENCES

1. *Tennessee River and Tributaries,* House Document 328, Vol. 32, Part I, 71st Cong., 2d Sess., Mar. 24, 1930, letter of transmittal and p. 1.
2. *Ibid.,* pp. 2, 6–7, 14.
3. *Ibid.,* p. 14.
4. *Ibid.,* pp. 6, 7.
5. *Ibid.,* p. 6.
6. Tennessee Valley Authority, *TVA Annual Report,* 1964, p. A4.
7. John Lord O'Brian, *Ashwander v. Tennessee Valley Authority,* 56 S. Ct. 466, 297 U.S. 288. Argument of John Lord O'Brian, Special Counsel for TVA, presented before U.S. Supreme Court on Dec. 19, 1935.
8. 306 U.S. 118; 59 Supreme Court 366; 83 Law Ed. 543.
9. Tennessee Valley Authority, *loc. cit.*
10. *Ibid.,* p. A27.
11. Edwin Vennard, *The Facts about the TVA Power Business,* EEI, 1966, pp. 3–4.
12. *Ibid.,* p. 5.
13. *Ibid.,* p. 6.
14. Public Law 17, 83d Cong., approved May 18, 1933, *TVA Annual Reports* through 1960.
15. Tennessee Valley Authority, *op. cit.,* 1961, p. A3.
16. *Ibid.,* pp. A5, A13, A14.
17. EEI, *Statistical Yearbook of the Electric Utility Industry for 1964,* p. 58.
18. Vennard, *op. cit.,* p. 14.
19. *Ibid.*
20. EEI, *A Study of the TVA Power Business,* 1965, p. 27.
21. Tennessee Valley Authority, *op. cit.,* p. 29.
22. General Herbert D. Vogel, *Proceedings of the American Power Conference,* Eighteenth Annual Meeting, Chicago, Ill., Vol. XVIII, 1956, p. 20.
23. Tennessee Valley Authority, *TVA Power, 1963–64,* p. 22.
24. Vennard, *op. cit.,* pp. 25–26.
25. 16 USCA, 831 n-4 (e), pp. 382–383.

Chapter 7

The Bonneville Power Administration

The Bonneville Project Act of 1937, which authorized the Corps of Engineers to complete, maintain, and operate the Bonneville Dam, navigation locks, and power plant on the Columbia River, also authorized the Bonneville Power Administration within the Department of the Interior.[1] The Administrator, appointed by the Secretary of the Interior, was directed to make all arrangements for the sale and disposition of the electric energy generated at the project not required for the operation of the dam and locks or navigation facilities. The act further authorized and directed the Administrator to provide, construct, operate, maintain, and improve such electric transmission lines and substations and facilities he finds necessary, desirable, or appropriate for transmitting the electricity available for sale to existing and potential markets.[2]

Where TVA owns and operates its electric generating and transmission facilities and is the sole supplier of certain specified municipal and cooperative distributors, the Bonneville Power Administration (BPA) is less clearly defined and is not necessarily the sole source of supply of its customers. During the first years of its existence, under the administration of J. D. Ross, it followed an aggressive policy of encouraging formation of public utility districts and other governmental units that could be given preference to Bonneville power.[3]

These activities caused difficulties which led Secretary of the Interior Ickes to develop a low opinion of Ross's abilities.[4] In 1939 he was replaced by Dr. Paul Raver, whom Ickes found to be a better administrator and who led BPA through its most important formative years.[5]

In 1940 BPA was assigned responsibility for marketing power from the Bureau of Reclamation's Grand Coulee Dam.[6] In 1944 it was made responsible for transmitting and marketing the surplus electric power generated at Hungry Horse Dam,[7] and the following year it was assigned to market the surplus electric power from all Corps of Engineers projects in the Pacific Northwest.[8] In 1953 BPA was given the task of marketing the surplus energy from the Bureau of Reclamation's Chandler Power Plant, Yakima Reclamation Project.[9]

BPA today

BPA is an integral part of the U.S. Columbia River Power System complex, which includes such activities as irrigation, flood control, navigation, fish and wildlife preservation, recreation, and electric power production.* In 1962 it marketed power produced at fifteen hydroelectric projects built and operated by the U.S. Corps of Engineers and the Bureau of Reclamation, all in the Columbia River Basin.[10] (Chart 7·1)

* U.S. Columbia River Power System is the term used by the BPA to denote the combined power activities of three agencies, the Corps of Engineers, the Bureau of Reclamation, and the Bonneville Power Administration.

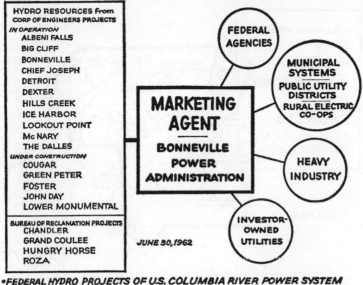

HYDRO RESOURCES From
CORP OF ENGINEERS PROJECTS
IN OPERATION
   ALBENI FALLS
   BIG CLIFF
   BONNEVILLE
   CHIEF JOSEPH
   DETROIT
   DEXTER
   HILLS CREEK
   ICE HARBOR
   LOOKOUT POINT
   Mc NARY
   THE DALLES
UNDER CONSTRUCTION
   COUGAR
   GREEN PETER
   FOSTER
   JOHN DAY
   LOWER MONUMENTAL

BUREAU OF RECLAMATION PROJECTS
   CHANDLER
   GRAND COULEE
   HUNGRY HORSE
   ROZA

FEDERAL AGENCIES

MUNICIPAL SYSTEMS
PUBLIC UTILITY DISTRICTS
RURAL ELECTRIC CO-OPS

MARKETING AGENT
BONNEVILLE POWER ADMINISTRATION

HEAVY INDUSTRY

JUNE 30, 1962

INVESTOR-OWNED UTILITIES

*•FEDERAL HYDRO PROJECTS OF U.S. COLUMBIA RIVER POWER SYSTEM
AND BONNEVILLE POWER ADMINISTRATION'S MARKETING OUTLETS*

Chart 7·1

In 1963 the Department of the Interior added the 61,000-square-mile upper Snake River drainage area to BPA's marketing area. This includes all of southern Idaho, and small adjoining areas in Wyoming, Utah, and Nevada. With this, the BPA marketing area now encompasses the entire Columbia River Basin and the remaining portions of Washington and Oregon.[11] (Chart 7·2)

The U.S. Columbia River Power System has grown from a total investment in its multipurpose projects in 1952 of $781.0 million to $2,402.7 million in 1962—a 208 percent increase.[12] (Chart 7·3) During this period, the number of Federal hydroelectric projects in operation increased from two to fifteen. The total installed electric generating capacity at these fifteen projects at the end of fiscal year 1962 was 6,489,250 kilowatts.[13] (Chart 7·4)

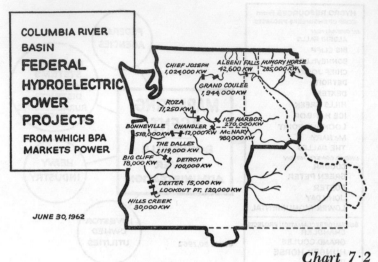

COLUMBIA RIVER BASIN **FEDERAL HYDROELECTRIC POWER PROJECTS** FROM WHICH BPA MARKETS POWER

CHIEF JOSEPH 1,024,000 KW
ALBENI FALLS 42,600 KW
HUNGRY HORSE 285,000 KW
GRAND COULEE 1,944,000 KW
ROZA 11,250 KW
ICE HARBOR 270,000 KW
BONNEVILLE 518,000 KW
CHANDLER 12,000 KW
McNARY 980,000 KW
THE DALLES 1,119,000 KW
BIG CLIFF 18,000 KW
DETROIT 100,000 KW
DEXTER 15,000 KW
LOOKOUT PT. 120,000 KW
HILLS CREEK 30,000 KW

JUNE 30, 1962

Chart 7·2

Chart 7·3

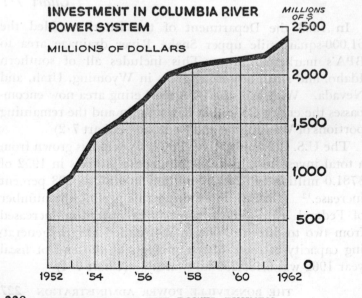

INVESTMENT IN COLUMBIA RIVER POWER SYSTEM

MILLIONS OF DOLLARS

MILLIONS OF $

2,500
2,000
1,500
1,000
500
0

1952   '54   '56   '58   '60   1962

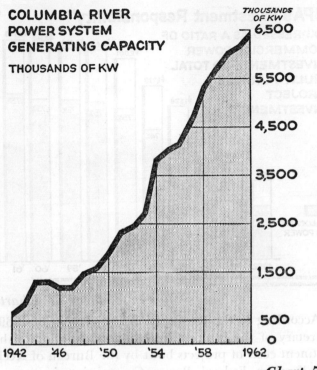

COLUMBIA RIVER POWER SYSTEM GENERATING CAPACITY

THOUSANDS OF KW

THOUSANDS OF KW

6,500
5,500
4,500
3,500
2,500
1,500
500
0

1942   '46   '50   '54   '58   1962

Chart 7·4

Of the total $2,402.7 million of public funds invested in the fifteen operating projects by the end of fiscal year 1962, the Comptroller General specifically identified $1,767.1 million, or 73.5 percent of the total, as commercial power facilities (Chart 7·5). In contrast, only about 26.5 percent of the total investment has gone to other functions of the U.S. Columbia River Power System, as follows: [14]

Function	Percent
Irrigation	16.54
Flood control	4.99
Navigation	4.86
Fish, wildlife, and recreation	.07

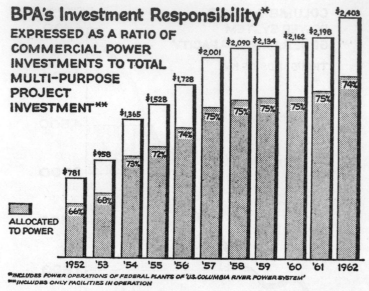

BPA's Investment Responsibility*

EXPRESSED AS A RATIO OF
COMMERCIAL POWER
INVESTMENTS TO TOTAL
MULTI-PURPOSE
PROJECT
INVESTMENT**

ALLOCATED
TO POWER

1952 '53 '54 '55 '56 '57 '58 '59 '60 '61 1962

*INCLUDES POWER OPERATIONS OF FEDERAL PLANTS OF 'U.S. COLUMBIA RIVER POWER SYSTEM'
**INCLUDES ONLY FACILITIES IN OPERATION

Chart 7·5

According to the Reclamation Project Act of 1939, the Secretary of the Interior is authorized to allocate the investment costs of projects built by the Bureau of Reclamation.[15] The Federal Power Commission is responsible for investment cost allocation of projects originating with the Rivers and Harbors Act of 1945.[16] However, no provisions are made in the Flood Control Act of 1944 for allocations of investment cost. The Corps of Engineers is making tentative investment cost allocations of Flood Control Act projects. The costs of the transmission facilities constructed by the Bonneville Power Administration are all allocated to power.

At the end of fiscal year 1962, BPA was supplying electric power to 119 industrial and wholesale customers. They included ten agencies of the Federal government, eighty-two non-Federal government power agencies and

REA-financed electric cooperatives, nineteen industries, seven investor-owned electric utility companies, and one Canadian utility.[17]

Total sales of electricity to these customers in fiscal year 1962 amounted to 29,157.2 million kilowatt-hours.[18] Distribution of these sales was as follows:

Customer	Percent
Federal agencies	9.3
Non-Federal government and cooperative-owned utilities	43.4
Industries	36.5
Investor-owned electric companies	10.8

Of the electric power sold by BPA in fiscal year 1962, more than half (52.7 percent) went to so-called preference customers, including Federal agencies, municipal electric systems, public utility districts, and electric cooperatives. More than one-third (36.5 percent) of the power sold by BPA in the same period was sold directly to industries. The remaining 10.8 percent of the electric energy sold went to investor-owned electric companies. Sales to investor-owned utilities decreased by 27 percent during the period, due mainly to completion of the companies' own facilities and purchase arrangements made with other sources.[19]

From sales of electric power and related operating revenues, BPA reported $74.6 million in total operating revenues for fiscal year 1962.[20] (Tables 7·1 and 7·2)

A deficit record

BPA has a responsibility by law to establish electric rates that will provide revenues to repay that portion of the investment in the Federal multipurpose projects which has been allocated to commercial power, together with its own transmission grid investment. In addition, power reve-

Table 7·1 Columbia River Power System and Related Activities: Statement of Commercial Power Operations for the Fiscal Years Ended June 30, 1962 and 1961

	1962	1961
Operating revenues:		
Sales of electric energy by Bonneville Power Administration:		
Publicly owned utilities	$33,938,933	$30,103,478
Privately owned utilities	7,214,228	9,638,672
Federal agencies	6,469,814	6,475,099
Aluminum industry	17,382,519	16,959,236
Other industry	4,048,550	3,818,059
Sales, at wholesale	69,054,044	66,994,544
Other operating revenues:		
Payments for coordination and downstream river regulation	1,114,645	1,748
Projects energy—use at site	123,636	106,876
Rental of electric property	4,337,675	2,715,957
Subtotal	5,575,956	2,824,581
Total operating revenues	74,630,000	69,819,125
Operating expenses:		
Purchased power	1,089,748	696,859
Operation:		
Specific power facilities	13,849,087	12,225,237
Joint facilities	2,020,098	1,496,827

nues are required to service a substantial portion of the irrigation investment in these multipurpose projects that is in excess of the repayment ability of the water users.[21]

As of July 1, 1961, BPA's gross power repayment responsibility amounted to $2,272.4 million. This included generating plants and transmission facilities then in service, including the estimated costs necessary to assure

Table 7·1 Columbia River Power System and Related Activities
(continued)

	1962	1961
Maintenance:		
Specific power facilities	5,497,838	6,441,853
Joint facilities	894,288	1,524,328
Depreciation:		
Specific power facilities	24,781,985	23,843,837
Joint facilities	5,232,237	4,841,924
Net loss on sales and abandonment of property	22,179	95,731
Total operating expenses	53,387,460	51,166,596
Net operating revenues	21,242,540	18,652,529
Interest and other deductions:		
Interest on Federal investment	36,597,773	33,475,455
Interest charged to construction	2,031,482*	667,527*
Miscellaneous income deductions, net ..	210,399*	15,342
Net interest and other deductions ..	34,355,892	32,823,270
Net loss from commercial power operations	13,113,352	14,170,741
Accumulated net revenues from commercial operations:		
Beginning of fiscal year	70,284,864	84,455,605
End of fiscal year	$57,171,512	$70,284,864

*Deduction

completion and the estimated irrigation assistance currently authorized. Of this total, only 13 percent had been amortized as of July 1, 1961, leaving an unamortized repayment responsibility of $1,978.2 million, including $1,-320.8 million for unamortized electric plant investment.[22]

Before 1958 BPA had made repayments ahead of schedule totaling some $78.8 million. Then for the five suc-

Table 7·2 U.S. Columbia River Power System
General Specifications, Projects Existing, under Construction and Authorized
June 30, 1962

Project	Operating agency*	Location	Stream	Plant installations		Date in service (initial unit)	Generation, fiscal year 1962‡
				Number of units	Total capacity, kw†		
Existing:							
Bonneville	CE	Washington-Oregon	Columbia	10	518,400	June 1938	3,461
Grand Coulee	BR	Washington	Columbia	18	1,944,000	September 1941	11,433
Hungry Horse	BR	Montana	South Fork Flathead	4	285,000	October 1952	796
Detroit	CE	Oregon	North Santiam	2	100,000	July 1953	338
McNary	CE	Washington-Oregon	Columbia	14	980,000	November 1953	4,859
Big Cliff	CE	Oregon	North Santiam	1	18,000	June 1954	97
Lookout Point	CE	Oregon	Middle Fork Willamette	3	120,000	December 1954	223
Albeni Falls	CE	Idaho	Pend Oreille	3	42,600	March 1955	176
Dexter	CE	Oregon	Middle Fork Willamette	1	15,000	May 1955	58
Chief Joseph	CE	Washington	Columbia	16	1,024,000	August 1955	4,446
Chandler	BR	Washington	Yakima	2	12,000	February 1956	40
The Dalles	CE	Washington-Oregon	Columbia	16	1,119,000	May 1957	4,985
Roza	BR	Washington	Yakima	1	11,250	August 1958	50

Project	Agency*	State	River	Units	Capacity (kw)†	Initial operation	Generation‡
Ice Harbor	CE	Washington	Snake	3	270,000	December 1961	537
Hills Creek	CE	Oregon	Middle Fork Willamette	2	30,000	May 1962	11
Subtotal					6,489,250		31,510
Under construction:							
Cougar	CE	Oregon	South Fork McKenzie	2	25,000	November, 1963	
Green Peter	CE	Oregon	Middle Santiam	2	80,000	April, 1966	
Foster	CE	Oregon	South Santiam	2	30,000	April, 1967	
John Day	CE	Washington-Oregon	Columbia	10	1,350,000	June, 1967	
Lower Monumental	CE	Washington	Snake	3	405,000	December, 1967	
Subtotal					1,890,000		
Authorized:							
Libby	CE	Montana	Kootenai	4	344,000		
Little Goose	CE	Washington	Snake	3	405,000		
Lower Granite	CE	Washington	Snake	3	405,000		
Subtotal					1,154,000		
Total, 23 projects					9,533,250		

*CE—Corps of Engineers; BR—Bureau of Reclamation.
†Nameplate rating.
‡Millions of kilowatt-hours.

cessive years—1958 through 1962—BPA operated at a deficit. By the end of fiscal year 1962, BPA's excess of funds returned over scheduled repayment had been reduced to $20.1 million—about a 75 percent reduction.[23] (Chart 7·6)

In fiscal year 1962, BPA failed by $17.7 million, or 19.6 percent, to meet that year's scheduled repayment responsibility.[24]

BPA would have had to increase its revenues by some 24 percent in order to have had revenue sufficient to meet its scheduled repayment responsibility. This obvious lack of adequate rates and revenues continues despite the

Chart 7·6

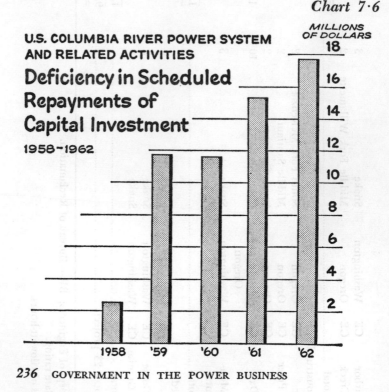

U.S. COLUMBIA RIVER POWER SYSTEM AND RELATED ACTIVITIES

Deficiency in Scheduled Repayments of Capital Investment

1958–1962

MILLIONS OF DOLLARS

GOVERNMENT IN THE POWER BUSINESS

fact that BPA pays no taxes and pays only 2½ percent or 3 percent interest on the unamortized electric plant investment in these projects by the Federal government. If BPA had been required in fiscal year 1962 to pay 5 percent on its electric plant in service and taxes equivalent to those paid by investor-owned electric companies, its deficit in its repayment responsibility scheduled for that year would have increased by $165.0 million and its revenues would have had to increase by 221 percent to fulfill its repayment responsibility.[25]

BPA's new payout schedule

In 1963 the Department of the Interior announced that it would apply to the U.S. Columbia River Power System the payout procedures currently being applied to Federal power projects in most other major river basins. It explained that

> Repayment for the Columbia River Power System by the Bonneville Power Administration hereafter will be computed on a "consolidated system basis." This means that when a Federal power installation has paid for itself, the dam will continue as a working partner, contributing financial support to all other elements in the system, including those irrigation investments chargeable to power revenues.[26]

BPA stated that it would reduce its annual obligations to the Treasury by about $7 million per year by adopting this new payout method.[27] Even so, when placed on a basis about comparable to investor-owned electric companies as a whole, BPA would have had a deficit in fiscal year 1962 of $158.0 million and would have had to increase its revenues by 212 percent to meet its scheduled repayment responsibility.[28]

BPA operated at a deficit from 1958 to 1962. As presently constituted, it cannot repay its full indebtedness because two vital ingredients in the true cost of electric power—taxes and the cost of money—are not fully accounted for in its repayment policies. The rate of return BPA pays on the public's investment in its electric plant and property is substantially less than the money was worth to the taxpayers from whom it was taken.

For a number of years power suppliers in the Pacific Northwest have been coordinating their activities through the Northwest Power Pool. This is an informal organization created through voluntary participation of investor-owned companies, non-Federal government agencies, and Federal facilities in the states of Washington, Oregon, Idaho, Utah, and Montana. The British Columbia Hydro & Power Authority in western Canada also participates in the pool. Each member manages its own system, but in such a manner as to harmonize with the others. The pool has helped provide consumers in the Northwest with reliable electric service, but such inequities as the preference given public utility districts and municipalities make its operation unnecessarily difficult. Problems such as this will continue as long as the inequities in cost of money and taxes exist.

More revenue for government

The fact is that government would gain more revenue from power development at hydroelectric dams if (1) the power plants were financed in the free market, thus saving government the cost of building them; (2) the government sold the falling water at the dam to the enterprise financed in the free market, which would be responsible for generating and selling the electricity; (3) full taxes were imposed on the enterprise; (4) the enterprise were regulated by government. If this course had been followed at the dams under the Bonneville Power Administration in 1962, the Federal government would have

REVENUE TO U.S. TREASURY FROM BONNEVILLE POWER ADMINISTRATION

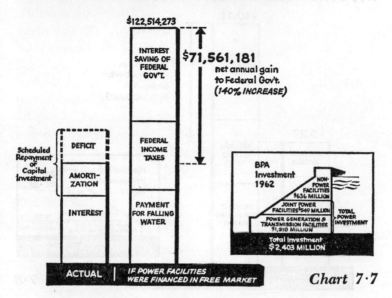

Chart 7·7

increased its income by about $72 million a year (Chart 7·7). The government could have carried out the flood control, navigation, and irrigation activities it now conducts in the area—and had more money with which to do it.*

A hypothetical case. Possibly this point can be illustrated better by a simple hypothetical example. Let us

*In fiscal year 1962, Bonneville Power Administration returned to the U.S. Treasury the following amounts:

Interest	$34,566,291
Amortization	16,386,801
Total	$50,953,092

If the power generation and transmission facilities were purchased at their stated original cost, the government would receive $1,218,-488,330, on which interest at 4 percent would amount to $48,739,533.

In the purchase of falling water, the companies would pay opera-

THE BONNEVILLE POWER ADMINISTRATION   **239**

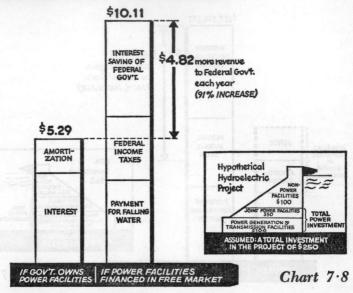

REVENUE TO U.S. TREASURY FROM A HYPOTHETICAL POWER PROJECT

$10.11

INTEREST SAVING OF FEDERAL GOV'T.

$4.82 more revenue to Federal Gov't. each year (91% INCREASE)

$5.29

AMORTIZATION

FEDERAL INCOME TAXES

INTEREST

PAYMENT FOR FALLING WATER

Hypothetical Hydroelectric Project

NON-POWER FACILITIES $100

JOINT POWER FACILITIES $50

POWER GENERATION & TRANSMISSION FACILITIES $100

TOTAL POWER INVESTMENT

ASSUMED: A TOTAL INVESTMENT IN THE PROJECT OF $250

IF GOV'T. OWNS POWER FACILITIES | IF POWER FACILITIES FINANCED IN FREE MARKET

Chart 7·8

---

tion and maintenance expenses, depreciation, and a 6 percent return on joint facility investments allocated to commercial power, of which the following amounts would accrue to the government:

6% return on joint facilities	$32,917,864
Depreciation on joint facilities	5,232,237
Total	$38,150,101

In addition, the government would receive federal income taxes on the operation by the investor-owned companies of the generation and transmission facilities purchased from the government amounting to $35,624,639, making total net annual payments to the government $73,774,740. The net annual gain to the government would then be as follows:

Payments for falling water	$ 38,150,101
Federal income taxes	35,624,639
Interest saving	48,739,533
	$122,514,273
Less payments made by BPA	50,953,092
Net annual gain to Federal government	$ 71,561,181

In addition, the companies would pay to state and local governments taxes amounting to $29,179,932.

assume a combination dam is built for which the flood control and irrigation features are financed by government and the power features are financed in the market. If we say that the total investment in the project was $250, the investment in nonpower facilities might be on the order of $100, the investment in power generation and transmission facilities might be about $100, and the remainder would be joint facilities, allocated to power. On this basis, the Federal government would get 91 percent more revenue each year than if it owned the power facilities itself (Chart 7·8).

REFERENCES

1. Bonneville Project Act of 1937 as amended, 16 USCA 832, 832a (a).
2. *Ibid.*, 16 USCA 832a (a), 832a (b).
3. See, for example, the *First Annual Report of the Bonneville Administrator*, House Document 86, 76th Cong., 1st Sess., 1939, pp. 49, 52–53, 57.
4. Harold L. Ickes, *op. cit.*, p. 53.
5. *Ibid.*, p. 43.
6. Executive Order No. 8526, Aug. 26, 1940.
7. Department of the Interior Order No. 1994, Sept. 26, 1944.
8. Department of the Interior Order No. 2115, Nov. 16, 1945.
9. Department of the Interior Order No. 2115, Amendment 1, May 15, 1953.
10. Bonneville Power Administration, *U.S. Columbia River Power System, 1962 Report*, p. 3.
11. Bonneville Power Administration, *U.S. Columbia River Power System, 1963 Report*, p. II; *Audit of Financial Statements of Columbia River Power System and Related Activities, Fiscal Year 1962*, report to Congress by the Comptroller General of the U.S., December, 1962.
12. Bonneville Power Administration, *U.S. Columbia River Power System, 1952 Report*, p. 9, *U.S. Columbia River Power System, 1962 Report*, p. 14.
13. Bonneville Power Administration, *U.S. Columbia River Power System, 1952 Report*, p. 26, *U.S. Columbia River Power System, 1962 Report*, p. 3.
14. Bonneville Power Administration, *U.S. Columbia River Power System, 1962 Report*, p. 14.

15. Public Law 260, 76th Cong., 1st Sess., H.R. 6984, USCA, Title 43, Sec. 485
16. Public Law 14, 79th Cong., 1st Sess., Mar. 2, 1945.
17. Bonneville Power Administration, *op. cit.*, 1962, p. 7.
18. *Ibid.*
19. Bonneville Power Administration, *U.S. Columbia River Power System, 1961 Report,* p. 9, *U.S. Columbia River Power System, 1962 Report,* p. 7.
20. *Ibid.*
21. 16 USCA 832, p. 415.
22. Bonneville Power Administration, *U.S. Columbia River Power System, 1961 Report,* p. 34.
23. Bonneville Power Administration, *U.S. Columbia River Power System, 1957 Report,* Schedule 3, *U.S. Columbia River Power System, 1962 Report,* Schedule 4; EEI, *A Study of the Bonneville Power Administration,* 1963, Appendix 5.
24. Bonneville Power Administration, *U.S. Columbia River Power System, 1962 Report,* Schedule 4.
25. EEI, *op. cit.*, pp. 7–9.
26. U.S. Department of the Interior Release, Apr. 17, 1963, No. 2694.
27. Bonneville Power Administration, *U.S. Columbia River Power System, 1962 Report,* p. III.
28. EEI, *op. cit.*, p. 12.

Chapter **8**

The Rural Electrification Administration

The TVA is a government corporation. The BPA is a
marketing agency of the Department of the Interior. The
Rural Electrification Administration (REA) represents a
third manner in which the Federal government acts in the
electric power business. It is primarily a lending agency,
set up during the 1930s for the worthy purpose of providing financing and various services that would speed the
process of bringing central-station electric service to the
farm areas of the nation.

The beginnings of the REA and the valuable role it
has played in farm electrification in this country are widely
misunderstood. To put the REA in proper perspective
it is necessary to go back before the turn of the century to
the first attempt to bring central-station electric service to
the American farm.

Rural electrification begins

At the turn of the century the electric industry in the
United States had fewer than 600,000 customers.[1] The
process of electrification was just beginning. The loca-

tion and size of some of the communities served, and articles appearing in various journals of the period, indicate that a few of these customers were farmers. Across the nation a handful of barns were lighted, a scattering of small motors were operated by energy from transmission lines.

What was probably the first successful utility company effort in taking electricity to a farm occurred in 1898 in northern California. A farmer named John Onstott was persuaded that electric power would help him on his 25-acre fruit ranch. He installed a 5-horsepower motor, and a power company built a line 2 miles long to serve his farm.[2]

At first, other farmers in the Sacramento Valley were slow to adopt electric power for irrigation pumping. But farther south, in the San Joaquin Valley, the idea spread more rapidly.

In 1899 A. G. Wishon, manager of the Mt. Whitney Power Company, surveyed the farms and orchards surrounding Lindsay, California. He found some twenty-five establishments operating pumping plants with gasoline or steam engines. Wishon staged a demonstration of electric pumping in the Lindsay schoolhouse. The discussion lasted until after midnight, but not one grower would commit himself to using electric power. They balked at the cost of the new equipment and at the company's plan for a yearly rate based on the horsepower of the motor installed. The growers wanted to pay for their power only when they used it.[3]

The next day Wishon went to San Francisco, talked a banker into loaning the company $25,000, and invested all the money in electric motors and transformers. When he got back home, he offered each grower one of the motors and a transformer under a contract which required no down payment, the principal to be paid in five annual installments at 6 percent interest. In 2 days he had sold all his equipment and his company had what it needed: a new market for its power. In 1902 Wishon became manager of the San Joaquin Power Company. Under his leadership the company set rate and line extension policies that encouraged the use of electric power for irrigation and other farm purposes. Thanks to his efforts, and those of men like him, a network of transmission lines spread over the southern San Joaquin Valley.[4]

The importance of irrigation. In its earliest days, the electric industry had brought its wires into homes and places of business in order to bring light. Lighting alone had not been enough, however. It was the advent of the electric motor, and particularly the application of electricity to interurban transportation, that put the first electric companies on a sound economic footing. In the Far West the immediate economic need was to irrigate land. Lighting and transportation were secondary problems. There, the use of electricity in pumping water improved the situation of many electric companies in rural areas all along the West Coast.

Throughout California, Oregon, Washington, and Colorado many central-station companies developed on the base of irrigation pumping and incidental farm loads. By 1909 the Northern Colorado Power Company had reached a point where it was selling more power during the summer than during the winter while most other companies in the country were selling more power during the winter months.[5] It was this fact that attracted the attention of the Rochester Railway and Light Company in upstate New York.

Most central-station companies knew that a great proportion of their generating equipment was lying idle for many months during the year. The Rochester Company, for instance, had a generating capacity of 28,000 kilowatts in 1910. This represented the amount necessary to take care of the heavy peak loads in November, December, and January. From April 1 to October 1, however, about one-fourth of this capacity was never called on. This meant that for 6 months an investment of $2.5 million was not being used. Like many companies, Rochester Railway and Light Company was searching for a market for this power. Rural electrification, as it was developing in the West, seemed to offer just such a market.[6]

A widening interest. At the thirty-third annual convention of the National Electric Light Association (NELA) in 1910, Herman Russell, president of Rochester Gas and Electric Company, told other utility men of his company's experience in rural electrification. A pumping plant has been installed on a fruit farm near Rochester, he said, and experiments are being conducted. A peach orchard has been irrigated with remarkable results. A number of farmers along the shore of Lake Ontario are installing pumping plants to supply water for irrigation. At Irondequoit, a market-garden town near the city, the company is supplying current at regular rates to more than forty motors, most of which are being used to pump water. Interest among the farmers is increasing, and the company is convinced that its campaign will soon bring a demand for extension of more lines into the country.

"I look forward to a time," he concluded, ". . . when the present enormous idle investment of our central-station companies will be employed in making our farms more productive and life more worth the living for both the farmer and the company—at good profit to each."[7]

The initial response to Russell's speech was enthusiastic. The convention chairman called it "one of the most important papers" of the session and commented that "it presents more possibility than anything that has been touched on." An immediate result of the interest aroused among some of the Eastern and Southern companies was the formation of a Committee on Electricity in Rural Districts. The report of this committee, an eighty-seven-page illustrated document presented to the NELA Convention the following year, was the first attempt at a systematic accumulation of data on rural electrification in the United States.[8]

The committee reported that it had been in correspondence with seventy-seven agricultural colleges and that a large majority had shown "considerable interest" in rural electrification. It also had begun to accumulate suggestions for ways electricity could be used on farms. Its first report listed thirty-eight farm machines which might be driven by electric motors.[9]

This pioneering committee made three recommendations in 1911 that were adopted by the NELA. They were:

1st. That the United States Department of Agriculture be urged to get out a bulletin on the use of electricity on the farm.

2nd. That a set of resolutions, similar to those adopted by the National Gas and Gasoline Engine Trades Association, but adapted to the special objects of this Association as regards the use of electricity in the rural districts, be prepared by a committee to be appointed by the chair, and that they be brought up for adoption by the Association; and that a committee be appointed to personally present an official copy of said resolutions to the Secretary of the Department of Agriculture at Washington, D.C.

3rd. That an investigation of types of farming machinery now being manufactured be made, with a view to securing adaptations which may be necessary in their design to render them readily adaptable to motor drive.[10]

The emphasis of the NELA committee during its first years was on the problem of markets. While irrigation provided a good base for development in the West and in some other areas, the utility men felt that additional uses for electricity needed to be discovered.

Demonstrations by train. In many parts of the country individual companies were working at showing farmers ways in which they could use electricity. In 1908 the University of California, in cooperation with the Southern Pacific Railroad, had fitted out a seven-car agricultural demonstration train. The train, exhibiting new techniques in farming and animal husbandry, toured the state repeatedly. In 1912, the Pacific Gas and Electric Company added an electrical exhibit to the train. There were demonstrations of irrigation pumping and domestic water-pressure systems, models of motorized farming equipment, and a home economics section that included electric washing machines and vacuum cleaners. The train proved to be so successful in stimulating interest that the electric company decided to develop a similar exhibit of its own. By the middle of April, 1912, the company had a fully equipped car touring the Sacramento Valley.[11]

The same summer, on the other side of the continent, the Edison Electric Illuminating Company of Boston sponsored a farm electrification "circus" which toured rural areas in Massachusetts demonstrating thirty-three electrically powered farm machines. As irrigation could not provide the market for electricity in New England that it did in the West, the Boston company stressed other uses for electricity and progressive farmers began to respond.[12]

Electrical manufacturers, too, were becoming aware of the possibilities of rural electrification. In 1911 the General Electric Company conducted a series of tests on a variety of farm machines under actual operating conditions. One of these, held on a farm near Dayton, Ohio, demonstrated that the cost of grinding 4,000 bushels of corn could be reduced from $308 to $160 by having electric power do the work on the owner's farm rather than having the corn hauled to a mill 2 miles away and hiring the service.[13]

The Lake County plan. At the same time, some electric power companies were doing research to find less expensive materials and equipment.[14] Then, in 1910 a Midwestern company decided to try an experiment. Experience had shown that a centralized electric utility company might be able to provide energy for light and power over a wide area more efficiently than could a scattering of small central station companies. The company set out to acquire the stations operating in a dozen rural villages in Lake County, Illinois. Samuel Insull, the company president, said it was probably "the poorest territory for the purpose of central-station distribution that it has been my fortune to operate in." [15]

The plants the company brought together were serving ten towns with a population of 15,395. They were the only towns in the county with electric service, and they had service only at night. By centralizing the operation and taking advantage of the diverse uses to which customers in the area could put electricity, the company was able to improve and extend service, reduce fixed and operating costs, lower rates, and earn a reasonable return on its investment. By 1912 there were twenty towns, with a total population of 22,188 people being served in Lake County. In addition, there were 125 customers, mostly farmers, outside the limits of any of the villages in the territory receiving electricity. This was the first real demonstration that electric service for small rural communities and farming areas, without the base of irrigation, was economically feasible.[16]

Reporting progress. Rural electrification was progressing. For the first time, in 1912, the U.S. Census Bureau report of central electric light and power stations included a section on electricity in agriculture. "The variety of uses to which electricity can be put on the farm is surprising," the report said. It cited the 1912 report of the NELA committee which enumerated fifty uses for electricity in the farm house itself, thirty applications for electric motors in the barn and field machinery, and twenty uses in the dairy. "The use of electricity on the farm," the report said, "has been pursued and developed with extraordinary rapidity in recent years. The chief reasons are the extension of power-transmission circuits from central stations in cities, and the establishment of distribution networks in connection with hydroelectric enterprises looking for patronage of every description." [17]

Although the First World War and the depression that followed it slowed down almost all rural economic and social developments, the expansion of rural electric service continued to progress. By the end of 1919 an estimated 100,000 farms were receiving electricity from central stations. Five years later, in 1924, the number had more than doubled.[18] Rural electrification was poised for a leap ahead. All it needed was a spark.

The CREA

The spark was provided by the Committee on the Relation of Electricity to Agriculture (CREA), which brought together farm organizations, agricultural schools, state agricultural departments, equipment manufacturers, and electric utility men. The central figure in the organization was Grover Neff of the Wisconsin Power and Light Company. Born and reared in an Indiana farm community, Neff had long been interested in rural electrification. When, in 1920, a group of farmers asked his company to extend service to them, he was delighted and quickly agreed. He was startled to learn, however, how little people in the industry knew about carrying out a job like this. There was no agreement about the materials necessary for adequate service. No one could tell him what the proper distance should be between poles, what kind of poles to use or what kind of wire, or exactly what voltage would be best.[19]

While his company was able to devise answers to these questions and construct a line for the farmers, Neff was left with the conviction that the industry-wide approach to rural electrification needed to be revitalized. At the 1921 convention of the NELA he pointed out to his fellow utility men that nearly 50 percent of the people of the United States and approximately half the unwired houses were located in rural districts. "The farmer," he said, "can, does and will use more current per customer than the customer in the city."[20]

"The rural business is very important to the utility," he continued. "The farmers are rapidly learning the value to them of electric service and are demanding it. I think, therefore, that the utilities and the electrical associations, and especially this Association, should take steps to develop a practical plan for financing farm lines and to ascertain the fundamental factors upon which to base a proper rate."[21] Three months later a new NELA Committee on Rural Lines was formed. The chairman was Grover Neff.[22]

The committee, consisting of representatives from thirty-one companies, conducted intensive surveys and gathered, analyzed, and exchanged a large quantity of data. By 1923 it was possible for a speaker at the NELA convention to say,

Our industry realizes its obligation to aid the farmer and stands willing to supply him with electric service whenever and wherever it is economical and feasible to do so.

There is no denying the fact that complete electric service on the farm brings with it great advantages, and as our systems of distribution spread out more and more, farms will come within the range of economic service. No engineering difficulties stand in the way. Every farm in the country could be reached, but in the present state of the art the cost of doing so would be so great that the rates which the farmer would have to pay for the service would be prohibitive.[23]

Facing the problems

Speaking for the Rural Lines Committee in 1923, Grover Neff noted that a dual problem had to be faced in the development of rural electrification: First, How could service be supplied to the farmer?; second, How could service be utilized by the farmer so that it would be profitable to him? "The farmer cannot be expected to use electrical energy unless he can profit thereby and likewise the central station cannot be expected to sell electric service to the farmer for less than its cost plus a fair return on the necessary investment," Neff said.[24]

With work on the technical problems of rural electrification well under way, the next step seemed to be finding more ways for farmers to use electricity in such a manner that it would increase farm incomes. To this end, Neff proposed that all groups interested in rural electrification join together in a cooperative effort.

In 1922, Neff, John Martin of *Electrical World,* and Arthur Huntington of Iowa Electric Light & Power Co., all members of the NELA Rural Lines Committee, had met informally with representatives of the American Farm

Bureau Federation to suggest that a joint effort be made to bring electric service to farmers at a more rapid rate. Out of this meeting the Committee on the Relation of Electricity to Agriculture was born. Other groups joined later, including the National Grange, the American Society of Agricultural Engineers, the American Home Economics Association, the General Federation of Women's Clubs, the National Association of Farm Equipment Manufacturers, the National Electrical Manufacturers Association, and various departments of the Federal government. Fifteen state committees were established, the CREA itself acting as a general coordinating agency and Dr. E. A. White of Evanston, Illinois, a man highly trained in agriculture, serving as its executive director.

The immediate program outlined by the committee consisted of four investigations: (1) a national farm power survey, (2) a foreign farm power survey, (3) a survey of central-station and isolated-plant service to farmers, and (4) experimental and research work on the uses of electricity in agriculture.

The farm power survey was conducted by the U.S. Department of Agriculture. Its purpose was to assemble all available data on the various sources of power in use on farms in the United States. The foreign farm power survey was carried out by the U.S. Department of Commerce through its Bureau of Foreign and Domestic Commerce. It was found that rural electrification in Europe was in about the same state of advance as in the United States. Rates to rural customers in European countries were no lower or more favorable than those in this country. The survey report noted, too, that in some European countries committees were trying to promote rural electric development.[25]

The survey of rural electric service was made by the

NELA. It was found that in eight states more than 10 percent of the farms had central-station electric service in 1923. The first four of these were California, Washington, Utah, and Idaho, where irrigation still provided the most important demand for power. In the next four—New Hampshire, Maine, Connecticut, and Rhode Island—line extensions had been favored by a relatively high density of rural population. Ohio, where 6.6 percent of the farms had central-station service, ranked thirteenth in the country. It was the highest-ranking state outside of the Far West or the Northeast.[26] In Indiana and a number of other states rural electrification committeees had been formed and promotional activities were under way.

The survey showed that in seventeen states less than 1 percent of the farms had central-station service. Twelve of these were in the South Atlantic, East South Central, and West South Central areas—the regions where farms were most scattered, where per farm income was lowest, and where little or no irrigation was used.[27]

The survey showed clearly how uneven the development of rural electrification had been. The CREA set out to correct this situation as rapidly as possible. To accomplish its mission, it developed a far-reaching program of research, experiment, and education.

Acting as the coordinating agency for the state committees, which had been increased to twenty-five by 1931, the national CREA saw to it that every known use of electricity on the farm was carefully reexamined and that new uses were developed. Exhaustive tests were made. Cost data were assembled. Results were accumulated and published in newsletters, bulletins, and magazines. In seven states rural distribution lines serving typical farm communities were selected or built as test projects. Utility companies, agricultural schools, equipment manufacturers, and farmers collaborated to operate these lines under controlled conditions. A reliable body of knowledge was being built up concerning the use of electricity on farms.[28]

The test projects, the model farms, and the laboratory work being carried on by the CREA and its state committees were only the nucleus of the work being done to advance rural electrification. Power companies in all parts of the country were alert to the opportunities of serving rural markets, and whenever any company built a new rural line, that line was as much an experiment as one of the CREA projects.

Like the construction methods being developed, the rate schedules and financing plans for rural electrification expressed local conditions and thus varied widely. By 1928, however, most companies had developed rural electrification to a point where their principal thought in designing rural rates was to encourage increased consumption. The year before, in its annual report, the NELA Rural Electric Service Committee told of a rural line that had been built to serve eleven farmers. The second month the average consumption was 160 kilowatt hours per farm. Many companies, the report noted, had individual farmers using 500 kilowatt-hours a month, but one small dairy farm held the record. During the last half of 1925 it had used 606 kilowatt-hours per month, and during the last half of 1926 it had increased this to 1,024 kilowatt-hours per month.[29]

The committee report told of a rural customer who had written to a farm publication that "My electric bill averages $22 a month and it is the most delightful bill I pay." As the committee concluded, these words meant a new day was arriving for the American farmer.[30]

The Great Depression

On September 26, 1929, Grover Neff was in French Lick, Indiana, speaking before the annual meeting of the Great Lakes Division of the NELA. "Utility companies of this division are giving more and more attention to the problem of extending electric service to the farmers in this territory," he said. "The development of this phase of the utility business is progressing at such a rate that within a few years all the farmers who live in reasonably well-settled districts and who want electric service will be supplied with it." [31]

But this peak of optimism, based on the booming prosperity of the 1920s, was not to last. Within 2 months the economic world had shattered. With characteristic stability, the electric utility companies were not affected by the Great Depression as quickly as many other industries. In 1930 the companies were able to raise and spend a record $785 million for construction. That year electric service was extended to 73,750 additional farms.[32]

As the Depression dragged on, however, sources of capital dried up. In 1931 the electric companies could spend only $485 million for construction, in 1932 only $260 million, and in 1933 a meager $145 million. Even during these three bleak years, rural electrification was edged forward: Another 63,650 farms were added from 1930 to 1933.[33]

The increasing difficulty the electric companies faced in finding capital for expansion was not the only factor which was slowing the progress of rural electrification. There had been a general farm depression in the United States throughout the 1920s. While the rest of the country had been prospering, American farmers had never really recovered from the post–World War I recession of

1920–1921 when gross farm income had dropped over $7 billion.[34]

After a decade of low incomes, and facing one of the worst depressions in the country's history, the farmers were in a bad way. Over 40 percent of the farms were operated by tenants. In 1930, and again in 1931, gross farm income declined by about $2.5 billion. All over the country, farmers were in serious financial trouble.[35]

To meet the hard economic problems of the day, the electric companies began developing new plans for rural electrification. Among these was the area plan, developed from the Illinois Lake County experiment of 20 years before, which worked well in areas where a small rural community with comparatively dense population or a group of large farms or an industrial plant could provide a nucleus. Such conditions were rarest in the farming sections that were yet unserved, but in some regions the plan was greeted enthusiastically.

Despite the achievements made in rural electrification in the face of the depression, nationwide progress was far short of what utility men and farm leaders hoped. The farmer's lack of purchasing power was the chief obstacle. To some, the best solution seemed to be long-term financing of farm lines. In this way the necessary high capital investment would be spread over many years. The funds and credit for the program could be supplied by the Federal government, these people suggested. The social need was such that Federal assistance would be of benefit to the whole nation.

Agitation for Federal legislation that would provide rural electrification with long-term financing at lower interest rates than private capital could provide began about 1933. A year later the National Grange and the American Farm Bureau Federation withdrew from the

CREA to ally themselves with this new movement. The utility companies were asked to join and the industry announced its willingness to cooperate.

A meeting with Cooke

In the fall of 1934 a group of Eastern utility executives met with Morris L. Cooke, Vice-chairman of President Roosevelt's newly created Power Policy Committee, to discuss the problems of rural electrification. They pointed out that the job of rural electrification had just started on a large scale when the Depression had slowed it down but that their companies were planning to renew their farm programs in 1935. They showed Cooke data indicating that 10.9 percent of the nation's 6.8 million farms were receiving central-station service. The field for expansion, they said, was enormous.[36]

In response to a request from Cooke, the companies began to prepare a report on rural electrification. Preliminary data were sent in November and December, 1934. The final report was submitted on January 24, 1935. It included tables for fixed and operating and maintenance costs for lines ranging in price from $800 to $1,200 a mile, with two to four customers per mile, and with 800 to 6,000 kilowatt-hours of annual consumption. In itself, the report was a thorough course in the economics of farm electrification based on some 35 years of electric company experience in the field.[37]

The report was carefully studied by the administration and, on May 11, 1935, President Roosevelt issued an executive order establishing a Rural Electrification Administration, with Cooke at its head. Congress immediately designated an emergency fund of up to $100 million for loans to utility companies, associations, and

cooperative organizations for farm electric development.*
At first, the REA was given broad authority to proceed
as it saw fit. Cooke immediately called in a group of
utility executives for consultation. In a meeting on May
20, 1935, he explained that since the electric companies
were serving 95 percent of the electrified farms in the
country, since the companies had physical facilities and
trained personnel, and since the primary objective of
the REA was to bring electricity to as many farms as
possible as rapidly as it could, he expected the bulk of
the Administration's appropriation would go to the
power companies. The remainder, he said, would go to
municipally owned utilities and farmer-owned distribution cooperatives. All the money would be loaned at
an interest rate between 2 and 3 percent. To facilitate
matters, he asked the utilities to conduct a new survey

*Executive Order No. 7037, May 11, 1935. The appropriation for
the REA was a part of the $4 billion Emergency Relief Appropria-
tions Act of April 8, 1935 (Public Resolution No. 11, 74th Cong.)
in which Congress earmarked a sum not to exceed $100 million for
rural electrification. A good deal of confusion developed from the
vague nature of the act. In early May, 1935, President Roosevelt
announced that $50 million would be allocated to the REA (New
York Times, May 8, 1935). On May 20, 1935, REA was allotted $10
million (Cooke and Nicholson, Hearings before the Subcommittee
of the Committee on Appropriations, 75th Cong., 1st Sess., Independent Offices Appropriation Bill for 1938, pp. 475–476). During
the summer of 1935, a struggle occurred within the administration,
particularly between Harold Ickes and Harry Hopkins, for control
of relief funds. At a conference held at Hyde Park on Sept. 12,
1935, President Roosevelt forced a compromise, but in so doing allocated all the remaining funds to projects other than rural electrification. To Cooke, it appeared that Roosevelt "took $90,000,000 away
from us." (See New York Times for the summer and fall of 1935,
particularly Sept. 12–19; Ickes, Secret Diary, for the same period;
and the hearings before the House Committee cited above, p. 475,
for Cooke's reaction.)

and to submit a nation-wide program that would make use of the available funds.[38]

A committee for the industry was quickly appointed with W. W. Freeman, of Columbia Gas & Electric Co., as chairman. On July 24, barely 2 months after Cooke had made his request, the committee submitted its plan.[39]

The industry program provided for construction of 78,180 miles of new rural lines during the fiscal year 1935–1936. These lines would serve 206,000 farmers and 79,000 non-farm customers. Another 66,000 customers, including 41,000 farms, were to be added to existing lines through loans financing service facilities. The average cost of the new lines, using durable construction, was estimated at not more than $963 per mile, and probably less. Transformers, meters, and services would add about $109 for each customer. The companies would be given long-term Federal loans to cover the cost.[40]

"In cooperation with the REA," the committee said, "we believe the privately-owned utilities can absorb the full $100,000,000 available under the Work Relief Appropriation for construction of additional rural facilities. The program can be started as soon as funds are available and pursued as rapidly as the prospects are sold on the government's financing plan." [41]

The proposal pointed out that the choice rural customers, such as the very large dairy farms and the large users for irrigation purposes, were generally receiving electric service already. The problem was to take service to as many of the smaller potential customers as possible. For this reason, the report stated, "the utilities consider the immediate urge for rural electrification as a social rather than an economic problem, and undertake to 'carry' the increased rural business outlined in this memorandum over the necessary long development period." [42]

Waiting for action. The committee and the companies settled down to wait for Cooke to take action on their proposal. After a week Cooke wrote thanking the committee for its efforts, commenting on various parts of the program, and suggesting that the companies might now present their applications for funds, piecemeal. At the same time, during the last week of July, he issued two press releases. One acknowledged receipt of the committee's report and commented that it now "seemed highly probable" the entire $100 million could be used effectively. The other belittled the companies' efforts and stated that "public bodies and the farm cooperative organizations have acted decidedly more promptly" in making applications for loans. In it Cooke announced that preferences for REA loans would be given to "applications from municipalities and other agencies of the state and to non-profit associations such as cooperatives." [43]

Nevertheless, Cooke remained friendly and gracious in his contacts with the utility men. Delay and lack of specific information, he told them, were simply due to governmental red tape. In view of statements by Senator Norris and a few others that they would oppose lending any money to utilities,* Cooke's violent opposition

*"Norris Opposes U.S. Loans to Private Utilities," Associated Press, Aug. 2, 1935.

About 25 years before President Eisenhower signed a bill directing the FPC to issue a license to the New York State Power Authority to construct and operate a power project on the Niagara River (see Chapter 2, p. 77), Franklin Roosevelt, then Governor of New York State, formed the organization he called the New York State Power Authority. One of Roosevelt's first appointments was Morris Llewellyn Cooke, who looked on it as "a glorious chance to take the lid off the public utility situation." (New York *World Telegram,* May 13, 1931.) Several of the men working with Cooke in New York during this period were later appointed to positions in the Federal government by Roosevelt. Among them were Basil Manly, who became Vice Chairman of the FPC in 1932; Leland Olds, who was named to the reactivation of the Ohio State CREA committee, and his previous activities with the New York State Power Authority, however, the companies felt they should proceed with caution.

Grover Neff was determined to apply for a loan. In order to learn the specific contracts, rates, etc., that would be approved by REA, the companies decided to follow his application carefully. In August, 1935, Neff, appearing for Wisconsin Power & Light Company, submitted an application for $260,000 to supply service to 642 rural customers. The company indicated that if its request should be approved, it would immediately apply for an additional $750,000 for extensions to another 2,000 farms. It was estimated that the electricity along these lines would be sold at an average of 6.44 cents a kilowatt-hour, with each kilowatt-hour over 100 per customer at 3 cents, and that at this rate the company would lose over $4,000 a year on the investment. The company was willing to absorb this loss in the hope that increased consumption would eventually make the extensions profitable.[44]

The application was under consideration for 3 months. On November 5, 1935, it was rejected on the grounds that the rates were too high. Disappointed, Neff wrote to Cooke suggesting that the Wisconsin Public Service Commission be allowed to set the rates. Whatever happened, he concluded, his company would continue to extend farm service to the limit of its ability. It was no use. Cooke did not bother to answer his letter.

Chairman of the FPC in 1939; and J. D. Ross, who held appointments as Chief Consulting Engineer of the Power Division of PWA, a member of the Securities and Exchange Commission, and Administrator of the Bonneville Power Administration. One of the staff members of the authority during this early period was Dr. John Bauer, a consulting economist, who became an associate editor of Carl Thompson's magazine *Public Ownership* in 1934.

The REA Act

Early in 1936 the REA, through the Norris-Rayburn Bill, asked Congress to authorize a 10-year program of rural electrification under which $400 million would be loaned for generating plants, transmission and distribution facilities, and wiring appliances, at a rate of not more than 3 percent. Loans were to be made for a period of 25 years and would be fully self-liquidating. All the expenses of REA as a lending, collecting, and administrative agency were to be fully subsidized by separate annual appropriations.

As originally drawn, the bill specifically excluded electric companies as borrowers. Eventually, however, a compromise was worked out: Investor-owned utilities would be allowed to apply for loans, but the Administrator was instructed to give preference to applications from governmental units and cooperative associations. In practice, this meant that few investor-owned companies could borrow from REA funds. Some companies persevered and were able to make use of REA loans to help build lines in rural areas. The Central Indiana Power Company was one of these.[45]

The intent of the act was clearly stated by Senator Norris. REA funds were to be used to bring electricity to areas not being served by the companies. "There will not be set up an organization and money loaned to it for the purpose of electrifying a rural area which is now supplied," Senator Norris said.[46]

As to rates, Sam Rayburn said, "The Rural Electrification Administration will have nothing whatever to do with the rates that may be fixed in these communities, for the simple reason that matter will be controlled by State law." [47] Cooke himself had said before congressional hearings the rate regulation "is an area in which we, under our conception of the law, have no authority. The setting of rates is entirely a State matter . . . I know, as administrator, that I am absolutely without power in the matter of fixing rates within the boundaries of a State." [48]

But in his letter to Neff rejecting the loan application, Cooke had written, "Only one obstacle prevents me from approving the application—the high rates of your company for rural consumers . . . shortly after the date of your application, a representative of this Administration called upon you to discuss the problems of your rural rate . . . But you refuse to consider a reduction of the rate now in force. I am, therefore, obliged to disapprove your application. I sincerely regret the necessity under which I act, and assure you that I will be glad to reconsider the application whenever you may decide to undertake a revision of your rural rate." [49] Despite what Cooke and others had said, the REA was using its loaning authority as a device to regulate rates.

The pace increases

Seeing that assistance from the REA would not be forthcoming, the electric companies set about reviving their farm programs themselves. Capital was becoming more readily available, in some cases at as low as $3\frac{1}{2}$ percent. With money obtainable and with farm income on the rise, the utilities took up the construction programs the Depression had stopped. During 1935 and 1936 service was extended to about 300,000 farms, including service through REA-financed organizations which brought electricity to some 6,550 farms.[50]

Morris Cooke and the REA were engaged in an active campaign to promote the organization of rural distribution cooperatives. Since these associations had no means to generate electricity themselves, they naturally turned to the power companies to buy energy at wholesale prices. The companies responded readily with rates that were considered to be sound, both from the point of view of helping develop the new rural projects and from the point of view of their economic effect on the companies themselves. The standard wholesale rates averaged about 2 cents per kilowatt-hour. REA contended that this was too high for many cooperatives. It threatened to build diesel generating plants that would make the companies' wholesale power unnecessary and vehemently denounced the electric companies for hindering progress of rural electrification.

After a series of discussions, an agreement was reached. The cooperatives were given special contracts under which the standard rates would be retained. However, these would be subject to certain discounts during the cooperative's development period. In effect, the

Chart 8·1

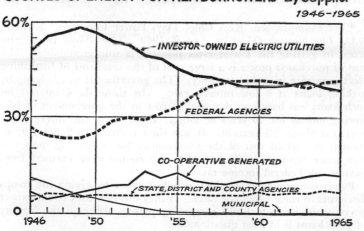

SOURCES OF ENERGY FOR REA BORROWERS—By Supplier

1946–1965

INVESTOR-OWNED ELECTRIC UTILITIES

FEDERAL AGENCIES

CO-OPERATIVE GENERATED

STATE, DISTRICT AND COUNTY AGENCIES

MUNICIPAL

60%

30%

0

1946   '50   '55   '60   1965

THE RURAL ELECTRIFICATION ADMINISTRATION *265*

companies agreed to absorb the losses which any business enterprise customarily experiences in its early years. On the other hand, the companies were not expected to incur any special investment, other than metering equipment, to serve this business. It seemed a happy solution to the problem. At present, most companies extend a special low rate to cooperatives. In 1965 over 38 percent of the energy purchased by REA borrowers was supplied by investor-owned companies (Chart 8·1).

Intermittently, the REA renewed its demands for further reductions of this rate. Each time, the tactics were much the same. The threat of generating plants financed by REA funds was used as a gun behind the door or, in a number of instances, as an accomplished fact. Again and again the companies were charged with standing in the way of electric service for the farmer.*

The fact is that the electric companies have steadily continued their program of rural electrification. Cooperating with farm groups, state and local farm bureaus, 4-H clubs, agricultural schools, manufacturers, and local electric cooperatives, the companies have played an im-

---

* For example, see "REA Chief Flays Power Concerns," Raleigh, N.C., *The News & Observer*, Aug. 9, 1940. The co-ops' intense interest in getting the lowest rates possible is understandable. The cost of purchased power is a large part of the total cost of furnishing electric service in a thin territory. The government was helping by making loans at a low interest rate. (In those days, interest on such loans was based on the average cost to the government of borrowing money for 10 years or more. Until 1944, the interest rate averaged about 2⅔ percent. It was then reduced to 2 percent, although the actual cost of the government for borrowing money is now more than twice that.) Also, the co-ops were excused from paying any Federal income taxes.

Power companies were asked to help further by giving the co-ops discounts in their wholesale rates. If they did not, they could expect government loans to build competing plants, although the legality of such loans is at least questionable.

portant part in the nation's agricultural development. In helping the farmer solve his labor problems electrically, they have aided in making farming less arduous and more profitable.

The deviation of REA

The REA Act states that loans may be made: ". . . for the purpose of financing the construction and operation of generating plants, electric transmission and distribution lines or systems for the furnishing of electric energy to persons in rural areas who are not receiving central station service . . ." And a rural area is defined by the Act to mean: ". . . any area of the United States not included within the boundaries of any city, village, or borough having a population in excess of 1500 inhabitants . . ." [51]

In this way, the act put limits on the authority of the REA to loan money for generating plants and transmission lines. When good wholesale central-station service was being provided, the act apparently did not authorize the lending of money to build a plant. In discussing this point when the act was being considered by Congress, Sam Rayburn, sponsor of the bill in the House, said:

. . . we are not, in this bill, intending to go out and compete with anybody. By this bill we hope to bring electrification to people who do not now have it. This bill was not written on the theory that we were going to punish somebody or parallel their lines or enter into competition with them. [52]

On the same point, Senator Norris emphasized that:

There is no intention of going into a farming community which is already supplied with electric current and forming farm organizations there and having them built up to go into competition . . . [53]

Senator Norris also entered a note in the record which read:

REA can make loans for generating plants, but we must be shown conclusively: (1) That energy is not available from any existing source. (2) That the proposed generating plant can produce energy at a lower cost than it could be obtained from any other source. (3) That the output of such plant will be used mainly for supplying energy for use in rural areas.[54]

The REA was formed for the worthy purpose of lending government help in getting electric service more quickly out to rural areas that didn't have it. Although the REA could have made use of the existing investor-owned power companies, another approach was taken. Rural cooperatives were formed to distribute electricity. The investor-owned power companies have played their part by providing many cooperatives with energy at special low rates and by working to extend their own lines into unserved rural areas.

Chart 8·2

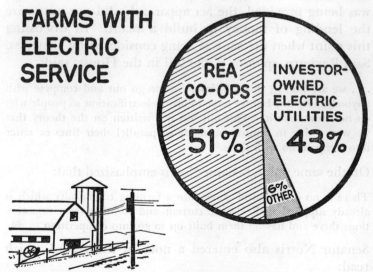

FARMS WITH ELECTRIC SERVICE

REA CO-OPS 51%

INVESTOR-OWNED ELECTRIC UTILITIES 43%

6% OTHER

Today, 98 percent of America's farms have electric service. Of these 51 percent are served by cooperatives, 43 percent by investor-owned power companies, and 6 percent by others.[55] (Chart 8·2)

Today, REA makes its loans almost exclusively to co-ops and only one out of every ten new co-op customers is a farmer. There are now some 1,000 REA-financed rural electric cooperatives serving about 5½ million customers.[56] (Chart 8·3)

The original purpose of the REA has already been accomplished. Virtually all the nation's farms have electric service. Despite this, REA is promoting the construction of unnecessary generating plants and transmission lines, to be financed by the government. The reason is fairly plain. When Congress said No to any further expansion of the TVA idea and to plants in the Department of the Interior such as those the Southwest Power Administration had for expansion of government power in the Southwest, advocates of the government power idea turned to the REA. Because REA gets blanket appropriations from Congress

139,500 NEW CO-OP CUSTOMERS ADDED IN 1965

9 NON-FARM to 1 FARM

Chart 8·3

THE RURAL ELECTRIFICATION ADMINISTRATION   *269*

and can appropriate money from these appropriations without specific approval of Congress, it has been possible to use REA funds to form super cooperatives that build generating plants and transmission lines that are not needed and that were not intended under the REA Act.

REA has already made loans to over forty generating and transmission cooperatives (called G&Ts) to finance generating plants and transmission lines. The total of such loans now amounts to $1.4 billion.[57] In 1965, more than 60 percent of all REA loan funds went to finance generating plants and transmission lines.[58] (Chart 8·4)

Criteria for G&T loans. Each year, after hearings and recommendations, Congress authorizes a certain number of dollars for REA loans. The exact amount varies from year to year. After the funds have been authorized, the

Chart 8·4

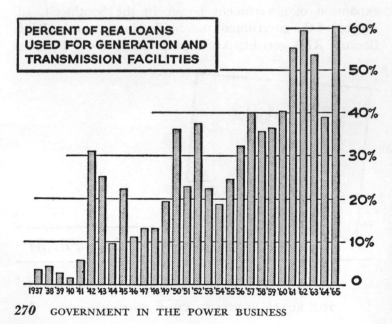

PERCENT OF REA LOANS USED FOR GENERATION AND TRANSMISSION FACILITIES

REA decides which applications shall be granted (Chart 8·5).

The pattern for obtaining REA loans to build generating plants calls for forming a generating and transmission (G&T) co-op, made up of a number of distribution cooperatives. The G&T sells its power to the member co-ops, using long-term power supply contracts as anchors for loans from the REA.

Before 1961, criteria for loans to G&Ts were as follows:

The Rural Electrification Administration will make loans to finance the initial construction of generation and transmission facilities only under the following conditions:

(1) Where no adequate and dependable source of power is available in the area to meet the consumers' needs, or

(2) Where the rates offered by existing power sources would result in a higher cost of power to the consumers than the cost from facilities financed by REA.[59]

Under these criteria it is clear that few loans to G&Ts could be justified. Adequate service was available to all cooperatives and the price was reasonable and fair.

Chart 8·5

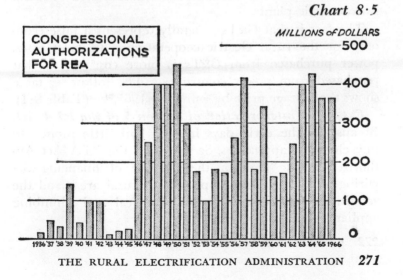

CONGRESSIONAL AUTHORIZATIONS FOR REA

MILLIONS of DOLLARS

THE RURAL ELECTRIFICATION ADMINISTRATION *271*

But in 1961 a third criterion was established: "Where generation and transmission facilities are necessary to protect the security and effectiveness of REA-financed systems." [60]

This new criterion has been criticized as being vague and indefinite. It is not clear what is meant by *security* or *effectiveness.* The co-ops can buy energy from the largest and most efficient power system on earth. The companies have reserve capacity of about 25 percent. The co-ops are secure in their future power supply. The service is under government regulation as to price, quality of service, and adequacy of supply. The co-ops have the benefit of a good discount when they buy power and they can enter into long-term contracts if they wish to do so. They are as secure as everyone else in purchasing central-station service.

The real effect of the third criterion is to make it easier to build power plants financed with 2 percent government money and free from Federal income taxes, which often can be used in combination with Federal hydroelectric plants.

The fact is that G&Ts generally represent a false economy for the rural electric cooperatives. In most cases, power purchased from G&Ts is more costly than that purchased from power companies. The following table shows the average price by source for 1965.[61] (Table 8·1)

Expanded interpretation of Section 5 of the REA Act. Because in the early days farmers had little money to buy electrical appliances, Section 5 of the REA Act Authorized loans ". . . for the purpose of financing the wiring of the premises of persons in rural areas and the acquisition and installation of electrical and plumbing appliances and equipment." [62]

**Table 8·1 Cost of Energy Purchased by REA Borrowers,
by Supplier
(Average Cost per Kilowatt-Hour, Fiscal Year 1965)**

Supplier	Average cost per kwhr, cents
Investor-owned companies	0.74
Cooperatives*†	0.83
Municipals‡	0.91
Federal agencies†	0.48
State, county, and district agencies‡	0.69

*Includes both co-op generation and purchases for resale.
†These projects are not required to earn a return equivalent to the market cost of capital, and pay no Federal income taxes.
‡These systems can finance with tax-exempt bonds, and pay no Federal income taxes.

The discussion of this section prior to passage of the bill showed that Congress had in mind loans to farmers and homeowners, to help them get equipped to use electric power. But today co-ops are in the money-lending business, using Section 5 as a jumping-off point. A law passed to answer the needs of a particular time has, at a later time, been applied so that the purpose for the law is being clouded and lost.

Perhaps the most bizarre loan under Section 5 was a $30,000 loan to the Jo-Carroll Electric Cooperative for reloan to the Chestnut Hill Resort, Inc., of Hanover, Ill., to buy snow-making equipment. *The Wall Street Journal,* reporting on the financing of the resort, noted that its owners "owe roughly $200,000 to bankers, finance companies and individuals, all of it in short-term loans of under two years' maturity at interest rates as high as 15 percent. The $30,000 REA loan, by contrast, is at four percent and is to be repaid quarterly over a ten-year period." One of the owners was quoted as saying, "We couldn't borrow more money anywhere, although we were offering to pay 18 percent interest." [63]

In hearings early in 1962, Representative Don L. Short told the REA Administrator, "You have gotten into a field where it seems to me that the REA is almost becoming a small business administration . . . I think that it deviates somewhat from the concept that most people have as to the purposes of the REA program." [64]

The House Agriculture Committee said of these Section 5 loans:

The committee heard testimony that loans under Section 5 of the act, which was intended to help farm and other rural people to utilize the electricity that the REA program was bringing to them, are now used to finance industry. The committee feels that REA's present interpretation of section 5 of the 1936 act is inconsistent with the original intent of Congress.[65]

Serving communities of over 1,500 population. The REA Act limits borrowers from serving communities with more than 1,500 population, but there are various ways in which a cooperative can come to serve towns larger than stated in the act. For one, a small town served by a co-op can grow until it exceeds 1,500 population. For another, a town under the 1,500 limit may be annexed by a larger adjoining town. Still another way is that a small town may enlarge its boundaries to take in additional area.

In most of these cases, of course, the cooperative is blameless, although here and there cooperatives have disregarded the limitation and tried to serve larger towns. Whatever the reason for breaching the requirements of the act, however, it is still against the will of Congress. Congress has spoken as to whether service to towns over 1,500 population should have a subsidy in cost of money and taxes, and has decreed that it shall not. In spite of this decree, co-op service to these larger towns still enjoys the subsidies meant for rural homes and farms.

Serving large industries. The whole idea of the REA program was to offer government aid in getting electric service into thinly populated areas where electric service could not be brought without some kind of help. It was hoped that in time the rural electric business in these areas could grow to the point where it could stand on its own feet. This has been occurring with the increased farm mechanization and new uses for electricity on the farm.

The present need for a subsidy for farm service is the reason for lending money at less than the actual cost to government when it borrows money. This is the justification for excusing the cooperatives from paying Federal income taxes that customers of investor-owned companies pay in their electricity bills. When an REA borrower takes on a large industry as a customer, problems arise.

Dual rate. When the power companies first offered discounts in their wholesale rates to cooperatives, many companies, instead of quoting a standard rate with a discount, simply designed a new rate which was less than standard. At the time, neither the companies nor the REA had any idea the cooperatives would sell the energy to anyone but ordinary rural customers. In other words, no one imagined that cooperatives would buy electricity at a special discount and then try to sell it, at prices less than the companies' standard prices, to aluminum plants or pipelines or oil refineries. But some of them did. Here was the most unfair kind of competition—taking advantage of a company's discount to undersell the company in supplying service to industry.

A remedy was needed. Some companies, in effect, said to their co-op customers, "The discount (or special low rate) is for energy which you resell to ordinary rural customers—not for energy which you might sell to big industry. We will sell you energy for industrial purposes and all that energy will be grouped together and billed at our standard rate for such purpose. You may charge the industry a rate like our standard rate, and because you buy in bulk, you will have a satisfactory margin."

This rate is called the dual rate—the standard price for all energy resold to industrial users and a discounted price for all energy resold to ordinary rural customers.

Other companies have said: "The REA Act contemplates government subsidies to assist in getting electric service more quickly to ordinary rural customers. No subsidy is intended for industry. Let us serve the industries as part of our regular utility obligation."

The present REA administration has said the dual rate must go. It has said, in effect: Let the co-ops use the special low rate to serve industry or we will bring forth our new criterion and rule the loan is not "secure" unless a government-subsidized power plant is built. The government-subsidized plant will then sell government-subsidized power to industry.

Some co-op people believe they should have the right to serve industry in order to have a balanced business and to offset the cost of providing service to farms in a thin territory. If that is so, the cooperative becomes a regular utility and should be on the same footing as any other utility. That is to say, it should finance in the free market, pay taxes like all other utilities, and be under government regulation. If co-ops are to continue to enjoy government subsidies, in all fairness they should not compete with those power suppliers which carry the burden of supporting the government with taxes and which finance in the free market.

Southern Illinois G&T. A good example of the economic waste that can occur from a G&T loan is the case of a loan approved by REA for the Southern Illinois Power Cooperative. The loan was in the amount of $25,800,000 for a 99,000-kilowatt steam generating plant and a 2,000-kilowatt diesel plant near Marion, Illinois, and for 354 miles of transmission lines.[66]

The co-ops that would buy the output of this plant had been buying all their power from two electric companies, Central Illinois Public Service Company and Illinois Power Company, under a contract at an average cost of from 8.1 mills to 8.5 mills per kilowatt-hour. (The price under the contract is slated to rise to between 8.5 mills and 9 mills per kilowatt-hour.)

In announcing the loan, REA said it would enable consumers to get power cheaper than under the contract rates offered by the power companies.[67] However, REA loans are made in secrecy. No one outside of REA is allowed to see the cost analyses upon which a loan is based. No one could question whether the cost of power from the G&T would be less than the cost of power from the companies.

People in the power companies made their own analysis of the costs. The G&T was given the benefit of all the lowest costs that could be attained with the type of equipment and kind of fuel available. Two percent was used as the cost of money, and the study excused the G&T from paying any Federal income taxes. Even on this basis, the analysis showed that the cost of power from the G&T would be 9.22 mills per kilowatt-hour, which was higher than the rate offered by the companies. *Adjustments for taxes and money costs.* Then two adjustments were made in the analysis. The first added in an amount for Federal income taxes now being paid by the power companies. After all, if the G&T is built, the Federal government will lose these taxes. With this adjustment the price of the G&T power became 12.77 mills a kilowatt-hour whereas the companies' wholesale rate would run some 8½ to 9 mills per kilowatt-hour.

A second adjustment reflected the actual cost to the government of borrowing money, not 2 percent. With this, the cost of the G&T power became 15.10 mills (Table 8·2).

Other special treatment. Co-ops are formed under state laws and are subject to state and local taxes as determined by the states' laws. Generally, however, co-ops are exempt from some state and local taxes and receive special treatment with respect to other such taxes. The net result is that cooperatives pay, on the average, a smaller share of their income in state and local taxes than do the power companies. It is clear why REA and some of the cooperatives want to keep their cost analyses secret.

The Southern Illinois G&T is not an isolated case. Analyses of other G&T loans have been made. As a rule, and without any adjustments at all, the retail cooperatives have to pay more for G&T power than for company power. With adjustments, the uneconomical nature of most G&Ts shows up clearly. A single plant or a small system is not economical, compared with the large interconnected systems and big units being used by the companies.

Table 8·2 Analysis of Power Costs for Southern Illinois Power Corporation

	Unadjusted	Adjusted for taxes	Adjusted for taxes and cost of money
Investment	$25,800,000	$25,800,000	$25,800,000
Production cost @ 3.3 mills	912,450	912,450	912,450
Trans. line operation & maint.*	115,000	115,000	115,000
Depreciation†	645,000	645,000	645,000
Taxes and insurance‡	361,200	1,341,600	1,341,600
Interest§	516,000	516,000	1,161,000
Total	$ 2,549,650	$ 3,530,050	$ 4,175,050
Kwhr delivered (000)¶	276,500	276,500	276,500
Mills per kwhr	9.22	12.77	15.10

*Trans. line operation & maint.— percent of trans. invest.	2.5%	2.5%	2.5%
†Depreciation— percent of total invest.	2.5%	2.5%	2.5%
‡Taxes and insurance— percent of total invest.	1.4%	5.2%	5.2%
§Interest— percent of total invest.	2.0%	2.0%	4.5%

¶Estimated deliveries in 1967, at 66,450 kw of demand and 47.5 percent annual load factor. Deliveries in excess of 66,000 kw would require additional investment for reserve.

There is no evidence that REA is willing to expose its economic analyses to public view. In fact, the REA has said that it "will treat . . . as administratively confidential . . . details of the economic and engineering feasibility and plans of the proposed project"—unless, of course, the Administrator feels he has to disclose them.[68]

The House Agriculture Committee, in its report on the

Food and Agriculture Act of 1962, expressed its disapproval of the secrecy which shrouds REA operations in these words:

Testimony revealed a growing public concern over the failure of the REA to disclose information on various phases of its operation. The public is entitled to know how public funds are being used, and the REA should approach the consideration of loans for generating facilities in a manner designed to provide as full public information as possible . . . Secrecy tends to kindle doubt, whereas public knowledge of the reasons for and justification of loans would go far toward dispelling criticism which threatens to bring the program into disrepute.[69]

The Senate Committee which considered the same Act said:

The Rural Electrification Administration should approach the consideration of such loans in a manner designed to provide as full public information as possible. Open and aboveboard consideration of loans, bringing together all pertinent facts in an objective manner, would preclude the possibility of charges that such loans were unjustified. Secrecy, on the other hand, might well tend to induce doubt that responsible action was taken. Public knowledge of the reasons for and the justification of loans might well go far in mitigating unjust criticism.[70]

An analysis of twenty-eight G&Ts. A study of the operations of twenty-eight REA-financed cooperatives indicates that their average wholesale rate for power is 8.8 mills per kilowatt-hour—which is 1.1 mills per kilowatt-hour higher than the average wholesale rate to all cooperatives of the investor-owned electric light and power companies (Table 8·3). When adjustments were made to reflect taxes now being paid by investor-owned power companies and the cost of money in the free market comparable to that paid by investor-owned com-

Table 8·3 REA Power-Type Borrowers
Revenue per kwhr Sold for Year Ended Dec. 31, 1964

	Revenue from sale of electric energy, dollars	kwhr sold, 000	Revenue per kwhr sold, mills
Arkansas Electric Cooperative, Corp.	2,029,815	442,604	4.6
Western Farmers Electric Cooperative	4,747,819	723,072	6.6
Arizona Electric Power Cooperative	1,830,656	246,223	7.4
East Kentucky Rural Electric Cooperative	5,777,559	773,584	7.5
East River Electric Power Cooperative, Inc.	3,257,276	430,891	7.6
Central Power Electric Cooperative, Inc.	2,295,005	296,356	7.7
L. & O. Power Cooperative	460,842	58,400	7.9
Associated Electric Cooperatives, Inc.	15,737,563	1,916,374*	8.2
(Kamo Electric Cooperative, Inc., Sho-Me Power Corp., M. & A. Electric Power Coop., Northeast Missouri Electric Power Coop., Central Electric Power Coop., N.W. Electric Power Coop., Inc.)			
Alabama Electric Cooperative, Inc.	3,135,120	375,921	8.3
South Texas Electric Cooperative	1,433,970	170,749	8.4
Northwest Iowa Power Cooperative	1,697,476	201,716	8.4
Brazos Electric Power Cooperative, Inc.	5,504,275	617,207	8.9
Plains Electric G&T Cooperative, Inc.	2,690,276	293,549	9.2
Southern Illinois Power Cooperative	1,758,725	191,646	9.2
Minnkota Power Cooperative, Inc.	4,141,352	440,986	9.4
Dairyland Power Cooperative	11,940,389	1,226,197	9.7
Corn Belt Power Cooperative	4,205,435	334,370	12.6
Wolverine Electric Cooperative, Inc.	1,950,484	150,001	13.0
S.W. Federated Power Cooperative, Inc.	1,514,652	115,164	13.2
Rural Cooperative Power Association	4,452,210	324,928	13.7
Northern Michigan Electric Cooperative, Inc.	1,795,390	117,602	15.3
Western Illinois Power Cooperative, Inc.	800,450	44,206	18.1
Total	$83,156,739	9,491,746	8.8

*Includes sales of 122,011,000 kwhr from distribution of Sho-Me Power Corp. system.

panies, the cost of G&T power became 12.8 mills per kilowatt-hour (Table 8·4).

That is, if these twenty-eight cooperatives paid the cost of money and taxes on the same basis as investor-owned companies, they would need to raise their revenues—and therefore their rates—more than 45 percent.

On the average, the cost of power purchased from the

Table 8·4 REA Power-Type Borrowers—Operating Revenue Deficiency*

	Operating revenue deficiency	% increase in operating revenue required	Adjusted revenue from sale of electric energy	Kwhr sold, 000	Revenue per kwhr, mills
L & O Power Cooperative	$ 67,576	14.7	$ 528,418	58,400	9.0
Western Illinois Power Coop., Inc.	282,967	35.4	1,083,417	44,206	24.5
Arkansas Electric Coop., Corp.	502,152	24.7	2,551,967	442,604	5.7
Central Power Electric Coop., Inc.	575,134	25.0	2,870,199	296,356	9.7
Northwest Iowa Power Cooperative	610,519	34.0	2,307,995	201,716	11.4
South Texas Electric Cooperative	1,028,473	71.7	2,462,443	170,749	14.4
Northern Michigan Electric Coop., Inc.	602,554	33.6	2,397,944	117,602	20.4
S W Federated Power Coop., Inc.	561,094	36.6	2,075,746	115,164	18.0
East River Power Cooperative, Inc.	583,093	17.2	3,840,569	430,891	8.9
Wolverine Electric Coop., Inc.	938,878	47.8	2,889,362	150,001	19.3
Plains Electric G&T Coop., Inc.	1,068,209	39.6	3,758,485	293,549	12.8
Arizona Electric Power Coop.	1,556,527	85.0	3,387,183	246,223	13.8
Alabama Electric Cooperative, Inc.	1,394,860	44.5	4,529,980	375,921	12.1
Minnkota Power Cooperative, Inc.	1,237,206	28.3	5,378,558	440,986	12.2
Rural Cooperative Power Assoc.	932,321	20.4	5,384,531	324,928	16.6
Southern Illinois Power Coop.	2,449,912	139.2	4,208,637	191,646	22.0
Brazos Electric Power Coop., Inc.	1,327,060	23.5	6,831,335	617,207	11.1
Corn Belt Power Cooperative	2,088,983	47.0	6,289,418	334,370	18.8
Western Farmers Electric Coop.	2,815,927	48.5	7,361,746	723,072	10.5
East Kentucky Rural Electric Coop., Corp.	3,643,180	62.3	9,420,739	773,584	12.2
Dairyland Power Cooperative	4,779,935	40.0	16,720,324	1,226,197	13.6
Associated Electric Coop., Inc.†	8,960,602	56.8	24,698,165	1,916,374‡	12.9
Total	$38,000,162	44.5	$121,156,901	9,491,746	12.8

*Operating results: the cooperatives had to obtain their funds in the free market at costs comparable to those paid by investor-owned electric utility companies and had to pay taxes comparable to those paid by the investor-owned companies.

†Includes Kamo Electric Coop., Inc., Sho-Me Power Corp., M. & A. Electric Power Coop., Northeast Missouri Electric Power Coop., Central Electric Power Coop., and N.W. Electric Power Coop., Inc.

‡Includes sales of 122,011,000 kwhr from distribution of Sho-Me Power Corp. system.

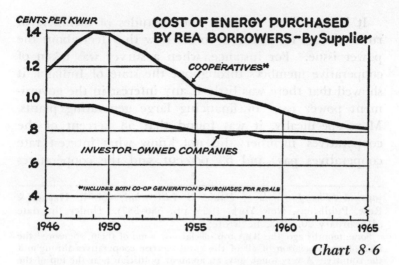

CENTS PER KWHR

COST OF ENERGY PURCHASED BY REA BORROWERS –By Supplier

14
1.2
1.0
.8
.6
.4

COOPERATIVES*

INVESTOR-OWNED COMPANIES

*INCLUDES BOTH CO-OP GENERATION & PURCHASES FOR RESALE

1946   1950   1955   1960   1965

Chart 8·6

generating plants financed by the REA has been more than 30 percent higher than the cost of power purchased from investor-owned companies (Chart 8·6).

What should be done?

During the past 30 years a great deal of progress has been made in developing rural areas. The rural electric cooperatives, the investor-owned power companies, and many others can share in the credit for bringing electric service to the farms of the nation. The problem is to maintain the progress that has been made and to keep the rural electrification movement from becoming embroiled in needless controversy.*

* One aspect of the change that has taken place in REA activities from the time of its founding to the present time has resulted from the formation in 1943 of the National Rural Electric Cooperative Association. This aggressive organization headed by former congressman Clyde Ellis has been a strong influence on the development of rural electric cooperatives in this country. An interesting view of the formation of this organization is given by Lilienthal in his

It is interesting to study the attitudes of members of rural electric cooperatives to see how they feel about the power issue. For instance, when a survey was taken of cooperative members throughout the state of Indiana, it showed that there was little if any interest in the government power issue or financing large generating plants. More specifically, it was found that 58 percent of the cooperatives' members did not know what interest rate cooperatives pay, and 63 percent said the cooperatives

---

journal (*The Journals of David E. Lilienthal*, vol. I., Harper & Row, Publishers, New York, 1964, pp. 586–587). Under the date of February 20, 1943, he wrote:

Some months ago, the REA top officials, or some of them, sponsored the idea of an association of all of the rural electric cooperatives throughout the country. A very tough guy, an amateur politician near the top of the organization, was the man who pushed it the most. His theory was very clear. If the farmers interested in rural electrification and members of these cooperatives, securing funds from REA, were organized into a national association, they could "put the heat on" members of Congress whenever the matter of rural electrification came up. Such an association was formed. The trustees were more or less handpicked by the REA's amateur politicos. Since the purpose was political, the trustees were men from the various cooperatives who had political background or ambition.

We were considerably disturbed by the way this national association was getting started, and by some of the *sub rosa* statements that were being made as to its purpose. On the surface the purpose was a perfectly appropriate one, for the exchange of information, the publication of a house journal, and matters of that kind. A few weeks ago the association held its first annual meeting in St. Louis. The speakers included prominent members of the Senate and the House interested in rural electrification. There was such a large and enthusiastic gathering that I rather assumed that my fears about the association had been falsely grounded.

Last week I had a long talk at breakfast with Harry Slattery, Administrator of REA. He was very frank to say that things had started off on a bad foot and that he was very much concerned as to what would happen to REA as the result of the formation of this association and the way it was already functioning. My guess is that he is finding that this politically inspired organization has already become a Frankenstein and is going to become increasingly important in the actual administration of the loans and policies of the REA, to say nothing of its personnel. He seemed to be surprised, although why, I am sure I don't know, that these trustees, selected because they were politicos, are now running true to form and want to use the REA for political purposes.

should be paying the same rate of interest the government pays for borrowed money. The survey also showed that 73 percent of the cooperatives' members did not know they were not paying the same taxes as investor-owned power companies.

There is a revolution taking place in the farming industry in this country, but it is not one which has anything to do with financing or ownership of power facilities. It is a revolution in the way of getting farm work done, as more and more jobs are being done with the help of electric energy. Both the investor-owned power companies and the rural electric cooperatives face a big challenge in the years ahead. With each group now providing electricity to about half the farms of the nation, the best interests of the American people will be served if all power suppliers can work together in harmony to increase the utilization of electricity.

To do this, the electric companies should continue to give adequate service to the cooperatives, at as low a price as possible, and plan to have plenty of power to meet the needs of the future. They should work with the cooperatives' members to make the best use of electric energy on the farm by continuing their research into new ways of mechanizing farm operations.

At the same time, the Federal government should re-examine the REA program to make sure it does not become involved in unnecessary and wasteful activities. Clear-cut criteria should be established for making REA loans in cases where they are needed, and public hearings should be held to make sure that all the facts are brought out. In the analysis of the economic feasibility of every generating and transmission cooperative applying for REA funds, the real cost of money should be used, whether or not a 2 percent interest rate is applied when the loan is made. Further, each analysis should adjust for taxes foregone or lost by using a government-financed power plant rather than an investor-owned plant. These simple procedures will enable the REA administrator to judge more accurately whether a loan is needed.

At the present time, requirements for extending and strengthening distribution systems of REA borrowers have leveled off at about $150 million per year and Congress has consistently provided appropriations in excess of this amount. As an increasing percentage of REA loans has been made to finance unnecessary generating and transmission facilities, committees of Congress registered concern and set down certain restrictions to keep REA loan activities in line with the purpose for which REA was founded. In 1966, the National Rural Electric Cooperative Association (NRECA) presented a plan for a Federal bank for rural electric cooperatives which apparently was an effort to free REA from congressional controls and to expand its lending power for generation and transmission facilities. Such a bank is completely unnecessary. Moreover, as Dr. Nelson Lee Smith, former Chairman of the Federal Power Commission, testified in hearings before the House Agriculture Committee on the proposal, ". . . it would also be without economic point, purpose or justification." [71]

Dr. Smith also stated that if the proposal for a Federal bank for rural electric cooperatives were to be enacted,

. . . the (REA) program developed to assist in the distribution of electricity to rural areas would be turned into a device whereby large integrated electric systems, sheltered from Federal taxation and supported by the use of Federal credit at or below its cost to the Government, and with no assurance of repayment, would be enabled to compete for customers and loads with investor-owned companies which must pay their full share of taxes, market rates for their borrowings, and returns to their stockholders.[72]

It seems only fair that REA borrowers should be subject to the same obligations as their neighboring electric utilities. However, co-ops and companies alike should keep in mind that the over-all effort in farm electrification today ought to be toward developing and promoting the greater use of electricity. Cooperatives and companies can work together toward this end. In so doing, they will be strengthening their common interest and minimizing their differences—and the American people will gain as a result.

REFERENCES

1. U.S. Bureau of the Census, *Central Electric Light & Power Stations, 1902,* p. 123.
2. C. M. Coleman, *PG&E of California,* McGraw-Hill Book Company, New York, 1952.
3. *Ibid.,* pp. 203–204.
4. *Ibid.,* p. 204.
5. H. Russell, "Electricity on the Farm and the Influence of Irrigation from a Central Station Viewpoint," *NELA Proceedings,* Vol. II, 1910, p. 201.
6. *Ibid.,* pp. 196, 203–204.
7. *Ibid.,* pp. 203–204.
8. *Ibid.,* p. 204; *NELA Proceedings,* 1911, Vol. I, pp. 448 ff.
9. *NELA Proceedings,* 1911, Vol. I, pp. 485, 520.
10. *Ibid.,* p. 524.
11. Coleman, *op. cit.,* p. 206.
12. *NELA Proceedings,* 1912, Vol. II, p. 266; *NELA Proceedings,* 1913, Vol. I, pp. 105–106.
13. *Ibid.,* pp. 266–269.
14. See, for example, *Electrical World,* 1911, pp. 1105, 1139.
15. Samuel Insull, *Central Station Electric Service,* Chicago, 1915, p. 358.
16. *Ibid.,* pp. 358–360.
17. U.S. Bureau of the *Census, CELPS, 1912,* pp. 154–156.
18. EEI, *Statistical Yearbook of the Electric Utility Industry, 1958,* Table 57, p. 65.
19. Forrest McDonald, *Let There Be Light,* The American History Research Center, Madison, Wisc., 1957, pp. 285–287.
20. *NELA Proceedings,* 1921, Vol. II, p. 851.

21. *Ibid.*, pp. 851, 852.
22. *NELA Proceedings*, 1922, Vol. I, pp. 104, 111. In 1924, the name of the committee was changed to "Rural Electric Service Committee."
23. *NELA Proceedings*, 1923, p. 204; *NELA Proceedings*, 1922, Vol. II, pp. 1279–1280.
24. *Ibid.*, p. 45.
25. *Ibid.*, 1925, p. 204.
26. NELA, *Progress in Rural and Farm Electrification*, New York, 1932, p. 5.
27. *Ibid.*
28. *Ibid.*, pp. 1, 11.
29. *NELA Proceedings*, 1927, p. 84.
30. *Ibid.*
31. Grover Neff, "President's Address," NELA, Great Lakes Division, 1929.
32. *EEI Statistical Bulletin*, 1952, pp. 51, 54.
33. *Ibid.*
34. U.S. Bureau of the Census, *Historical Statistics of the U.S., Colonial Times to 1957*, Washington, D.C., 1960, p. 283.
35. *Ibid.*, pp. 278, 283.
36. Memorandum from W. W. Freeman, Chairman, to members of the National Committee on Rural Electrification. Wisconsin Power & Light Co. farm file.
37. *Report of the National Committee on Rural Electrification.*
38. W. W. Freeman to Grover Neff, May 27, 1935; Freeman memorandum, Oct. 9, 1935, in Wisconsin Power & Light Co. farm file.
39. National Committee on Rural Electrification to Morris L. Cooke, July 24, 1935, copy of letter in EEI files.
40. *Ibid.*, p. 2.
41. *Ibid.*, p. 5.
42. *Ibid.*, pp. 1, 6.
43. Morris L. Cooke to W. W. Freeman, July 31, 1935; *REA Release No. 20*, July 22, 1935; *REA Release No. 21*, July 31, 1935.
44. Circular letter, Edwin Vennard to executives of the Middle West Utilities Co., Aug. 17, 1935; "Wisconsin Power & Light Application for Power Loans," both in Wisconsin Power & Light Co. farm file.
45. Morris L. Cooke to Grover Neff, Nov. 5, 1935; in EEI file. Neff to Cooke, Nov. 11, 1935; in EEI file.
46. *Congressional Record*, 74th Cong., 2d Sess., Feb. 25, 1936, p. 2751.
47. *Congressional Record*, 74th Cong., 2d Sess., Apr. 9, 1936, p. 5283.

48. *Hearings before the Committee on Interstate and Foreign Commerce, House of Representatives, on S. 3483,* 74th Cong., 2d Sess., March, 1936, p. 51.
49. Morris L. Cooke to Grover Neff, Nov. 5, 1935.
50. *EEI Statistical Bulletin,* 1952, p. 54.
51. Rural Electrification Act of 1936, Sec. 4 & 13, Public Law 605, 74th Cong., May 20, 1936.
52. *Congressional Record,* 74th Cong., 2d Sess., Apr. 9, 1936, p. 5283.
53. *Ibid.,* Feb. 25, 1936, p. 2752.
54. *Ibid.,* Feb. 26, 1936, p. 2901.
55. EEI, *Electric Utility Industry Statistics in the United States for the Year 1958* (latest accurate data available).
56. *REA Bulletin* 1-1, *1965 Annual Statistical Report,* Table 3, p. 7.
57. *Report of the Administrator, Rural Electrification Administration,* 1965, Table 2, p. 27.
58. *Annual Report of REA Administrator,* 1965, p. 6.
59. *REA Bulletin,* 20-6, Jan. 30, 1957.
60. *REA Bulletin,* 20-6, May 31, 1961.
61. EEI, *REA Items,* April, 1966, p. 10.
62. Rural Electrification Act of 1936, Sec. 5, Public Law 605, 74th Cong., May 20, 1936.
63. The *Wall St. Journal,* Apr. 6, 1962.
64. *Hearings before the Committee on Agriculture, House of Representatives, on H.R. 10010, Food and Agriculture Act of 1962,* 87th Cong., 2d Sess., Serial AA, Part 2, p. 328.
65. *Report of the House Agriculture Committee on H.R. 11222, Food and Agriculture Act of 1962,* House Report 1691, (87-2), May 16, 1962, p. 72.
66. U.S. Department of Agriculture Loan Announcement 1205, Mar. 1, 1960.
67. *Ibid.,* p. 2.
68. *REA Bulletin,* 20-12, Apr. 5, 1962.
69. *Report of House Agriculture Committee on H.R. 11222, Food and Agriculture Act of 1962,* House Report 1691, (87-2), May 16, 1962, pp. 71-72.
70. *Report (1365) of Senate Committee on Agriculture and Forestry on S.R. 1365, Food and Agriculture Act of 1962,* 87th Cong., 2d Sess., Apr. 27, 1962, p. 24.
71. Nelson Lee Smith, *Hearings of the House of Representatives Committee on Agriculture on H.R. 14000, H.R. 14837,* June 2, 1966.
72. *Ibid.*

Chapter 9

Cost of money and taxes

One difference between investor-owned electric companies and companies in other businesses is that utilities operate in a fishbowl, under the close scrutiny of regulatory bodies. State commissions or local authorities exercise control over their rate schedules and, in many instances, over construction of their facilities. Regulatory agencies supervise their accounts and records, their rules and regulations. Furthermore, the companies are analyzed continually by security analysts and institutional investors. Inefficiently operated companies would soon lose favor among them.

The rates charged by government-owned power suppliers, on the other hand, are rarely regulated. Having the benefit of low-cost government funds, government-financed agencies do not pay the market price of money, and they are excused from Federal income taxes as well. During the early 1930s, when Federal activity in the power business was being vigorously advocated, income taxes and property taxes were not a major cost of doing business. Today they are. The discrepancy in tax payments between government power and investor-owned power has grown as a result. In 1960, the electric companies, which had 74 percent of the industry investment, paid 97 percent of the industry's taxes. Government-financed power operations, on the other hand, which had 26 percent of the industry investment, paid only 3 percent of the taxes.

The difference in taxes

The effect of the difference in tax payments, particularly when added to the subsidy government power agencies receive in the cost of money, surprises many people. As has been noted earlier, in the electric power business it takes an investment of about $4.45 for each $1 of annual gross revenue. Because of this high investment ratio, taxes and the cost of capital take a large portion of gross revenue. Annual taxes on investor-owned companies are about 5 percent of the utility plant investment. The annual cost of money in the market is about 6 percent of the investment, the return people expect when they invest their money in the power business. Together, taxes and the cost of money take about 11 percent of the investment, and 11 percent of $4.45 is 49 cents. In other words, for an investor-owned company about half of each $1 of gross revenue is required to pay these two items of cost. A power supplier that is freed of the burden of paying the full cost of money and taxes thus is relieved of about half the cost of furnishing electric service.[1]

People sometimes ask why government power projects should pay taxes to government. "It is just government paying taxes to itself," they say. But government never pays taxes, people do. Through income taxes and through the taxes contained in the prices of things they buy, people bear the burden of government. When government power projects avoid taxes, it means their customers are not paying their fair share of the cost of government. The difference has to be made up by someone else.

Surveys of public opinion show that most people are completely unaware of the tax discrimination which exists in the electric power business. When they are informed about it, however, three out of four say the government agencies should pay the same taxes as the companies.[2]

There are many ways to compare the taxes of the governmental segment of the industry with those of the investor-owned segment. It may be done on the basis of customers served, revenues, kilowatt-hour generation, power-producing capacity, electric utility plant, and others. In 1963 the Edison Electric Institute made a study using the basis most closely related to tax payments: investment in electric utility plant.*

A random sample of twenty-five investor-owned companies showed that 81 percent of their taxes was related to investment. The breakdown was Federal income taxes, 53 percent; other income taxes, 3 percent; † property taxes, 25 percent. In addition, it was reasoned that investment or ownership represents the control of the factors of production. It is because of government investment in the electric utility industry that many tax

* In the study, ownership was defined as the original cost of plant and equipment in use or under construction. Ordinarily, a plant under construction is not subject to property taxes. However, because the plant under construction was not known for all government power operations, it was not excluded where it was known. The result was that a lower tax rate was applied in determining equivalent taxes for government power operations.

† Income taxes are based on taxable income, which is determined by investment.

problems arise. However, because revenues have often been used for comparison in the past, a companion study was also made on that basis.

Investment in the electric utility industry by sectors and subsectors as of June 30, 1960, is shown in Table 9·1.

Table 9·1 Investment in the Electric Utility Industry for the Year Ended June 30, 1960

Sector	Investment	
	Dollars, millions	Percent
Electric companies	44,110	74.3
Government operations:		
Non-Federal	6,200	10.5
Federal:		
Bureau of Reclamation	1,088	1.8
Tennessee Valley Authority	2,054	3.5
Columbia River Power System	1,607	2.7
Southeastern Power Administration	410	0.7
Southwestern Power Administration	230	0.4
REA borrowers	3,590	6.1
Total industry	$59,289	100.0%

Classified as to ownership by its two major sectors, the electric utility industry appears in Table 9·2.

Table 9·2 Investment in the Electric Utility Industry for the Year Ended June 30, 1960

Sector	Investment, millions
Electric companies	44,110, or 74.3%
Government and REA borrowers	15,179, or 25.7%
Total	$59,289, or 100.0%

In the study, taxes were analyzed for two periods. The first period was for the selected year 1960. Here, the results revealed that the Federal government and borrowers from the Rural Electrification Administration owned 15 percent of the electric utility industry's total investment but paid only 1 percent of the taxes. During the second period from 1937 to 1961, the taxes for the electric companies amounted to $28 billion. In contrast, the taxes of the Tennessee Valley Authority (TVA) for the same period amounted to only $73.5 million. If TVA had been taxed on the same basis as the electric companies, it would have paid taxes of $1,014.3 million.

The two major taxes paid by the electric companies are

Table 9·3   Taxes of Electric Companies for the
Year Ended June 30, 1960

	Dollars in millions
Electric utility plant	$44,110.0
Gross operating revenues*	9,910.0
Taxes:	
Federal income	1,254.7†
All other	1,016.1
Total taxes	$2,270.8
Tax ratios	
Investment basis:	
Federal income taxes	2.84%
All other taxes	2.30%
Total taxes	5.14%
Revenue basis:	
Federal income taxes	12.7%
All other taxes	10.3%
Total taxes	23.0%

* Including sales for resale such as sales to other electric companies.
† Including about $200 million of deferred taxes.

property taxes and income taxes. Property taxes are related to investment in plant and equipment. Income taxes are related to income earned on the investment in plant and equipment. Thus, both major taxes, property and income, are related to investment. Again, a great discrepancy exists between the tax rate of TVA and the tax rate of the electric companies.

Equivalent taxes for government power operations were determined by applying the tax ratios found for the electric companies to the electric utility plant or gross operating revenues of the government power operations for the selected year 1960. Table 9·3 shows these tax ratios for the electric companies expressed as percentages.

The tax deficiency for the government power opera-

Table 9·1 Taxes on Government Power for the Year Ended June 30, 1960, Plant Basis (in millions of dollars)

	Actual taxes*	Equivalent taxes	
		Federal income†	Total‡
Non-Federal	$42.4	$176	$319
Federal:			
Bureau of Reclamation	.6	31	56
Tennessee Valley Authority	7.1	58	106
Columbia River Power System	0	46	83
Southeastern Power Admin.	0	12	21
Southwestern Power Admin.	0	7	12
REA borrowers	20.2	102	185
Total	$70.3	$432	$782
Actual taxes	....	....	70
Tax deficiency	....	....	$712

* Including payments in lieu of taxes.
† 2.84% of electric utility plant.
‡ 5.14% of electric utility plant.

tions for the selected year 1960 was $712 million as computed on the plant basis (Table 9·4).

The tax deficiency can also be calculated on a revenue basis. On this basis the tax deficiency for the government sector for the selected year 1960 was $636 million. If the revenue from government operations had included an amount for cost of borrowed money equivalent to that paid by electric companies, this estimated tax deficiency of $636 million would have been much higher.*

* In the study, equivalent taxes represent the estimated taxes which would be paid if electric companies operated government investments. The equivalent taxes were calculated on both the electric utility plant basis and the gross operating revenues basis.

The plant basis refers to year-end electric utility plant. For the selected year 1960, electric company taxes for the year ended June 30, 1960, as a percent of plant at June 30, 1960, were used in determining the equivalent tax rates for government power operations. On the revenue basis, taxes as a percent of revenues for the year ended June 30, 1960, were employed.

Although the revenue basis is often used, the procedure is more complicated if properly applied because the revenues of the electric companies include a sufficient amount to pay all the operating expenses and all taxes but the revenues from government power operations do not. Therefore, in calculating equivalent taxes on the revenue basis it is first necessary to add to the government power revenues the equivalent taxes before applying the tax rate found for the electric companies. This requires the solution of simultaneous equations. For example, an electric company could be chosen with a tax rate of 25 cents per dollar of revenue. When this tax rate is applied to a government power operation which pays little or no taxes, 25 cents must be added to each dollar of revenue before the tax rate can be properly applied. Thus, a dollar of revenue from a tax-free government operation would have assigned to it equivalent taxes of 31¼ cents (1.25 times .25 = 31¼ cents instead of only 25 cents).

The equation for the determination of taxes for government power operations employing the revenue method is only applicable for *total* taxes. The equation for determining equivalent *Federal income* taxes is even more complicated, but equivalent total taxes having been calculated equivalent Federal income taxes can be determined by applying the ratio of Federal income taxes to total taxes.

Table 9·5 Taxes on Government Power for the Year Ended June 30, 1960, Revenue Basis (in millions of dollars)

	Gross operating revenues*	Equivalent taxes	
		Federal income†	Total‡
Non-Federal	$1,368.1	$219	$396
Federal:			
Bureau of Reclamation	56.7	9	17
Tennessee Valley Authority	240.7	39	70
Columbia River Power System	68.9	11	21
Southeastern Power Admin.	20.7	3	6
Southwestern Power Admin.	15.0	2	4
REA borrowers	663.8	106	192
Total	$2,433.9	$389	$706
Actual taxes	....	....	70
Tax deficiency	....	....	$636

* Gross operating revenues include sales for resale such as sales to other government power operations. For example, the Southwestern Power Administration receives about 97% of its revenues from sales for resale and about 3% from other sources, mostly government agencies. If sales for resale had been excluded in the revenue basis of determining equivalent taxes for government power operations, the Southwestern Power Administration would be assigned almost no equivalent tax.

† 12.7% of adjusted gross operating revenue.

‡ 23.0% of adjusted gross operating revenue.

The average tax rate of 5.14 percent for the plant basis means that the electric companies pay taxes on the average of $5.14 for each $100 of plant investment. Some companies pay more than average and others pay less, but the tax rates of the companies cluster about the average. There is a greater variation in tax rates on the revenue basis; when charted, it appears to be bimodal (having two peaks). Also, the range of tax rates of the companies is wider for the revenue basis than for the plant basis. The closer relationship between taxes and investment in the electric utility industry make the plant basis seem preferable.

The cost of money

The discrepancy between the taxes of investor-owned companies and government power suppliers is not difficult to understand. An appreciation of the importance of the subsidy capital and cost of money to the growth of government power in this country requires some introductory discussion.

The use of money has a price that can be measured, just as the price of any other commodity can be measured. In the United States, as in any market economy, this price may not be constant, but at a given time and for like employment it will be the same regardless of who employs it. When governments enter the marketplace it is possible for this basic economic fact to become obscured. The power of government can shift the normal currents of the market and cloud attempts to analyze values or compare alternative methods of using a society's investable funds. The result can be that capital is used inefficiently and long-lasting harm is done to the public interest.

The place of savings. Any society must have capital in order to grow. It is one of the essential elements of production, and it can be formed only by diverting the products of labor and natural resources away from consumption and toward investment, that is, by saving.

Ultimately, the source of all saving is the individual. Banks, business, and governments serve to facilitate the process. They provide the environments that allow, induce, compel, or discourage saving by individuals. While they may direct the use of capital, they cannot form it.

When savings are invested toward future production, either directly by individuals or through financial institutions, they become the basis for capital formation. But people can save only if they are able, if they have the will, and if they are permitted to produce more than they find essential to their well-being. In some societies this may mean a person can save anything over the minimum required to maintain life; in others, it may mean he must first attain an acceptable standard of living. In any case, his saving may be either forced or free. The pyramids of Egypt, being built by slave labor, were created by a kind of forced saving. In nations like the U.S.S.R., capital formation today is almost entirely a result of compulsory saving while in societies like the United States saving is relatively voluntary.

In a free society, people save for a variety of motives. Some save to have money for emergencies. Others save for security. Some save to improve their economic status and to enjoy luxuries they could not have without an accumulation from their current incomes. Others save for the satisfaction of building an estate. And a certain number save for the sheer pleasure of being in a position to traffic in money. The motives may be laudable or superficial, but, combined with the temperament of the saver, they largely govern the use to which savings are put and, consequently determine the reward demanded.

Whether an investor acts for himself or as a manager of funds accumulated in a financial institution, he seeks out those opportunities that seem most suitable to his situation. In one degree or another he balances liquidity, safety of principal, annual return, and opportunity for growth. The breadth of the market brings together investors having different requirements and would-be employers of capital of varying kinds and characteristics, to the end that the available funds are matched with the available investment opportunities.

The market cost of money. To compete successfully,

an employer of capital must satisfy the requirements of the market.

In general, each employer of capital competes in a particular segment of the capital market for a given supply of funds, although there can be some ebb and flow between market segments. Mortage-loan requirements for new housing, for example, compete with real estate development and in varying degrees with corporate requirements for new plant and equipment. When the Federal Treasury or a municipality seeks to obtain funds in the market, it meets competition for the type of funds it is seeking and, at the same time, provides competition to others.

The market cost of money is determined by the demand for each particular kind and character of capital employment in relation to its supply. It is difficult to evaluate this cost in over-all terms, for investors impute different values to the different characteristics of investment opportunities. As a result, the monetary rewards they demand for investable funds vary. However, the diversity in the needs and temperaments of millions of people having funds to invest provides a balance among the funds available to the market, and the relative market cost of money for the predominant employments of capital funds can be measured by several widely accepted indices. The prime interest rate of commercial banks, real-estate mortgage-loan rates, the average rate of return of bellwether stocks, the average market yields of government and corporate bonds outstanding, and yields of new government and corporate issues all indicate the cost of new money to an employer of capital.

Investable funds are fluid. They can move into or out of an enterprise, depending on its ability to demonstrate productivity and to yield a satisfactory return that is commensurate with the risks involved. It is this movement of funds that determines the allocation of resources in any nation. Directed by the guiding hand of productivity, the result is the most efficient possible resource allocation. When funds are directed by artificial means, without regard for relative productivity, the economy stands to suffer from the ensuing inefficient allocation of its resources.

Government finance. To provide security of person and home, members of an organized society are usually willing to levy taxes on themselves. These taxes form the basic source of revenue to a government and are the basis for its credit.

Most governments have been given the right to borrow money when tax revenues fail to meet requirements. So long as the nation is solvent its government can, by a capital levy if necessary, assure that its obligations will be paid at maturity. Consequently, obligations of governments are usually sold at yields well below those of nongovernmental entities of like character and maturities.

When a government borrows from its own constituents, away from the banking system, the impact on the national economy is the same as if the government had been able to tap the same source of funds through taxation. Under these circumstances, government borrowing is no more nor less than another method of taxation, the interest cost being simply that which is required to direct the flow of funds. However, when a government borrows through the banking system it increases the supply of money and exposes the currency to an erosion in values which then, in effect, becomes a capital levy.

In general, interest rates are the price that is required to bring forth investable funds in amounts sufficient to satisfy requirements. This is not necessarily true for government. For example, for a number of years interest rates in the United States were held to an artificially low level by the simple device of the Federal Reserve System purchasing government bonds in the market at par. Refinancings took the form of short-term paper which was sold to banks. The operations monetized the Federal debt, producing the same result as if the government had printed money. In other words, through manipulation of the supply of money, the government controlled interest rates. The average cost to the Federal government or to the American people of borrowed money was not reflected by the coupon rate at which outstanding government bonds were sold. The return offered was not indicative of that which was necessary to induce people to save. These funds were not obtained from savings. They were manufactured by government fiat, and in effect eroded savings.

When the Federal Reserve System removed its support of the government bond market, interest rates sought their own level as determined by supply and demand in the free market. U. S. Treasury bonds, which had been supported at around 2½ percent, dropped in value and currently yield above 4 percent—still below the cost of money to corporations because of the element of sovereignty in government.

In this country, income and savings are channeled into the Federal Treasury by compulsion—that is, through taxes—or by a desire for maximum security. But a case could be made that, in the last analysis, all funds acquired by the Federal government are compulsory savings. If the government requires funds and its tax revenues are not sufficient, it borrows. When it borrows it can, by use of the banking system, create the necessary funds to assure the success of its bond issue. The entire operation becomes so interwoven with the over-all management of the money supply that the coupon rates on the government bonds lose their significance. They no longer show the cost to the economy of funds appropriated by the government.

Cost/benefit ratios. The difficulty is compounded, and becomes a matter of more than academic concern, when the Federal government invests a part of its funds in proprietary enterprises—functions that are ordinarily performed by individuals or groups of individuals, such as corporations, and that provide commodities or services that are characteristically commercial rather than social. The benefits of these functions are measurable in terms of the gains and comforts they bring to the individual, and may be performed so that the individual rather than the community pays the cost of benefits received.

Governments throughout history have performed proprietary functions in varying degrees, depending on their political and economic philosophies. In the U.S.S.R., the government performs almost all proprietary functions. In the United States with its tradition of free enterprise, the economic endeavors of the community have been left largely to individuals, acting alone or in voluntary association.

In a totalitarian state, such as the U.S.S.R., where the government is the sole employer of capital, return on capital usually has been ignored. The state creates capital through enforced savings, merely by not rewarding its constituents in accordance with their productivity. The individual has no choice. The state retains what he might have saved by consuming less than he produces. In recent years, however, Soviet economists have come to realize that in order to allocate their nation's resources efficiently, the so-called interest factor must be recognized.

In the United States, where the Federal government has

been increasingly going into proprietary enterprises, the relationship of interest cost to potential economic benefits is acquiring even greater importance.

A statement on the subject by the executive branch of the Federal government, titled *Policies, Standards, and Procedures in the Formulation, Evaluation and Review of Plans for Use and Development of Water and Related Land Resources,* provides that in formulating plans Federal agencies should use interest rates "based upon the average rate of interest payable by the Treasury on interest-bearing marketable securities of the United States outstanding at the end of the fiscal year preceding such computation, *which, upon original issue, had terms to maturity of 15 years or more.** [italics added]".[3] Use of this formula gives such weight to securities issued prior to 1952 that the over-all rate is less than 3 percent. In a recent feasibility study prepared by the Southwestern Power Administration, an interest rate of 2⅝ percent was used. The Department of the Interior used an interest rate of 2⅞ percent in its report to the President on the Passamaquoddy Project.[4] Even assuming that 2⅞ percent were a free-market appraisal of the cost to the U.S. government of borrowed funds under the formula, it would represent an historical cost of money and not the cost of new money. But, of course, 2⅞ is far below the market cost of money, even to the government itself.

The Rural Electrification Administration, of course, loans funds at an interest rate of 2 percent. This is an arbitrarily set rate, apparently not intended to have any relation to the true cost of money.

Allocation of resources. The relative merits of capital expenditures should be determined by the true economic costs of comparable alternatives. Only in this way can the most economical allocation of the nation's resources be achieved. Neither the historical nor the current yields on government bonds provide the proper criterion for sound judgments.

The economic costs of any undertaking, assuming equal quality of management and equal efficiencies of operation, are the same regardless of the type of organization performing the function. For instance, as an economic enterprise an electricity undertaking should provide the same investment opportunity regardless of the type of ownership. The knowledge of converting energy is in the public domain. The technology and operating practices of the industry are available to anyone. Engineers, accountants, and other personnel of comparable ability may be employed both by investor-owned companies and by government-financed power agencies. It takes the same type of equipment, costing the same amount of money, to generate a kilowatt-hour whether the machinery is operated by a corporation or by a government agency. The market is the same and there is no difference in the risk in the market.

Given a free money market—a market which is not compelled nor induced by the prerogatives of a sovereign power—the cost of money for the electric utility business has been demonstrated to be on the order of 6 to 7 percent, after full account has been taken of provisions for either continuing the enterprise by renewals, or by amortization of the investment, and for taxes necessary to provide such earnings. This is the return, free from the support of any credit other than that of the enterprise itself, which investors demand for funds employed in the electric utility business.

This was demonstrated when, in 1960, the Tennessee Valley Authority sold $50 million of bonds in the free market. Although some $1.2 billion of taxpayers' funds had been invested in TVA over the years, when the American people had a free choice they demanded a return of 4.4 percent—despite the fact that the entire obligation to the Federal Treasury was subordinated to the debt service of the bonds sold to the public.[5] At the time these bonds were marketed, triple-A bonds offered by investor-owned electric utility companies were selling to yield about 4½ percent, or for about the same cost the market demanded for TVA's bonds.[6]

TVA has authority to issue $750 million in bonds.[7] Assuming the entire $750 million were issued, TVA would have an "equity" cushion of $1.2 billion of appropriated investment behind these bonds, or a debt ratio of 38 percent. In addition, it still has access to the Federal Treasury. But the market evaluated the cost of money to TVA to be about the same as that of a top-grade electric utility company bond. Were TVA required to pay the free market rate for its equity funds (The subordinated appropriation investment of the Federal government), the over-all cost of money would be in the range of 6 percent, or no different from that of the electric companies.

Sound criteria. As the Federal government enters deeper into the nation's economic activities, the need for sound criteria for judging the economic feasibility of proposed government projects is brought into sharper focus. The appropriate interest rate for discounting future values is of major importance among these criteria.

But no matter what type of ownership is involved, it would seem reasonable that any criteria for determining the economic feasibility of an undertaking should include the free-market cost of money demanded by investors for such an undertaking. These criteria, of course, would include not only the after-tax return, but also the taxes required to be paid to earn such a return and provisions for the amortization of the investment in accordance with the established practice of the market.

Given sound criteria, people might still elect to have some form of government provide them with electric service. But with sound criteria they could base their choice on judgment rather than emotion, and their judgment would be based on facts rather than misunderstandings.*

* I am particularly indebted to John Thornborrow of the Edison Electric Institute for the analysis, data, and much of the language in the foregoing discussion of the cost of money.

REFERENCES

1. EEI, *Let's Look at Government in the Power Business,* 1966.
2. Opinion Research Corporation, 1967.
3. "Policies, Standards and Procedures in the Formulation, Evaluation and Review of Plans for Use and Development of Water and Related Land Resources," letter to the President from the Secretaries of Agriculture, Army, Interior, and Health, Education and Welfare, May 15, 1962, p. 28.
4. *The International Passamaquoddy Tidal Power Project and Upper St. John River Hydroelectric Power Development,* report to President John F. Kennedy from Secretary of the Interior Stewart L. Udall, July 1, 1963, p. 40.
5. Tennessee Valley Authority, *TVA Annual Report,* 1961, p. A9.
6. *Moody's Public Utility Manual,* 1961, p. A5.
7. *Tennessee Valley Authority Act of 1933,* as amended by Public Law 86–137, Aug. 6, 1959, Sec. 15d, p. 306.

Chapter 10

A change in attitude

Efforts continue to increase the REA-financed generating plants and transmission lines, to build electric transmission systems, under the Department of Interior, and to expand other government power activities, but the force of public opinion is no longer behind them. Advocates of government power remain vigorous and active, but government power is no longer growing at the rapid rate it once knew. What has happened to bring about this change? Why is the public attitude different from what it was in the 1930s and 1940s when government power was growing very rapidly?

All modern and progressive business enterprises endeavor to secure and to hold the good will of their customers. This is especially true in the public utility business. Customers of a utility company cannot shop around for electric service as they can for groceries or clothing, for example. The utility is a permanent part of the community, with government acting as the regulator.

Factors affecting attitude of the public

In any business enterprise there are three primary factors that affect the attitude of the customers and the public.

1. *Quality of service and price.* The product or the service should be good and the price should be fair.

2. *Performance.* The business functions of the enterprise should be performed in a fashion that is pleasant and not irritating to the customers.

3. *Public understanding.* The customers and the public should have an understanding of the company's business affairs. Lack of knowledge is a factor contributing to ill will.

All three of these factors have a bearing on the question of whether a customer would prefer to obtain electric service from an investor-owned company or from a government power enterprise. Each of the factors has had a bearing on public attitude over the past 25 years, with the result that now most people prefer to have electric service rendered by investor-owned companies. A brief examination of each of the three factors will illustrate why this is so.

Quality of service and price. Most people agree that the quality of electric service has been excellent. For the average customer, reliability of service runs above 99.98 percent. People have witnessed the fact that all demands for electricity have been met in times of war and peace. When they want more electricity it is always there.

People have witnessed the gradual evolution to larger and larger generating units interconnected with heavier and heavier transmission lines at higher and higher voltages. The large units of 500,000 to over 1,000,000 kilowatts now being installed appeal to the imagination. People realize the economy of scale these machines provide and that many power plants serving the smaller municipal systems are not nearly so large or efficient as those of the power companies. People have become more conscious of this difference. They realize that small individual municipal power systems cannot afford to install the very large power plants that are now being installed by the interconnected power systems. More and more municipal systems are shutting down their small power plants in favor of purchasing energy from the large interconnected systems.

The rapid development of atomic power also has been a contributing factor to public understanding of the industry's performance record. Until 1954 nuclear knowledge was devoted almost exclusively to manufacture of a bomb. Within 10 or 12 years the power industry and others, through very extensive research efforts, learned to control the fission reaction and to utilize the heat to produce electricity. People are conscious that power companies are now installing atomic power plants in order to bring about further economies.

The public generally has associated hydroelectric power with government power although, as has been pointed out earlier, power companies also operate hydroelectric power plants. The public has also associated hydroelectric power with cheap power although modern steam turbines with conventional fuels are able to produce electricity more cheaply than most of the later hydroelectric power installations. But now atomic power is coming, and in the public mind that also is associated with cheap power. Actually the rapid growth of atomic power is making most new hydroelectric installations obsolete, especially where the atomic power plant is used in conjunction with pumped storage plants. All these elements have helped associate the idea of low-cost power with investor-owned companies.

People have witnessed the lowering of the average price of electricity while practically all other commodities are rising in price because of inflation. The performance of the investor-owned companies in giving good service at a fair price has been a primary factor affecting public attitude and in assuring satisfied customers.

Performance. While it is essential for a business enterprise to furnish good service at a fair price, this is not enough. If the enterprise is to build and to hold the good will of the customers it must do more. There are myriads of contacts between a power company and its customers. Messages in advertisements, releases, letters, bills, and contracts have an effect on customer attitudes. There is person-to-person contact with meter readers, billing clerks, servicemen, telephone operators, linemen, and the management. It is not possible to name them all, but all are equally important.

With this in mind, power companies regularly check the way they carry out their activities. Are all employees who come face to face with customers trained in courtesy? Are the meter readers neatly dressed? Are the company's cars and trucks maintained in a neat fashion? Are the drivers trained in safety and courtesy? Are all the messages from company to customer examined carefully for accuracy and courtesy? Is the tree-trimming policy reasonable? Is fair treatment given in attaining rights-of-way? Is it possible for a customer with a complaint to meet privately with the complaint clerk? Are complaints promptly followed and satisfied? Is the customer given all possible and reasonable opportunity to pay his bill before service is cut off? Are delinquent notices and cut-off notices courteously worded? Has the company trained experts to assist their large industrial, commercial, and other customers in the best use of their equipment? Are customers assisted in getting proper and prompt repairs of equipment? Does the company maintain good relations with manufacturers, dealers, distributors, and contractors?

Is appropriate consideration given to the effect of the company's product and service on the environment? Does the company play its proper role in civic affairs? Does it help bring industry to the community? Does it help develop the area? Does it play its proper role in support of local charitable and welfare and educational institutions? Does it help solve the local public problems? Does the company treat employees fairly in wages and in fringe benefits? Does it keep them informed so that they like to work for the company and so express these views to their friends?

Modern public relations involves constant examination of all the functions of the company to be sure proper consideration is given to public attitude.

Public understanding. It would seem logical to assume that if a company produces a good, product, or service and sells it at a fair price and performs in a way so as to encourage good will, that should be sufficient to create a good attitude in the public mind. Unfortunately, logic does not always prevail where people are concerned.

The fact is that if people are not properly informed, their attitude may be bad even though service is good and performance excellent. For example, the price of the service may be low, but if people think it is high then it may as well be high as far as the effect on their attitude is concerned. The price must be low and the people must understand that it is low. Performance must be good and people must understand that it is good. People must understand that efforts are being made to better the service and to keep the price low. This knowledge breeds understanding and understanding breeds good will.

One good way to find out what people's attitudes are is to visit with them, but it is expensive to visit all of a company's customers. Moreover, a visit by a company representative does not always result in fully accurate answers. Sometimes people tend to hold back from expressing their irritations to a company representative. A survey by an independent party generally is more accurate. But no matter how it is done, a survey requiring a call on every customer is a very costly and time-consuming undertaking.

During the mid-thirties a new and valuable tool became available to businessmen. It was no longer necessary to guess what people think and know, or to ask every person individually. It was found that a small sampling, properly balanced, would give the information, on the average, of the whole community.

It has been wisely said that a man's judgment on any subject is no better than his knowledge of that subject. All the research in this field of sampling public opinion disclosed a strong correlation between attitude and knowledge. Many institutions, including power companies, began using this opinion sampling process as soon as they realized its value. In the field of performance, it became possible to identify those functions that irritated people and to do less of them. The surveys also disclosed the functions that were pleasing to people, and the companies tried to do more of these.

Obviously, the same tool could be used in sampling the knowledge and attitude of employees. In this way the whole complicated field of employee relations was elevated to a higher and more scientific plane. Grievances could be discovered before they became acute. Here, too, there was relationship between knowledge and attitude. Uninformed employees tend to be the most dissatisfied. They transmit their feelings in their contacts with the public. Better-satisfied employees help contribute to public understanding.

The middle thirties

During the middle thirties when the tool of public opinion sampling became available, business in general was somewhat in the doghouse. The Great Depression was hanging on. Unemployment was high. Many incomes were low. Banks had failed. A big utility holding company went into bankruptcy. The administration was not wholly friendly toward the business community. Electric utilities were singled out for severe attack. It was a time for deep and comprehensive self-analysis of all business performance and for a thorough analysis of public opinion. A group of electric utilities in the Middle Western states decided to use the new sampling tool in this process. They made a survey which covered parts of about seventeen states. Questions concerning a number of basic industries, including electric utilities, were included in the survey. Attitudes toward the electric utilities were not especially good. It also was clear that people were so uninformed about the power business that it was having a bearing on their attitudes.

These companies decided to run advertisements in the principal newspapers of the areas they served, stating facts the ignorance of which had a bearing on belief in government ownership or operation. The ads ran for about 2 years. Then a new survey was made. The expressed belief in government ownership of power facilities dropped from something over one-half to about one-third.

Other power companies, having heard of this research effort and of the results it showed, suggested that a committee be formed to bring the facts about the power industry to the American people all across the nation. In 1943, a national survey of public opinion was made. It was found that about 55 percent of the American people favored government ownership of power facilities, and the chief reason they gave was to get lower rates. The companies knew that the price of electricity had been going down, and felt the trend could continue. They knew, too, that government power rates did not include a full share of taxes or cost of money. When they tested public opinion, they found that about 80 percent of the people did not know that the average unit price of household electricity was almost half what it had been 15 years before. Here was a serious misunderstanding. The companies felt that their customers and their investors should know the full facts of the situation before trying to decide which type of ownership they preferred.

With this in mind, the companies set up a national advertising program to keep people informed.

Steps are taken

The decisions to do these various things were made locally, by individual companies. The implementation has also been on a local basis, with companies working to improve their performance and public understanding. Where there have been problems common to a number of companies, however, associations have been formed. In this way, a group of companies make up the Electric Companies Advertising Program (ECAP), which acts through signed advertisements in national media. Similarly, a group of companies formed the Electric Companies Public Information Program (PIP), to help see that the facts about the investor-owned electric utility industry are brought to the attention of national magazines and others. Another organization, the National Association of Electric Companies (NAEC), represents the industry's point of view in Washington. The Edison Electric Institute, the industry's national trade association, does not carry on activities of these kinds, although as a fact-finding body it does provide information which is available for all to use.

The intensive sales and marketing efforts of electric utility companies have also had an important effect on public attitudes during this period. The more benefits of electricity that are made available and the more the economy is developed with the help of electric energy, the more people have come to appreciate the aims and activities of the electric power suppliers.

It is equally true that the public information activities of the companies have had a relation to their sales. When customers or potential customers believe a power supplier is doing a good job and understand that the service being provided is reliable and low in price—and that the long-term price trend is down—They are more likely to choose electric energy than some other energy form in a competitive situation.

Results of the program

The national advertising program began in 1943. Two years later a major insurance company made a survey of public opinion and asked the public what in their opinion was the most economical service or product that they purchased. Electricity headed the list.

The advertising program has been going on continuously ever since. The people are told about the affairs of the power business so they can understand it better. They are told of the companies' efforts to meet all power needs, of their great expansion programs, of the development of atomic power, of the large interconnected systems, of the research efforts, of the companies' civic and community affairs, and of how the average price over the long term keeps on going down. This program for imparting knowledge and facts about the power business has been an important contributing factor to the change in public opinion.

A resurvey is made of public opinion every 2 years. This helps the companies improve their performance and helps guide the advertising. Key questions are asked so as to check progress. One question always relates to public attitude on government ownership. Over the years there has been a marked decline in the attitude of favoring government ownership and an increase in favoring investor-ownership (Chart 10·1).

There is still some confusion on the part of many people about the distinction between investor ownership and government ownership. At one time, government ownership was called *public power* and investor ownership *private power*. These terms are confusing. To most people, *private ownership* means something owned by an individual or a family while *public ownership* means something owned by a great many people. Actually power systems are owned by the public. Research indicates that people better understand the term *investor ownership* as describing enterprises financed in the free market. *Government ownership* describes enterprises financed through government.

A number of power companies use the name of their city or state in their corporate name. This can lead to

Trend in OWNERSHIP SENTIMENT

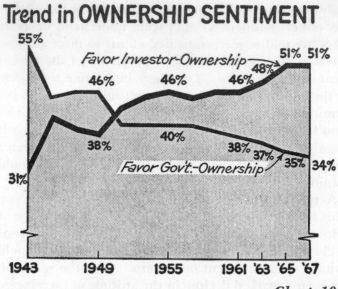

Chart 10·1

confusion. Some people served by these companies believe they are being served by the city or the state. A survey disclosed that 24 percent of the customers of the investor-owned companies think they are being served by some form of government operation. When these people give their preference on the question of government ownership or investor ownership, they generally name the kind of ownership they think they have. Apparently they are satisfied with the service, the price, and the way the power system is being conducted. They think they are being served by the city or state and so they say they are in favor of government ownership.

To eliminate this problem and to get answers to the principal question, the surveyers ask: "Suppose you had a choice between ownership by the Federal government or by an investor-owned company, which would you prefer?" The answers to this question are four to one in favor of investor ownership (Chart 10·2).

Another key question asked in the surveys is: "Can you think of anything that you don't like about your electric service?"

Ninety-one percent of the people now express themselves as not being able to think of anything they don't like about their power service. Nine percent have some complaint and state it. Even the major power interruption in the Northeastern part of the nation in November, 1965, had little effect on the high level of satisfaction.

Why government power?

With 91 percent of the people satisfied with their electric service and four out of five people expressing themselves as being in favor of investor ownership, it is apparent why the growth of government power has slowed down.

The question might well be asked, Why, if a substantial majority of the American people do not want government ownership, why does it continue at all? It is a good question.

It is a fact that government lends money or appropriates money for government power projects and charges interest rates less than the value of the capital. This is one reason for the continuance of government power. It also is a fact

Chart 10·2

WHEN ASKED ABOUT FEDERAL OWNERSHIP....

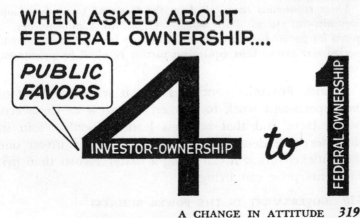

PUBLIC FAVORS INVESTOR-OWNERSHIP **4** *to* **1** FEDERAL OWNERSHIP

that government power projects are not charged federal income tax. Some day there will be equal treatment on these important matters, there will be a more equitable division of our national resources, and government power will go down in history as one of the interesting experiments in America.

Isn't this in reality what Congress has been saying about TVA? There have been many proposals to build TVAs in other areas, and in fact in all parts of the country. In each case the Congress has said No. In effect, Congress has said, "It has been an interesting experiment, but let us not build any more."

Senator William Proxmire, Chairman of the Joint Economic Committee of Congress, has been one of those concerned over the way Federal funds have been invested. In an article on this subject, "Approach to Economy," (*NAM Reports,* Jan. 15, 1968, p. 5.) he wrote:

Competent economists have testified before our Joint Economic Committee that the economic profession agrees that, when the government invests funds at a return of 3 or 4 or 5 percent, these funds are mostly misallocated. This is because the same money could be invested in private enterprise with returns ranging between 10 and 20 percent (before Federal income tax) which would clearly enrich the American economy more rapidly and promote a far greater degree of growth.

These economists have called on the Congress to apply an opportunity-cost system which would say "no" to Administration requests for government investment unless the invested money would receive a return at least equivalent to that received by private enterprise.

Senator Proxmire concludes that it will take a lot of hard, persistent work to awaken Congress to these economic facts, and that business leaders should "join in the chorus of demands on Congress not to invest one more nickel unless it can bring a better return than private enterprise can bring."

Chapter **11**

Where we stand

And so here we are. The use of inanimate energy is growing and electricity is providing a larger and larger share of the energy supply. Our use of electric energy is doubling about every 10 years.

We have in this country the finest, most advanced electric power system on earth. In war and peace, it has met all the nation's needs for electric energy with an ample reserve capacity, and the electric utility industry is planning and building to be sure that the nation's power needs are met in the years ahead.

As we have seen, two principle methods have been developed in this country to provide the large amounts of capital needed to build and operate electric power systems: (1) independent investor-owned companies and (2) agencies of government. For several years the proprietary role of government in the power business has remained relatively stable. About 80 percent of the electric utility customers in this country are served by investor-owned companies. The remaining 20 percent get their electricity from government-owned or government-financed agencies.

In the early days of the electric utility industry, the most common government agency to have a proprietary role in the electric utility business was the municipality. In the course of time, the number of these municipally owned systems has decreased despite several attempts to reverse the trend. Today, the Federal government plays a more important role than ever in the power supply picture. Several Federal agencies are in the business of producing or selling electric power and others make subsidized loans (and sometimes outright grants) to certain types of power suppliers.

The REA today

One of the Federal lending agencies is the Rural Electrification Administration (REA). The background to the formation of this powerful agency is outlined in Chapter 8. Here, it is sufficient to say in summary that the REA has served a worthy purpose in helping bring central-station electric service to farms more quickly than would otherwise have been possible. To get the job done, a number of subsidies were provided REA borrowers, including loans at 2 percent interest and exemption from Federal income tax. Most people agree that these subsidies should be continued for distribution cooperatives where they are needed. However, considerable controversy has grown up over REA loans which finance facilities for unnecessary generation and transmission facilities. Congress has increasingly criticized these practices and has attempted to restrict them.

Questions also have been raised about the REA practice of using the subsidies to serve large industries and non-rural customers which need no subsidy.

In 1966, in a maneuver to get around congressional restrictions, proponents of REA loans proposed a Federal bank be established to provide supplemental financing for rural electric systems. One proposal would have involved $1 billion of government funds, another $750 million. In addition, capital from other sources would have ranged from $8 billion to substantially more than $10 billion. In these proposals, no congressional restrictions or Federal regulatory control would be provided for borrowers from the bank. Billions of dollars would be used at interest rates below the market cost of money for the construction of Federal-income-tax-free generating and transmission facilities which would duplicate or displace investor-owned electric power company facilities which pay their full share of taxes.[1] While REA was formed to provide necessary subsidies to build rural distribution lines, the new financing plan would provide unnecessary subsidies for generating plants and transmission lines, and serve all kinds of customers, not just rural customers. It seems necessary to continue some subsidies to provide for the growth of distribution cooperatives, but no subsidy is required beyond these.

While it might be desirable for some of the REA-financed cooperatives to finance themselves without drawing further on the Federal Treasury, the bank proposals as they were presented did not appear to provide a sound approach to a transition to free-market financing and failed to pass in Congress.

Are cooperatives public utilities?

One of the serious questions raised during the discussions of the proposed bank was whether or not a rural electric cooperative ought to be viewed as a public utility. Traditionally, a public utility in our country has certain definite characteristics. It is assigned a certain territory to serve. It is required to provide service to all those in the territory who request it. It is required to provide service that is good and adequate. And it is generally regulated by government. We assume, also, that the utility has a responsibility to finance its activities in the free market and to pay a full share of taxes. Cooperatives, on the other hand, are formed for the purpose of serving their members. They do not have an obligation to serve non-members who happen to be in their area. When people argue that the cooperatives need to serve industries in order to improve their earnings, they are arguing in effect that the cooperatives ought to be acting like public utilities.

If the cooperatives are not public utilities and are simply groups of people supplying power to themselves, they have a right to build their own power plants, just as a hotel or large industry has the right to build and operate its own electric generator rather than purchase energy from an electric utility. However, under these circumstances there would seem to be no justification for the government providing a subsidy to build the plant, any more than there would be justification for the government lending funds at below cost to a hotel or industrial organization which prefers to have its own generator. Without the subsidy, the hotel, the industrial organization and the cooperative would be making their decisions on an economic basis. Most users of electric energy have found that the economics of the electric power business lead toward purchasing energy from large interconnected systems rather than from isolated operations. The REA Act provides for government help in building generating plants only in those cases when central-station service is not available. Today, it is available almost everywhere.

On the other hand, as a public utility, a cooperative would have to take on certain responsibilities. It would need to secure a certificate of convenience and necessity from an appropriate regulatory body before building transmission lines or generating plants. Issuance of these certificates is at the heart of the regulatory body's responsibility to protect the public against duplication of electric power supply facilities. Duplication means an overinvestment is being made and must inevitably result in a higher price to the consumer. The regulatory body decides whether or not it is in the public interest for a new power plant or transmission line to be built. If there is ample power-producing capacity in the area and there is no public interest to be served in building a plant, the commission is supposed not to allow it.

The Colorado-Ute case. This principle has been upheld again and again in the courts. One example is the case of the Hayden generating plant, constructed by the Colorado-Ute Electric Association, Inc., with the help of REA loans. In this case the cooperative began building a 150,000-kilowatt power plant while the question of whether or not it could build the plant was still in litigation. In fact, the plant was completed before the question was decided and the Colorado Supreme Court could rule it should never have been built.

A Colorado statute passed in 1961 declares that electric cooperatives are public utilities and so are subject to the jurisdiction of the state's regulatory commission. Another statute provides that no public utility shall begin the construction of a new plant without first having obtained a certificate from the commission that public convenience and necessity require its construction. In reviewing the case the Colorado Supreme Court found:

1. adequate electric service is already available in the State of Colorado for the needs and necessities of the proposed new customers of Colorado-Ute; therefore

2. the construction of the Hayden Plant, requiring an investment of approximately thirty million dollars, is not necessary to supply any present or foreseeable future electric requirements, and Colorado ratepayers should not be required to support it; and

3. affirmance of the district court's judgment and the decisions of the Commission would sanction a duplication of existing electric facilities which are adequate to supply the needs of the public; and

4. the affirmance of the district court and Commission decisions by this court would be inconsistent with the doctrine of regulated monopoly and would . . . render regulation "wholly ineffective and meaningless." [2]

The U.S. Supreme Court refused to review this decision and the cooperative was left with the problem of disposing of a $30.5 million power plant which had been illegally constructed.[3]

This is an example of effective government regulation of a public utility. It shows the value of a regulatory system which provides for review of commission decision in the courts. It may be that solutions to the controversies surrounding the REA-financed cooperatives can be found through this kind of regulatory process.

Changes at Bonneville Power Administration

There are indications that some in the government power agencies recognize that the small systems, such as the municipally owned and REA-financed power suppliers, are best served by purchasing power from a large interconnected system rather than generating electricity themselves. In the Pacific Northwest, as was noted in Chapter 7, the investor-owned companies, Bonneville Power Administration, and the other government-owned and government-financed systems work closely together through the Northwest Power Pool. In 1963 a decision was made within the Department of the Interior to reallocate more of the cost of Grand Coulee Dam to flood control.[4] The effect was to reduce the percentage of the cost allocated to power production and thus to reduce the amount BPA would have to earn from the sale of power. At the time, BPA was operating in the red. There was pressure to increase rates to cover costs. But instead, an administrative decision was made that simply reduced the costs to be covered.

The difficulties at BPA were instrumental in a far-reaching Department of the Interior action in 1964. Although BPA was not earning its repayment requirements, it had surplus power that was going begging. There was no market for this excess energy in the Pacific Northwest. In California, however, the population was growing rapidly and the demand for electricity increasing. The investor-owned companies proposed that they build transmission lines and other facilities that would make it possible for them to purchase Bonneville power and bring it to the people of California. The city of Los Angeles, which is served by a municipal electric system, would receive a share of the power, they said.[5] The Department of the Interior objected and, after threatening to build a transmission line of its own from Bonneville to Los Angeles, it agreed on a compromise calling for a combination of lines to be built by the companies, the city of Los Angeles, and the Federal government.[6]

The Department of the Interior's decision concerning the BPA-California intertie was the subject of considerable debate in Congress. At present most of the construction plans of the Department's marketing agencies are subject to congressional review, item by item. The Department, however, has been urging that "revolving funds" be established for these agencies. Some people fear that this might do away with close congressional review of Federal power projects.

The Yankee-Dixie plan

In 1965 a group of cooperatives and municipal systems in the Northeast formed the Yankee-Dixie Power Association and proposed building at least four large mine-mouth generating plants which would be interconnected by a complex network of extra-high-voltage lines connecting load centers in a twenty-two-state area from New England to Florida and as far west as Illinois.[7]

The proposal has not gained the support it needed to get under way as its sponsors had hoped. It is an example, however, of the new approaches being taken to development of government-financed and government-subsidized power projects.

Passamaquoddy

The history of Federal interest in the possible development of electric power from the tides of Passamaquoddy Bay, a small body of water off the Bay of Fundy and located almost entirely in Canadian territory, presents another example of the differences between traditional approaches to government power development and the new kinds of approaches being taken.

The idea of harnessing the great tides at Passamaquoddy has fascinated a succession of engineers for many years. Study after study was made, but it has always been proved uneconomical. In 1925 the state of Maine reported that construction of a power plant at Passamaquody was too costly. In 1933 the FPC said that development of a power plant would cost $2\frac{1}{2}$ times the cost of building a comparable steam-electric generating plant. In 1934 the

Canadian International Commission rejected the idea. But the following year President Roosevelt approved allocation of $10 million in work relief funds to start the project. By 1936 some $7 million had been spent on the project and to house construction workers, but Congress called a halt to the activity by refusing to appropriate further funds.[8]

In 1941 the Federal Power Commission made another study of the project and reported that the "Passamaquoddy tidal power cannot compete successfully at this time with river hydroelectric power potentially available in the State of Maine, or with power from modern, efficient steam electric plants." Late in 1948 the idea was referred to an International Joint Commission, this time representing Canada and the United States. After two years the Commission reported that a proper study of the proposal would cost more than $3 million. The two governments asked the Commission to undertake the study in 1956 and for 4 years and 8 months experts examined every aspect of the idea. The result was a report stating that "the tidal project, either alone or in combination with auxiliary sources, would not permit power to be produced at a price which is competitive with the price of power from alternative sources." The matter seemed to be closed.

But it was not. Just a month later the President directed the Secretary of the Interior to see what changes in fuel, engineering, and financial costs would be needed to make the project economically feasible. This was done. Engineers from the Department of the Interior found that when they combined the Passmaquoddy project with a proposal for construction of a conventional hydroelectric project on the St. John River 175 air miles away, the combination appeared economical. In 1963 the Department issued a report so stating. It stated that the cost of the development would be $1,117,445,400, which would provide 1¾ million kilowatts of installed capacity, of which 1 million kilowatts would be peaking capacity for *only 1 hour per day*. There was one difficulty. The Canadian government said it did not want any part in the activity.[9]

Again, the project seemed to have come to a standstill. Then, in July, 1965, the Department of the Interior changed its recommendations drastically. It suggested that the Passamaquoddy portion of the project be put aside for a time and asked approval for construction of a hydroelectric plant on the St. John. Ninety-five percent of the cost of the project was to be allocated to power with the remaining five percent allocated to recreation and flood control. The President recommended that this new form of the project be authorized, and it passed the Senate. The House, however, refused to approve the project and suggested that a survey be made of alternative methods of providing power in the area. The Senate did not agree and insisted on immediate authorization. No compromise was possible. The parliamentary situation made it impossible for members of the House to vote on the proposal separately from an omnibus public works authorization bill and it was eventually approved. However, in 1967, the Senate gave in to House demands that all funds for the project be dropped from the fiscal 1968 public works appropriation bill.[10]

Here is a case in which Congress considered subsidizing a power plant for New England when all the capacity can be financed in the market. It is not a flood control project. Navigation is not involved. Ninety-five percent of the project costs are allocated to power, and it is not economically feasible.[11]

As it was passed, the project included a large dam at the Dickey site on the St. John River and a second dam at the Lincoln School site for regulating the water flow from

Dickey. The Dickey Dam would have eight generators with a total capacity of 760,000 kilowatts, and the Lincoln School dam would have two generators with a total capacity of 34,000 kilowatts. The total cost, including 400 miles of transmission lines needed to carry the energy produced to the market, would be $314 million. The average price for the kilowatt-hours produced, based on the Department of the Interior estimates, would have to be over 15 mills per kilowatt-hour. The plan would be that some of the power would be sold at 7 mills per kilowatt-hour to preference customers in Maine and the remainder sold at a higher price as peaking power in the Boston area.[12]

If the New England electric companies will be producing baseload and peaking power in 1973 equivalent to the proposed project for $3.1 million less than Dickey-Lincoln costs, as they assert they will, Department of the Interior will have to market its electricity at an annual deficit of this amount to be competitive. The Chairman of the Electric Coordinating Council of New England, Albert A. Cree, calculated the cumulative deficit on this basis to be $363 million in 50 years with $3\frac{1}{8}$ percent interest added.[13] Mr. Cree has also pointed out that if taxes were included in the cost of the project, the tax costs would be $5.2 million a year, according to testimony presented by the Corps of Engineers. The 50-year tax loss, with interest at $3\frac{1}{8}$ percent, would be more than $600 million. This amount, together with the cumulative deficit of $363 million, would raise the true economic cost to the taxpayer to $963 million. The Department of the Interior estimates the flood control benefits of the project at $40,000 a year and the area redevelopment benefits at $409,000 a year. In 50 years, these benefits would total $22.5 million. The question is, Are they worth a price of $963 million?[14]

One reason the Dickey-Lincoln project was considered

was because New England has had to pay higher than average prices for fuel. It is not near raw fuel sources and freight rates are high. But development of atomic power has changed all that. New England can now be on a par with other areas in fuel costs. The combination of atomic power plants and pumped storage plants makes Dickey-Lincoln obsolete before it is built.

An attempt to regulate Federal power

In any Federal river development project an attempt is always made to show that the sum of all the benefits will at least equal the sum of all the costs. Net revenues that might be derived from the sale of power are counted among the benefits.

The Comptroller General has repeatedly called attention to the fact that the Southwestern Power Administration has not been meeting its repayment schedule.[15] He also reported to Congress that in the 6 years through 1963 the Bonneville Power Administration's power operations showed a total deficit of more than $50 million and that at existing unregulated rates the repayment of the cost of the Bureau of Reclamation's projects in the Missouri River Basin will not be completed until almost the turn of the twenty-second century.[16]

Under the Flood Control Act of 1944 the power-marketing agencies of the Department of the Interior are directed to submit their rates to the Federal Power Commission for approval. In 1966 the Comptroller General of the United States made a report to Congress on the effectiveness of this procedure as follows:

The Department of the Interior sold hydroelectric power and energy, generated at and not needed in the operation of three projects under the control of the Department of the Army, to the Tennessee Valley Authority during the period December 1948 to December

1964, although the rate schedules for the power and energy were specifically disapproved by the Federal Power Commission (FPC) in May 1958. Also, the Department of the Interior, in January 1961, agreed to an amendment to a power-marketing contract with the Arkansas Power & Light Company under which the Government received $822,000 less in revenues during 1961 than would have been received for the same amount of hydroelectric energy under the contract provisions in effect prior to the amendment. The Department did not consider the amendment to constitute a rate change and therefore did not submit the amendment to the FPC for confirmation and approval. When we brought this matter to the attention of FPC, the Chairman informed us that, in FPC's opinion, the amendment did constitute a rate change which required FPC's approval. The Chairman, however, stated that our advice of the matter was FPC's first notice of the amendment and that the Flood Control Act of 1944, under which the power is marketed, does not provide FPC with retroactive authority.

Section 5 of the Flood Control Act of 1944 (16 USC 825a) provides that rate schedules for the marketing of hydroelectric power and energy by the Secretary of the Interior from projects under the control of the Department of the Army become effective upon confirmation and approval by FPC. The act, however, does not state what action can or should be taken when power and energy are marketed at rates that have been disapproved by FPC or at rates which have not been submitted for confirmation and approval.

We believe that the circumstances indicate that, if FPC is to effectively confirm and approve rate schedules for the marketing of hydroelectric power by the Secretary of the Interior from projects under the control of the Department of the Army, section 5 of the Flood Control Act of 1944 will have to be amended.[17]

New arenas

More and more, decisions affecting the future of government in the power business are being made by the administrative departments rather than by the Congress. Probably one of the most important of these was made by the Corps of Engineers during the 1940's when the possibility of forming a Missouri Valley Authority was being discussed. Until that time the Corps had taken the position that large multipurpose dams were not effective in controlling floods. The Bureau of Reclamation and the Department of the Interior took the opposite view. The Missouri Valley proposal brought the controversy to a head. The Bureau urged establishment of a valley authority. The Corps opposed the idea. Eventually, representatives of the two organizations worked out what became known as the *Pick-Sloan Plan*. While it did not call for establishment of a valley authority, it did suggest that a series of multipurpose dams be built along the Missouri River. This has been done, and a substantial amount of electric energy is being produced as a result.[18]

A similar controversy grew up in the 1960s over a proposal by the Bureau of Reclamation that a dam be built at Marble Canyon on the Colorado River. Conservationists rose up against the plan, saying that the dam would flood part of the Grand Canyon, an irreplaceable natural resource. Although Congress approved the project, it did not receive the endorsement of the Department of the Interior. When a leading conservationist suggested construction of "Federal profit-making thermal generating plants" as an alternative, the Department agreed to study the possibility of building coal-fired or nuclear power plants to help pay for other aspects of the project.[19]

Atomic power. There are other new arenas and directions in which the advocates of government ownership are interested. One of these is the development of atomic power.

The electric utility industry was given permission to develop atomic power for the generation of electricity in 1954, with the passage of the Atomic Energy Act. By 1966 there were fifty-five nuclear generating units in various stages of operation, construction, or planning. These units have an aggregate capacity of slightly more than 27 million kilowatts, which is greater than the total electric generating capacity of most nations. In the relatively few years since 1954, thanks to the efforts of the utility industry, equipment manufacturers, the Atomic Energy Commission, and others, the use of nuclear power for production of electricity has come of age.

Government power agencies and cooperatives have been interested in the development of atomic power from its earliest days, but they have not received preference in this field. A generating and transmission cooperative in Minnesota, a power district in Nebraska, and the city of Piqua, Ohio, had atomic power plants in operation prior to 1966. Other nuclear projects were being planned by similar bodies. One of these is a dual-purpose plutonium production reactor, built by the Atomic Energy Commission in Hanford, Washington. Although the companies in the area offered to buy the power produced at this plant, Congress directed the Atomic Energy Commission to sell the steam produced by the reactor to the Washington Public Power Supply System (WPPSS), an organization of public utility districts and cooperatives. However, the legislation included a provision that a share of the power produced at Hanford should be sold to the companies.

Recently some have advocated that small government-financed power systems should own shares of the large nuclear power plants being built by investor-owned power companies. They say government should see that this is done so that customers of these small systems can share in the economies of scale represented by the nuclear plants. Of course, these economies are available to any system purchasing power from one of the large interconnected power systems. If this suggestion were followed, the government-financed systems would be purchasing energy from the newest plants in the system, avoiding the costs of the older and less efficient plants. This does not seem fair. One of the principles of utility regulation is that a customer should be served by the entire system, not just a part of it. This same principle should be applied to nuclear power plants.

The development of large nuclear power plants has opened a possibility that they might provide the power necessary for desalinating seawater and brackish water. That is, it might prove economical to construct large multipurpose plants which would desalinate water and at the same time produce electric energy for sale. The desalination process is very costly and it has been suggested that the revenues from sale of the electric energy might help pay this cost. In 1965 the state of New York announced plans to build prototype desalination plant, but rather than sell the related electric power itself, it plans to sell it to the Long Island Lighting Company for distribution.

Principal reasons for government power

Through the years there have been four reasons which have been given most frequently for spending tax money to build electric power plants:

1. Some say America's power needs are so great that there is need for government financing as well as free-market financing. But, as was shown in Chapter 5 there is nothing to indicate all the electric power the nation needs in the future could not be financed in the market.

2. Some say government power is cheaper and thus provides a yardstick by which to measure the investor-owned companies. But a yardstick is valid only if it includes all the elements being measured. As the studies of TVA, BPA, and REA, described in Chapters 6, 7, and 8, indicate, government power is not cheap power. It is power sold

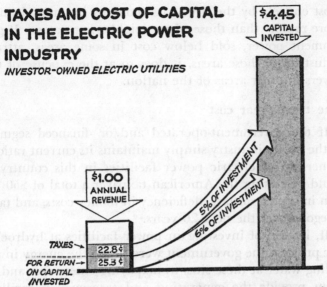

TAXES AND COST OF CAPITAL IN THE ELECTRIC POWER INDUSTRY

INVESTOR-OWNED ELECTRIC UTILITIES

$4.45 CAPITAL INVESTED

$1.00 ANNUAL REVENUE

5% OF INVESTMENT

6% OF INVESTMENT

TAXES → 22.8¢

FOR RETURN → 25.3¢
ON CAPITAL
INVESTED

Chart 11·1

below cost. The cost of capital and taxes makes up about half of every $1 of gross revenues of investor-owned electric utility companies (Chart 11·1). Unless these elements are included, comparisons with investor-owned companies are not valid.

3. Some say the sale of electric power by government brings income which helps pay for other functions, such as flood control. But studies show that when government produces electricity, the power facilities do not pay their own way. As a result, they cannot help pay the cost of other functions.

4. Some say cheap government power will help the economic development of an area. But there is no indication that areas with government power grew faster than similar areas served mainly by investor-owned companies. As indicated in Chapter 6, although Tennessee is served al-

most entirely by the TVA, its economy has not advanced more rapidly than those of its neighboring states. If government power, sold below cost in some areas, attracts industries to those areas, it does so at the expense of taxpayers in other areas of the nation.

The twenty-year cost

If the government-operated and/or -financed segment of the power industry simply maintains its current ratio of ownership of electric power facilities in this country, it could be costing the American taxpayer a total of $50 billion in capital outlays, deficiency in money costs, and taxes foregone over the next 20 years.[20]

If, instead of investing in power facilities at hydroelectric projects, the government were to sell the energy in the falling water at these sites to taxpaying enterprises and let them provide the generating and transmission facilities needed to get the energy to market, the government's income would be increased. In fact, there would have been $72 million more available to government for irrigation, flood control, navigation improvement, recreation, and other good purposes if this method had been followed at the dams under the Bonneville Power Administration in 1962.

General conclusions

There is nothing to indicate that government financing is needed to supplement free-market financing for the power facilities the nation requires.

There is nothing to indicate that subsidized power rates increase economic development.

There is nothing to indicate that government power is really cheaper than investor-owned power. In fact, if government power projects paid taxes and cost of money as investor-owned companies do their rates would have to be as high as or higher than comparable companies in the same part of the country.

There is nothing to indicate that government's sale of power at a multipurpose dam helps pay for other functions. Actually, the evidence all points to the fact that government would gain more income to pay for these other functions by finding ways for the power facilities at such projects to be financed in the free market.

Opinion measurements show that when given a choice between investor ownership of power facilities and Federal ownership, the public favors investor ownership by four to one. Why, then, does government power continue?

What should be done?

At this time there seems little chance that a complete change will be made to free-market financing of existing government power projects. The earnings of the government projects are not adequate to interest investors. If any interest were to be shown and if any of the projects were to be financed in the market, it is likely that they would be required to pay taxes at the level of any investor-owned company. However, the government projects do not have sufficient revenue to pay such taxes.

Possibly the first step in meeting this problem would be to require that government power projects begin paying for the capital they need in accordance with the real value of the capital and that they begin paying taxes on the same basis as investor-owned companies. It may be wise to bring the principle of independent government regulation into play by putting government power projects under the same regulatory bodies that oversee investor-owned companies. These experienced bodies can see that the broad public interest is protected.

The regulatory bodies should be instructed to find the value of government power facilities devoted to electric utility service, to determine a reasonable return on this capital, and to determine the taxes that should be applied in order to make these taxes equivalent to those paid by investor-owned companies. It may be that these taxes may have to be calculated on some basis such as the percentage of gross plant account. Regulatory bodies should also be instructed to check the rates of government power projects so that there will be sufficient earnings to pay their fair return to the taxpayers, as well as to pay their fair share of taxes.

Even though this would appear to be an equitable solution, it will not be easy to accomplish.

As a beginning to correcting the present inequity among American citizens on this power problem, there should be a reexamination of the criteria now being used to determine economic feasibility of future government power projects. In determining feasibility it would appear that the criteria should employ an evaluation based on the market cost of capital and taxes equivalent to those paid by investor-owned companies.

The choice: government or market financing. In the final analysis the choice between government financing and market financing is affected by a multitude of economic and noneconomic considerations. The history of power development in the United States of America, however, provides data which should be studied by all who are interested in economic progress.

First of all, the evidence indicates that it is possible to build and operate a large and very advanced electric power supply system which is able to provide electricity reliably and economically to all areas of the nation and all classes of customers by depending on free-market financing.

Second, experience leads to the conclusion that even the best-intentioned attempts to make use of government as a vehicle for financing electric power supply result in the inequity that subsidies inevitably produce—some of which may at times be desirable. However, the subsidization can lead to unnecessary confusion in analyzing alternative methods of allocating resources and to an increased accumulation of economic power in governmental hands. In a free-market economy this may have serious results. In any nation it reflects a decreasing reliance on the individual, on his economic freedom, and eventually on his freedom in other areas.

In this country, despite the forces working to expand the activities of government in the electric power business, the percentage of government-owned power-producing capacity, which grew so sharply during the 2 decades following 1930, has been leveling off. This, of itself, attests to the growing understanding of the American people of the ability of the investor-owned companies to continue their outstanding record of performance and of the problems and inequities produced by government power.

In providing the large sums needed to finance power facilities, each society must devise its own answers to the alternative methods available. Where capital is readily available within the economy, the choice is between government financing, free-market financing, or some mixture of the two. If the traditions and beliefs of the nation point to government control of the economy, the choice is relatively simple: the tendency would be to government financing. If the society believes in free-market financing, the choice may become more complicated, but under these conditions it would seem wise to make use of volun-

tary investments to the greatest extent possible. Where
capital is not available within the economy, assuming the
existence of the other elements necessary to growth, the
same choice exists. Either government may direct its tax
funds to construction of power facilities or outside capital
may be used for financing.

Society benefits most when capital for power facilities is
raised in the free market. When this occurs, no investment of government funds is required and government is
able to direct its attention to other important areas, at
the same time possibly gaining considerable tax income.
The nation's resources are allocated more efficiently.
But, most important, the individual citizen, as taxpayer, as
power consumer, and as investor, gains economically and
in the individual freedom that is inherent in the free-
market approach.

REFERENCES

1. *Hearings before the Committee on Agriculture, House of Representatives, on REA Legislation,* 89th Cong., 2d Sess., p. 206.
2. *The Western Colorado Power Co. and Public Service Co. of
   Colorado v. The Public Utilities Commission of the State of
   Colorado and Colorado-Ute Electric Association,* Supreme Court
   of Colorado decision, pp. 16–17.
3. Oliphant Washington Service, *Washington Memo,* Oct. 24, 1963.
4. *Hearings before a Subcommittee of the Committee on Appropriations, House of Representatives, on Public Works Appropriations Act for 1965,* 88th Cong., 2d Sess., Part 2, p. 241.
5. Southern California Edison Co. Release, Jan. 14, 1963.
6. Senate Document 89 (88–2), July 29, 1964.
7. Yankee-Dixie Power Association Incorporated, "The Yankee-
   Dixie Coordinated Plan for Providing Low Cost Power to the
   Eastern United States," June, 1966, pp. 9–12.
8. Charles Avila, "The Quoddy Follies of 1964," *EEI Bulletin,*
   July, 1964.
9. *Ibid.*
10. *Conservation of the National Resources of New England,* House

Document 236, 89th Cong., 1st Sess., July 12, 1965; *Congressional Quarterly Weekly Report*, Jan. 12, 1968, p. 38.

11. *Federal Spending Facts*, Bulletin No. 228 of the Council of State Chambers of Commerce, Washington, May 30, 1966, p. 1.
12. *Ibid.*, p. 2.
13. *Ibid.*, p. 4.
14. *Ibid.*, p. 4.
15. Comptroller General of the U.S., *Audit of Southwestern Power System (Dept. of Army) and Southwestern Power Administration (Dept. of Interior) by Comptroller General of U.S., Fiscal Years 1960 & 1961*, letter of transmittal, p. 1.
16. Comptroller General of the U.S., *Audit of Missouri River Basin Project, Fiscal Years 1959 & 1960*, p. 26.
17. Comptroller General of the U.S., *Report of Compilation of General Accounting Office Findings and Recommendations, Fiscal Year 1965*, pp. 137–138.
18. *Congressional Record*, 88th Cong., 2d Sess., Vol. 110, Part 6, Apr. 15, 1964, pp. 8101–8102.
19. *Christian Science Monitor*, Oct. 4, 1966; *Business Week*, Oct. 8, 1966.
20. EEI.

Index

Pensacola, 56
dam, 57, 58
People's Legislative Service, 36
Pick-Sloan Plan, 334
Plants, isolated, 11
Possum Kingdom Dam, 78, 124
Power-marketing agencies, 144
Power Policy Committee, 258
power, private, 317
public, 317
Preference, 89, 98, 99, 114, 116,
120, 128
Production, expense, 41
level of, 4
Projects, county, 51
Central Nebraska Public
Power & Irrigation Dis-
trict, 63
district, 51
Loup River Public Power Dis-
trict, 63
Platte Valley Public Power &
Irrigation District, 63
state, 51
Public attitude, factors affecting,
309
Public lands, 135
Public opinion, tax discrimina-
tion, 292
Public Ownership, 262
Public Ownership League, 36,
38–40, 139
Public Service Board of Vermont,
77, 81
Public Service Company of Okla-
homa, 58, 59, 61
Public utility districts, 51
PWA (Public Works Administra-
tion), 33, 34, 39, 54, 56,
63, 64, 68, 70–72, 115, 117

Raker Act of Dec 19, 1913, 128
Rankin, John, 103, 110
Raushenbush, H. S., 33, 100, 110
Raver, Dr. Paul, 54, 226
Rayburn, Sam, 263, 267
REA (Rural Electrification Administration), 28, 54, 58,
59, 64, 75, 76, 79, 81, 113,
115, 123, 127, 139, 144,
231, 243, 294, 304, 322,
336
Act of 1936, 128, 263, 267, 324
intent of, 263
section 5, 272
deviation of, 267
dual rate, 275
energy purchased by borrowers,
266
Reclamation, Act of 1902, 88, 99
Act of 1906, 88, 99, 128
Act of 1939, 128
Reclamation, Bureau of, 28, 93,
114, 118, 131, 133, 135,
139, 226, 332, 334
Reconstruction Finance Corporation, 62, 68, 72, 78, 206
Reed, Stanley, 97
Regulation, 31
Rivers and Harbors Act of 1945,
230
Rochester Gas and Electric Company, 246
Rochester Railway and Light
Company, 245
Roosevelt, Franklin D., 27, 38,
58, 68, 77, 94, 102, 105,
109–111, 115, 118, 258,
261, 329
Ross, John D., 64, 116, 139, 226,
262